IMAGES
of America

SENECA FALLS

I0792667

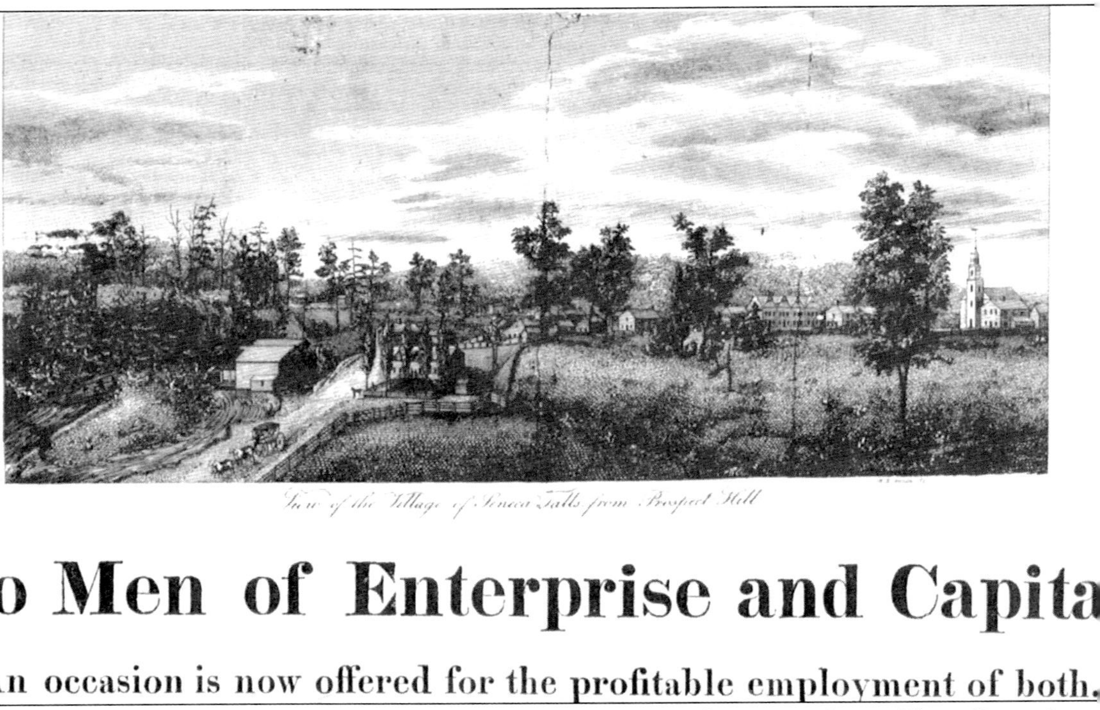

This 1817 engraving is of the Seneca Turnpike as it crosses the Seneca River. The village of Seneca Falls is in the background. This illustration was used on a broadside advertising land for sale by the Bayard Land Company. This land was part of the military tract that was offered to the soldiers of the Continental Army. Those not wishing to live in the wilds of New York sold their lots to investors. (Seneca Falls Historical Society.)

On the cover: Ken Wayne at age 29 and his 5-year-old son Bill get set to take Ken's 82-year-old grandfather for his first airplane ride in the summer of 1930. Bill would also become a pilot. This photograph was published in the *Seneca Falls Reveille* on March 15, 1967. (Seneca Falls Historical Society.)

IMAGES
of America

SENECA FALLS

Frances T. Barbieri and Kathy Jans-Duffy

ARCADIA
PUBLISHING

ISBN 978-0-7385-6588-0

Published by Arcadia Publishing
Charleston, South Carolina

Printed in the United States of America

Library of Congress Control Number: 2009921630

For all general information contact Arcadia Publishing at:
Telephone 843-853-2070
Fax 843-853-0044
E-mail sales@arcadiapublishing.com
For customer service and orders:
Toll-Free 1-888-313-2665

Visit us on the Internet at www.arcadiapublishing.com

To all of those who came before us
and collected and preserved the history of Seneca Falls

Contents

ACKNOWLEDGMENTS

The Seneca Falls Historical Society was founded in 1896 by a small group of men and women who wanted to preserve the story of a small Upstate village in New York. Over the years, several hundred volunteers and scholars have worked to preserve the history and to tell the story of Seneca Falls and the people who made it a vital part of New York, the United States, and the world. The Seneca Falls Historical Society's archives, library, and photograph collections have been called a treasure of information for the many researchers who have spent time delving into the history of the area. The staff and volunteers over the years have maintained these wonderful collections to tell the story of the men and women who made Seneca Falls known worldwide. Unless otherwise noted, all of the images used in this book are from the Seneca Falls Historical Society.

Thank you to Rebekah Collinsworth at Arcadia Publishing for her suggestions, patience, and understanding. Also, a thank you goes to the board of trustees of the Seneca Falls Historical Society for their support of the project.

INTRODUCTION

In 1779, Gen. John Sullivan was ordered by Gen. George Washington to remove the Cayuga Indians from the Finger Lakes region of New York. The Cayugas had sided with the British during the Revolutionary War, and it was decided that they should be removed from the area by sending them to Canada. Job Smith was the first European to settle in the area. The rapids in the Seneca River provided an opportunity to establish portage business in 1787. The second settler was Lawrence VanCleef, who, while on the Sullivan Campaign, became impressed with the land along the Seneca River. In 1789, VanCleef settled near Smith and built the first log cabin in the area. Smith was a roving spirit and was soon on the move again, leaving the portage business to VanCleef. When locks were built in 1815, the portage was no longer needed, and VanCleef opened a tavern. The Parkus family took over the operation of the tavern shortly after they arrived from Connecticut. In 1794, Robert Troup, Nicholas Gouverneur, Stephen N. Bayard, and Elkanah Watson, known as the Bayard Land Company, purchased 100 acres of land along the north side of the Seneca River. The next year, the Bayard Land Company sold one fifth of the original purchase including waterpower to Col. Wilhelmus Mynderse. He became an active partner in the company and was made their business agent at Seneca Falls.

Between 1792 and 1795, the legislature reorganized several counties in the central and western part of the state. Albany was the original colony, then Montgomery was derived in 1772; Herkimer came in 1791, and Onondaga in 1794. Cayuga County was organized from Onondaga in 1799, and Seneca was then derived in 1804. Seneca County became the county between Cayuga and Seneca Lakes and was divided into four towns, Junius, Fayette, Ovid, and Romulus. It was not until 1829 that Junius was divided into Junius, Waterloo, Tyre, and Seneca Falls.

Colonel Mynderse wasted no time improving his personal holdings. In 1796, the fist mill was put into operation, known as the Red Mill because of the color it was painted. Mynderse also built a double log house on a hill overlooking the mill with a store located in one end, the first store in the area. By 1816, the Bayard Land Company owned all of the waterpower on both sides along this section of the Seneca River as well as 1,450 acres of land.

The Bayard Land Company maintained control with very few improvements except for a few farms, the two mills, and a borough of about 300 inhabitants. It was unfortunate that the company would not further develop the waterpower. When offered $10,000 in 1816 for 10 acres of land and waterpower sufficient for 10 runs of millstone on the south side of the river, the company refused on the grounds that another flouring mill would injure the operation of the existing mills. This refusal to develop the natural resources and waterpower capable of 150 runs of millstone deprived Seneca Falls of early growth. Nevertheless, the village managed to overcome this handicap to become a leader in ideas and manufacturing.

As Seneca Falls grew, it became a crossroads for settlers heading west along the canal and Seneca Turnpike and later the railroad. When the restrictions on waterpower were lifted, manufacturing increased very quickly; men of enterprise and capital flourished. With prosperity came new ideas: abolition, temperance, Sunday school reform, and women's rights.

With the emergence of manufacturing came wealth and, for some of the women, free time. This wealth and freedom allowed many women to question why they could not own property, have custody of their own children in a divorce, or keep their wages they earned. Women and men gathered in Seneca Falls for the first women's rights convention in July 1848. The issue of slavery and its abolition was also raised by both men and women, and the Underground Railroad was established in Seneca County. Several freedom seekers stayed in Seneca Falls and owned thriving businesses.

The goods and products of the mills and factories in Seneca Falls were known worldwide. Pumps and bells made by Cowing, Downs, Rumsey, and Goulds have been found all over the world. Silsby Pump Company went on to make rotary steam fire engines that were used across the United States. In the early 20th century, Seneca Falls even produced an automobile, the Iroquois. Among the household goods manufactured in Seneca Falls were flat irons, cast-iron sinks, buttons made from the palm nut, rulers, and Venetian blinds.

From the very first settlers, who were of Dutch, German, and English heritage, Seneca Falls has relied on immigrants to work on the canals and in the factories and shops. The first wave came from Ireland to work on the Cayuga-Seneca and Erie Canals. They stayed to work in the foundries to produce and share in the wealth of Seneca Falls. Many of the young women worked as domestics for the wealthy families or owned millinery or dress shops. Sons of the Irish factory workers became policemen, firemen, and even politicians.

The next wave of immigrants, the Italians, came in the first part of the 20th century to work in the factories, and they became grocery store and shop owners and politicians.

Today Seneca Falls is still a small village in the heart of the Finger Lakes that offers a friendly greeting to all visitors—proud of its past, optimistic about its future.

One

After the Bayard Land Company

In 1825, the Bayard Land Company gave up their hold on the waterpower, and Seneca Falls was allowed to grow and flourish as it should have years earlier. Men of enterprise and capital were drawn to this area by the beauty and the abundance of farmland, waterpower, and the rivers and lakes for navigation. Men and their families came from the eastern seaboard, downstate New York, and from many countries in Europe. These were hardworking men with unusual skills. Some were inventors, some were farmers, and some had artistic skills that soon found a place in a busy community. Seneca Falls did become a leading manufacturing center, and the name Seneca Falls was equated with quality.

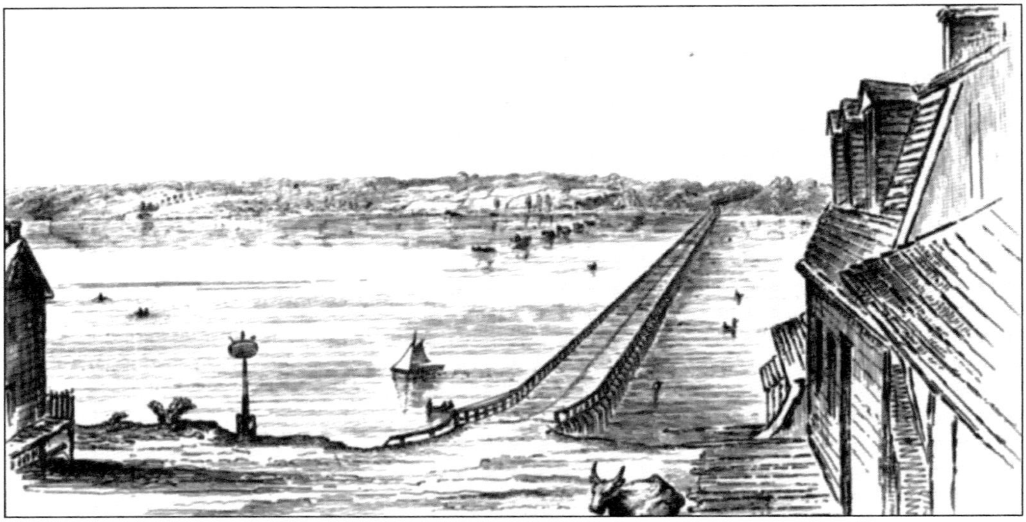

The toll bridge across Cayuga Lake was built between 1799 and 1800. This wooden bridge across the northern portion of Cayuga Lake was one and a quarter miles long. The cost of construction was $150,000. Damaged several times by icy winters, it was costly to repair, and was finally abandoned in the 1850s. The tollhouse, made of fieldstone, was a private home until the 1940s when it also was demolished.

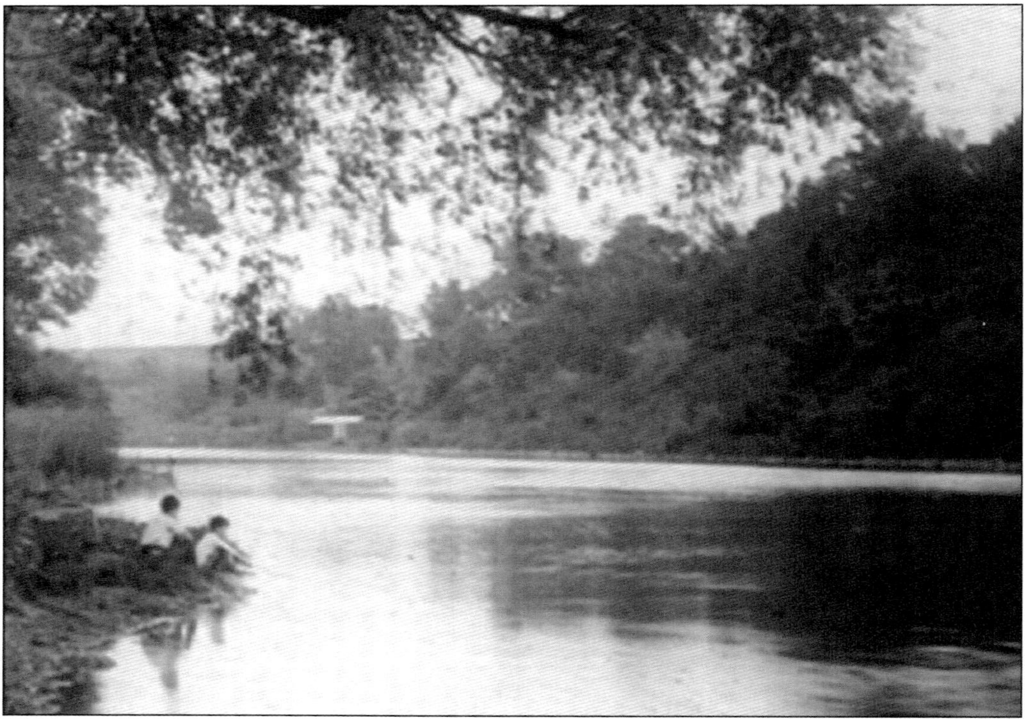

The Seneca River is seen on a summer day, where young boys have boy adventures. This river connects Seneca Lake on the west to Cayuga Lake on the east. There is a 40-foot drop in the river from one side Seneca Falls to the other. Grace Woodworth, a local photographer, took many photographs of the Seneca River and the surrounding countryside.

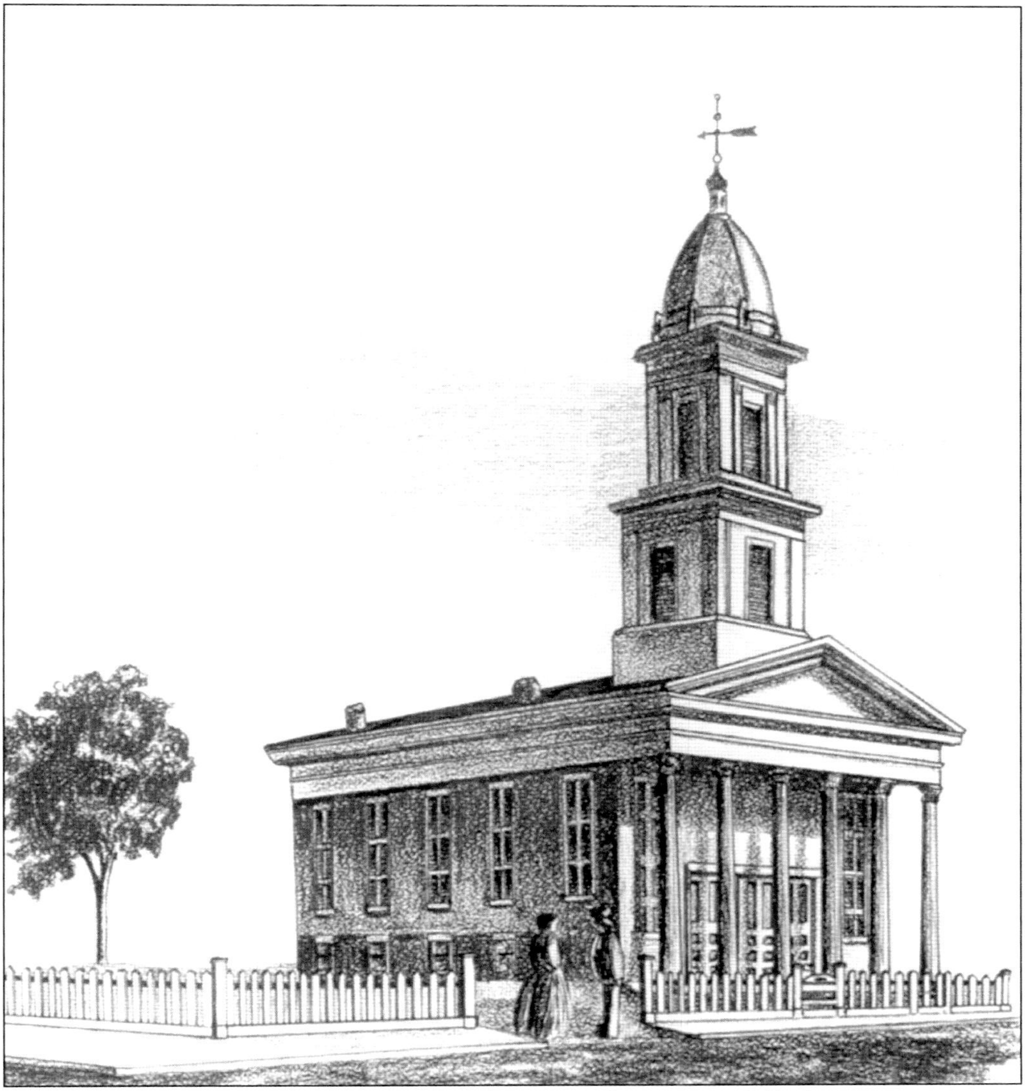

The Presbyterian church is the oldest church organized in Seneca Falls, being two centuries old. It was formed in 1807, only three years after the county was founded. The first minister was Rev. John Stuart. Originally the services were held in a school on Cayuga Street just two blocks from the present location. The present site was given to the congregation by Col. Wilhelmus Mynderse. On September 17, 1817, a wood building was erected. On September 12, 1871, the cornerstone for the present church was set; the original church building was moved to State Street and became a social hall.

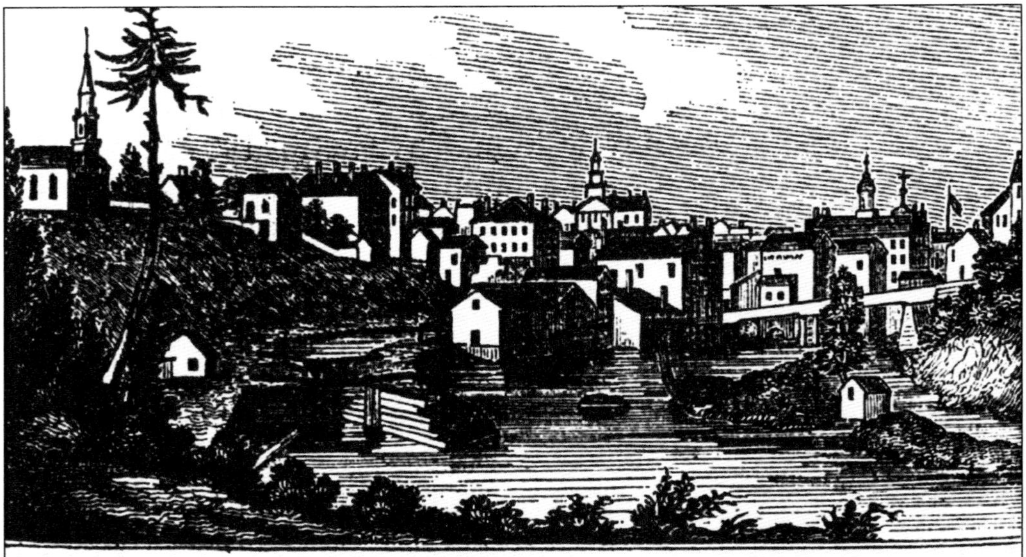

East view of Seneca Falls village.

This wood cut depicts Seneca Falls in 1832 shortly after being formed from Junius. The scene shows the canal, the river, and the several churches that had been built. The canal was in use a few years before the Erie Canal was completed.

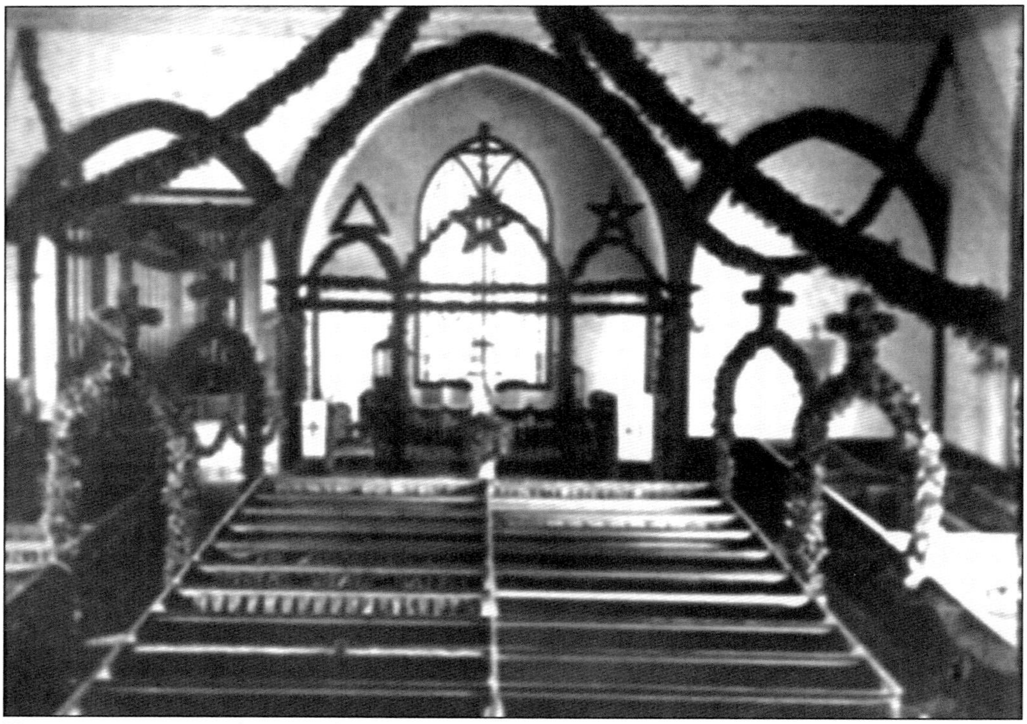

Here is an interior photograph of the original Trinity Episcopal Church, decorated for the Christmas season. It has been said that Trinity Episcopal Church was one of the first churches to use fresh greenery to decorate for Christmas.

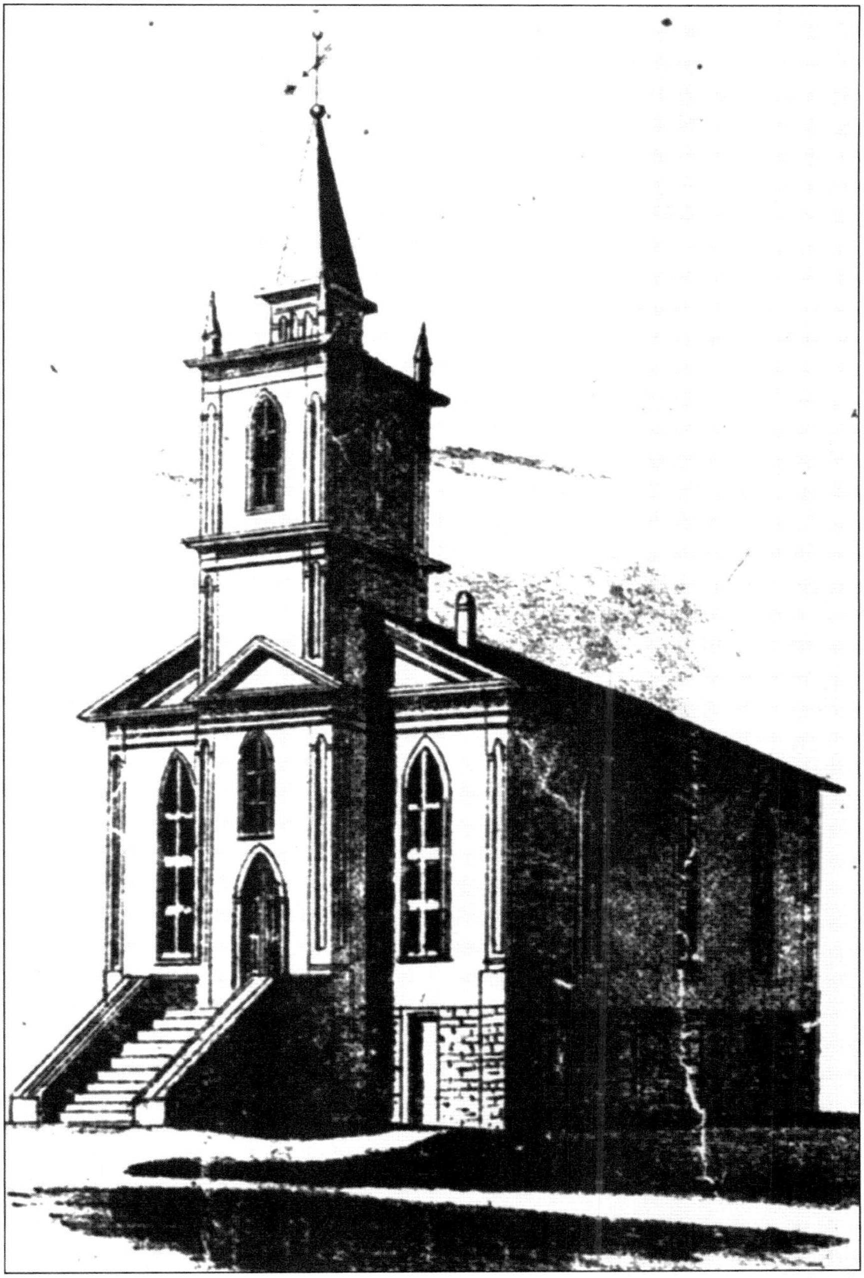

The Trinity Episcopal Church was organized January 13, 1831. While the first church edifice was being built, services were held above the post office. On November 18, 1833, the cornerstone of the first church was laid. The new building boasted a basement of stone and a superstructure of wood on Bayard Street. This was the church where Elizabeth Cady Stanton sent her sons to Sunday school. Even though she was not a regular churchgoer, she felt that the boys should have some exposure to religion. The boys were most impressed with the red "dress" that the priest wore. The building served the young congregation well until the new cornerstone was laid June 2, 1886, on lower Fall Street. Up until a few years ago, the original building was used as a ruler factory.

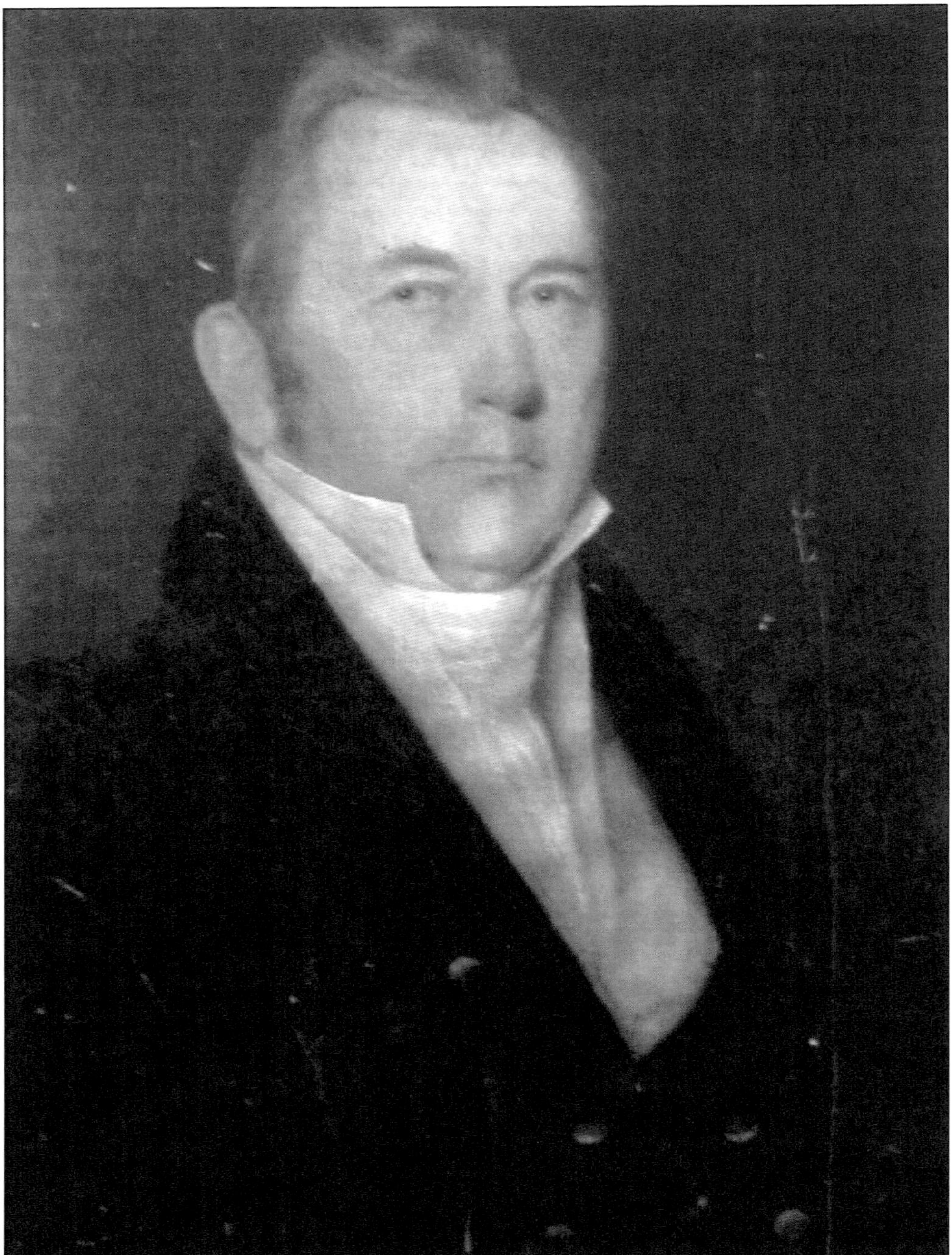

Col. Wilhelmus Mynderse, born in Albany on July 11, 1767, arrived in what was to become Seneca Falls as an agent of the Bayard Land Company in 1795. Under his leadership the first gristmill and sawmill were built in this part of the state, known as the Red Mills because they were painted red. As Seneca Falls grew, Mynderse donated land for churches, a school, and a park. Mynderse was known as a fine-looking, courteous, and cultured gentleman, and he fully realized the resources of Seneca Falls.

This daguerreotype is of Jane Clark, who was the first European to be buried in Restvale Cemetery. Clark named the cemetery because she found it extremely restful and located in a lovely vale. She died shortly after this portrait was taken. Cemeteries were becoming more than just places to lay loved ones to rest. They were designed as parks where one could spend a pleasant afternoon in a peaceful setting.

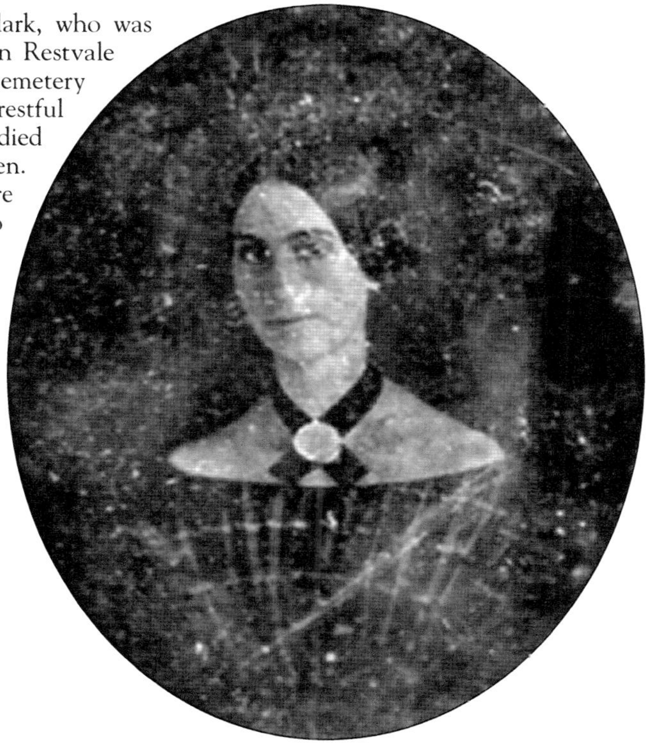

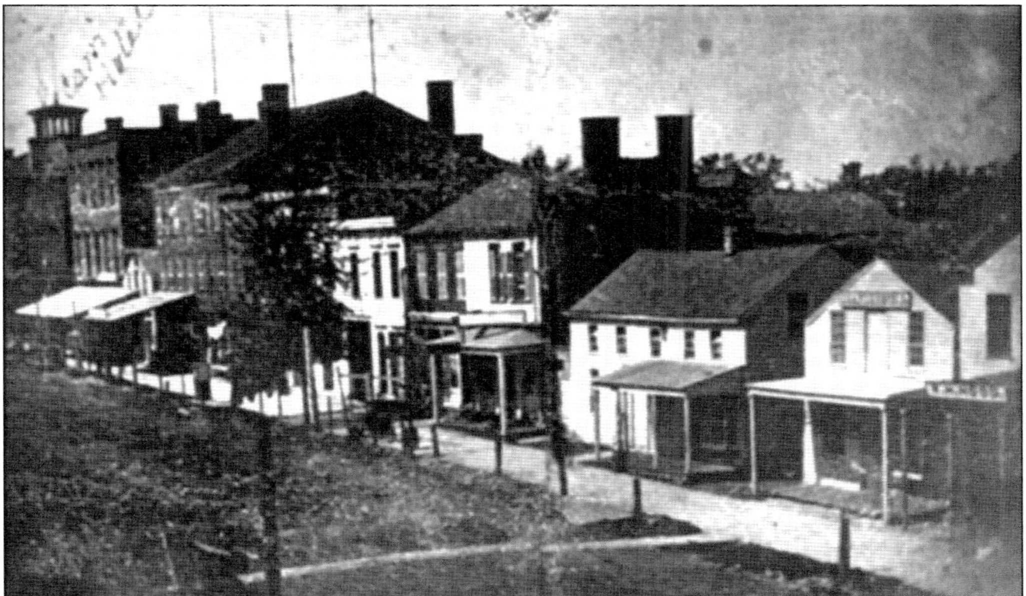

One of the earliest photographs taken of Fall Street in Seneca Falls, this dates from the 1860s and is of the north side of the street near the corner of State Street. One can just see the edge of the Carr Hotel on the left. Seneca Falls experienced rapid growth during the Civil War with the government contracts for socks and the grain that was milled for the Union army.

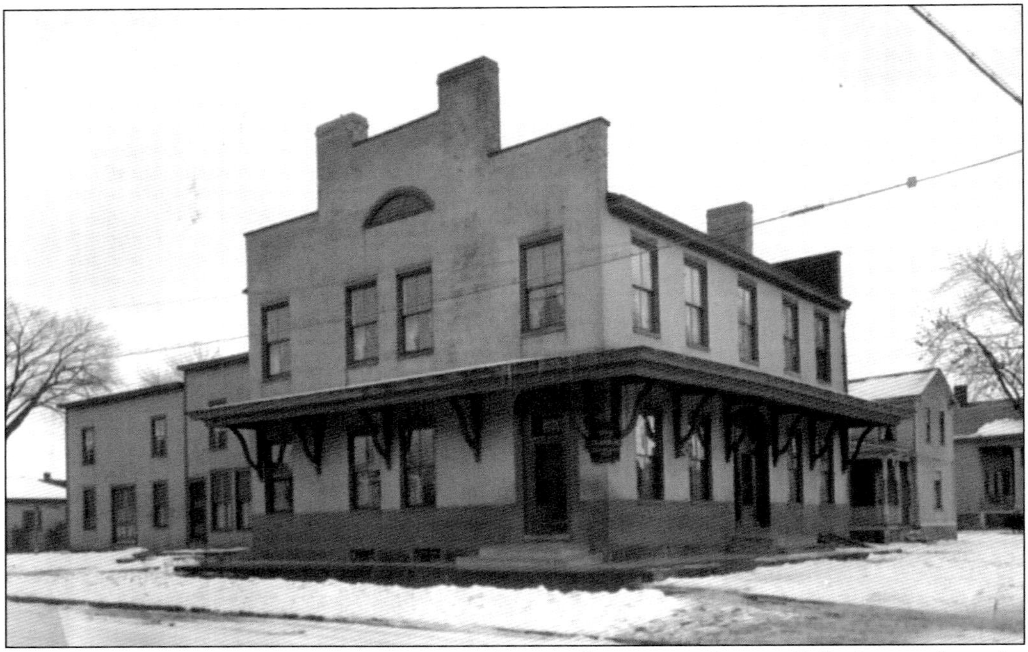

The Franklin Hotel is one of the oldest buildings still in use in Seneca Falls. Located on the south side of the Seneca River near Judge Gary V. Sacketts block of buildings, it was also used as a trolley stop for the Geneva-Cayuga Lake Railroad. The exterior of the building has changed very little since it was first constructed.

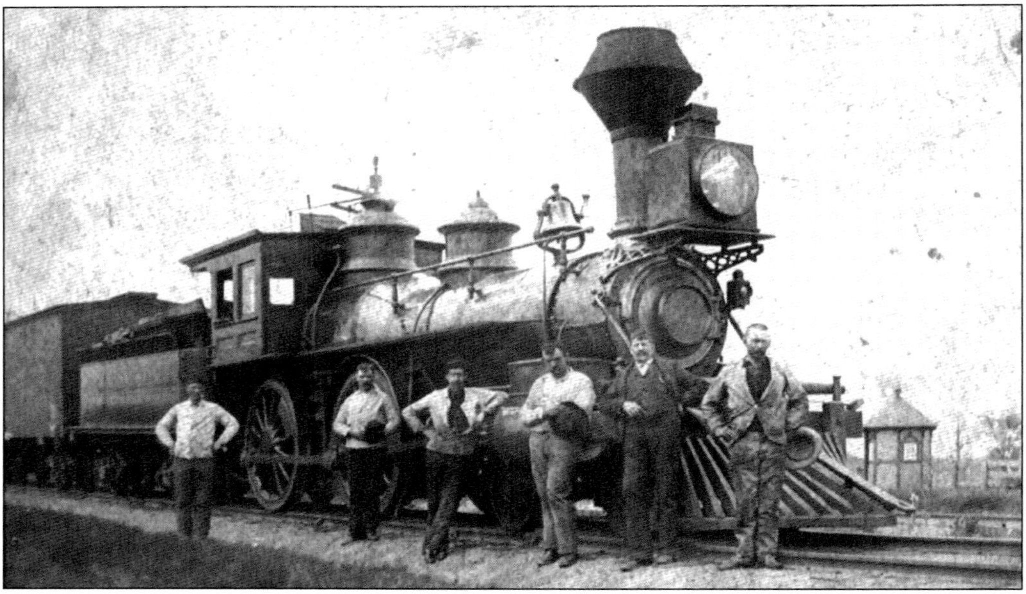

This steam engine is very similar to the engines used by the trains that first came through Seneca Falls in 1841. The railroad followed the rivers, Native American trails, and canals through Seneca Falls. Any one wishing to go west in the 1840s came through Seneca Falls. Immigrant trains were full as they made their way to the new lands in the Midwest and the gold fields of California.

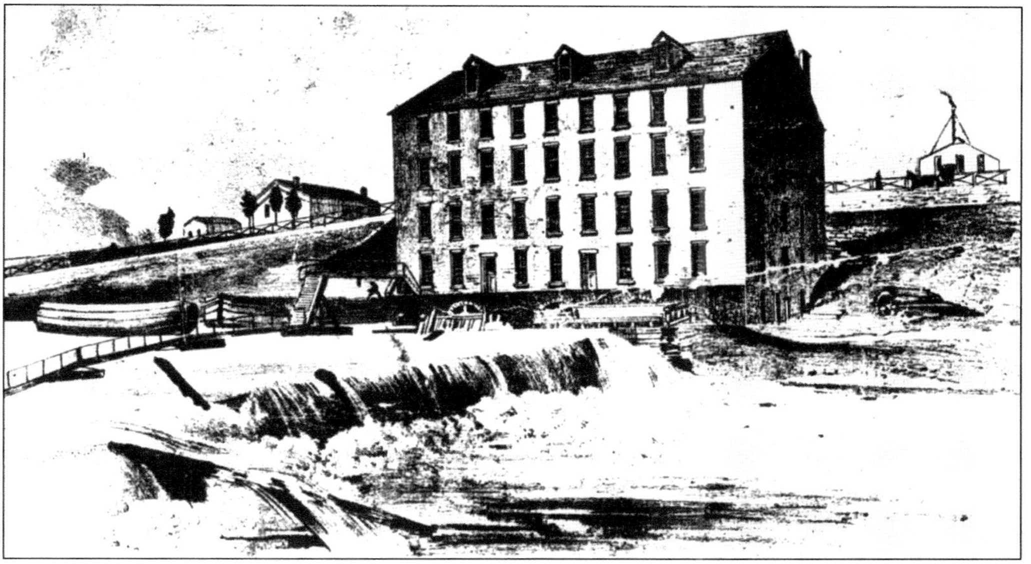

Arnett (or City) Mill was one of the early stone mills on the Seneca River at the foot of Water Street. This picture is from an 1859 map; many local buildings are depicted on the margins of the map. The mill stood until the 20th century when it was demolished.

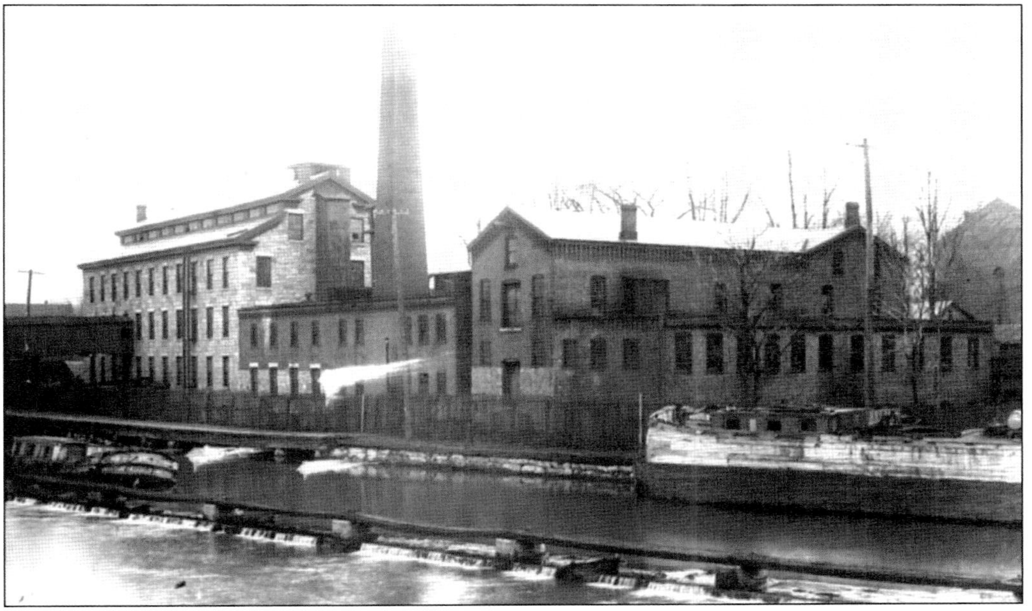

Seneca Woolen Mill was built in 1844 by a group of local businessmen led by Gary V. Sackett. The total cost of construction was $7,500. The mill was bought and sold several times and changed names over the years. The mill closed in 1995 and is now expected to become the new home of the National Women's Hall of Fame.

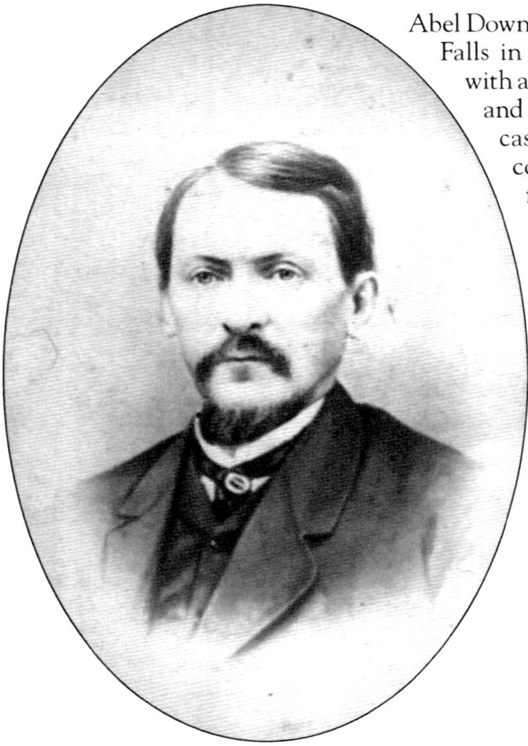

Abel Downs was the first to manufacture pumps in Seneca Falls in 1840. These early pumps were mainly wood with a cast-iron spout. In 1844, with John W. Wheeler and Smith Briggs, he started to manufacture cast-iron pumps. The shop was located on the corner of Green and Ovid Streets and was the first in Seneca Falls to use a steam engine to drive the machinery.

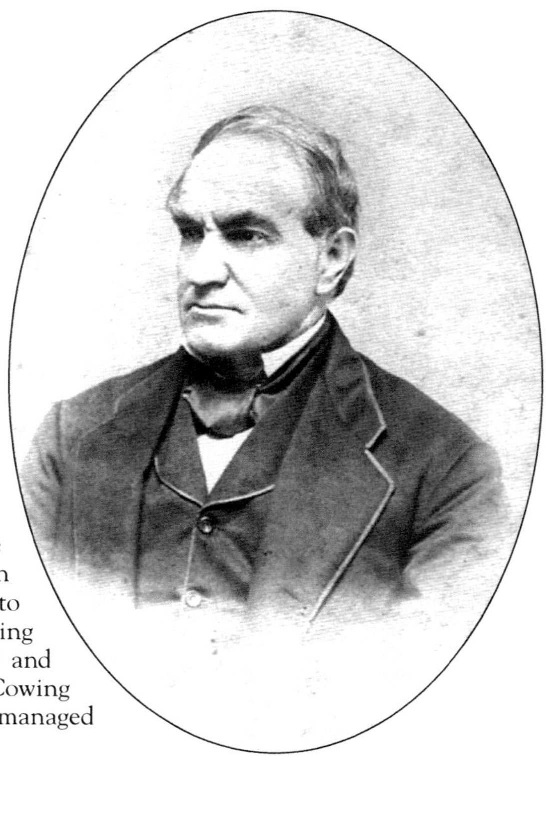

John P. Cowing, born in Seneca in 1807, was the youngest of 21 children. Moving to Seneca County in 1840, John, his wife Elizabeth Malay, and their three children bought Paine and Caldwell, and began to manufacture wooden pumps. In 1858, Cowing and his sons built a large six-story factory and manufactured fire engines. Though Cowing suffered several financial setbacks, he always managed to rebuild on a greater scale.

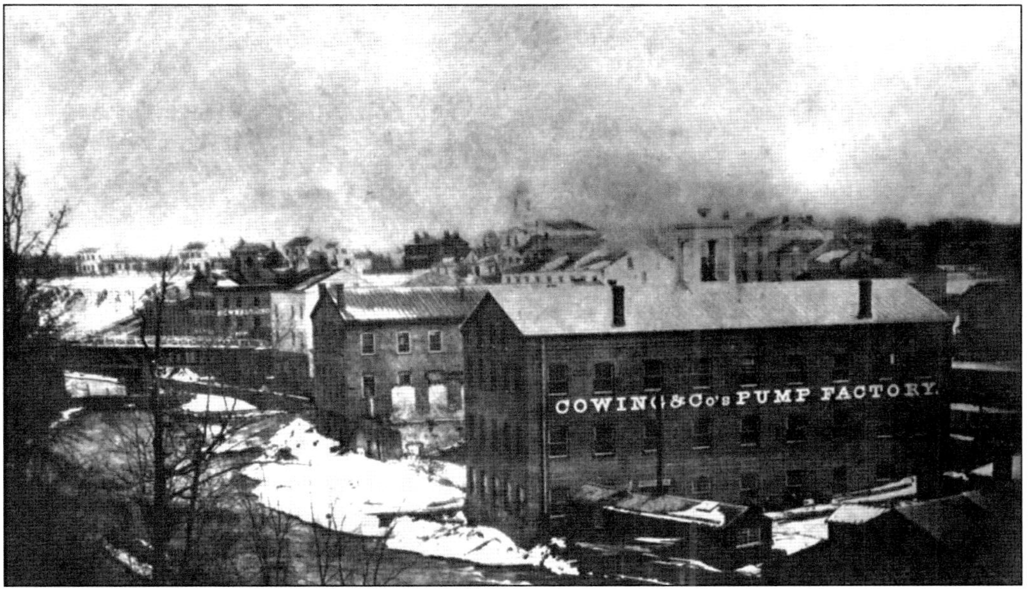

Cowing and Company was originally started in the old Marshall and Adams clock factory after the clock business had folded. John P. Cowing and Henry Seymour built the business up and were then joined by John A. Rumsey in 1849. Seymour retired in 1859; John P. took his sons Philo and George into the business. John A. Rumsey retired in 1864, and the Cowings carried on the business until 1875.

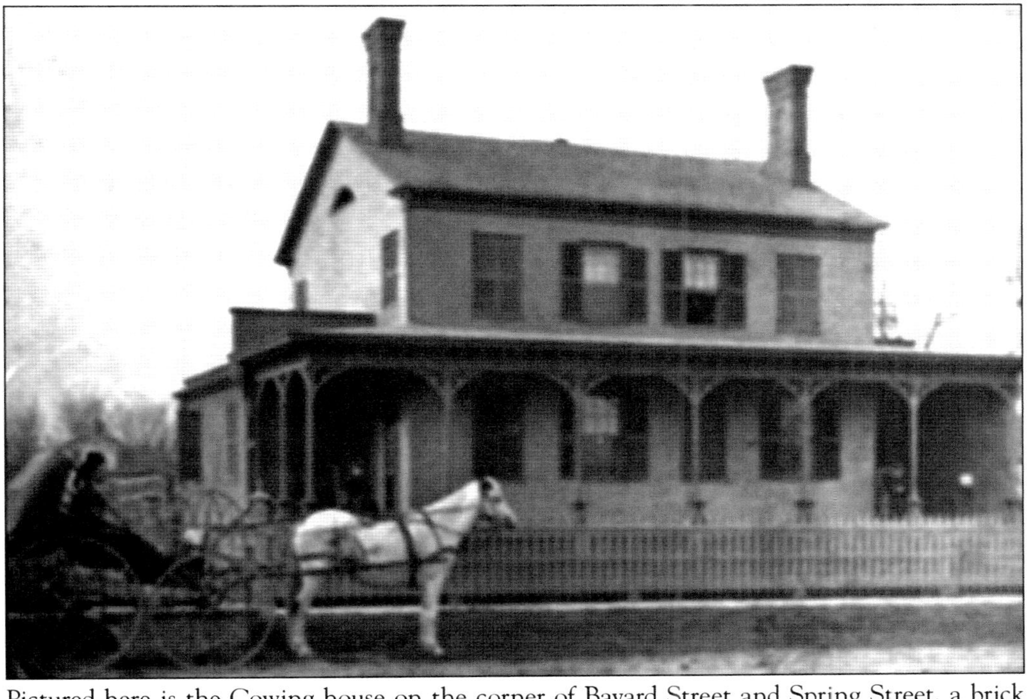

Pictured here is the Cowing house on the corner of Bayard Street and Spring Street, a brick Federal-style building that is still standing. The house overlooks what was once the flats, where Cowing and Company was located.

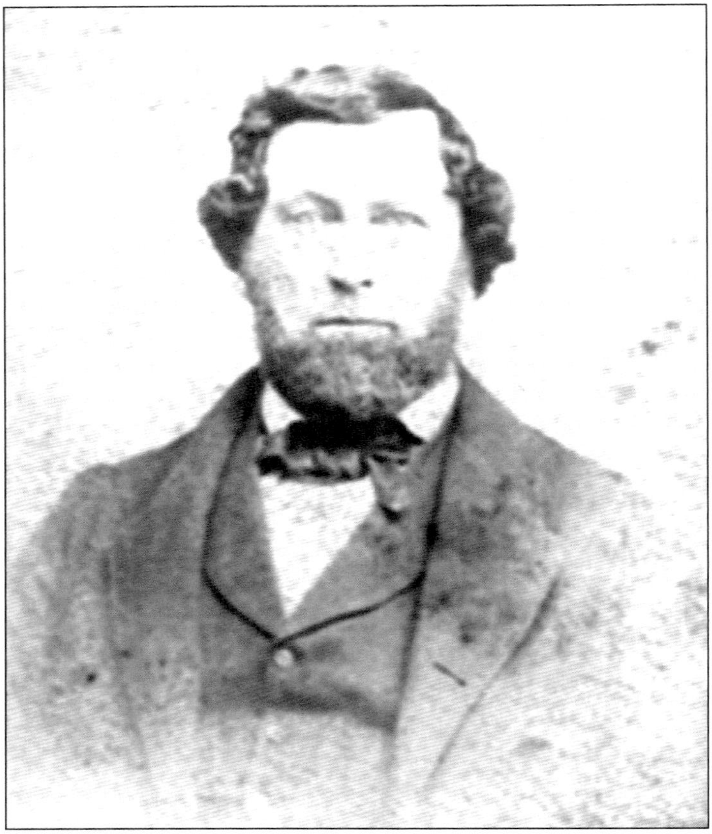

Thomas Carr, born in England 1807, came to America in 1836. Upon arriving in Seneca Falls, he took up farming and brewing. In 1856, Carr bought the Clinton House on the corner of Fall Street and State Street and renamed it Carr's Hotel. Carr was also street commissioner of Seneca Falls and had many trees planted in the village park as well as laying out Restvale Cemetery.

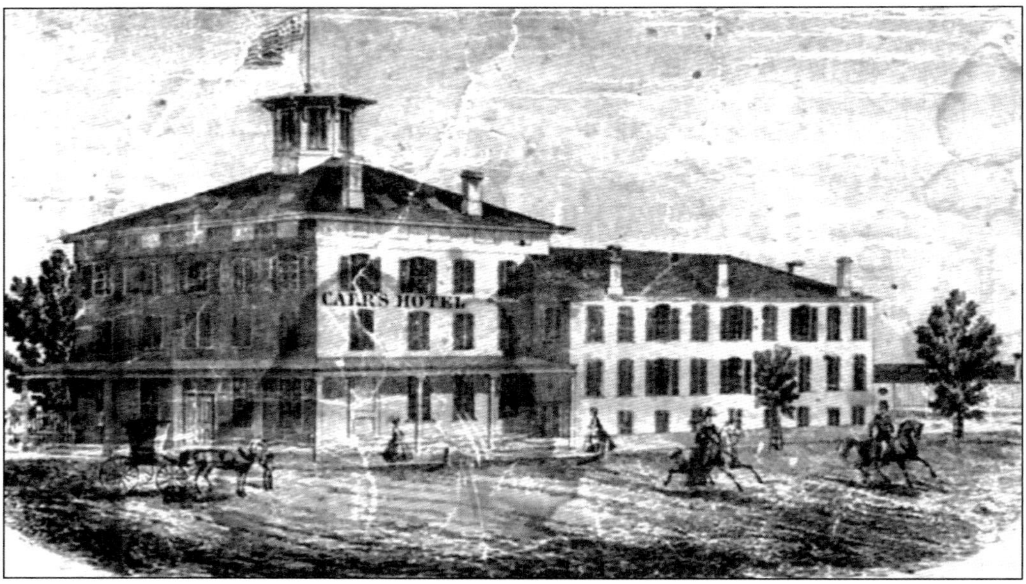

Carr's Hotel was the second hotel on that location; the first was the Clinton House, which was a stage stop on the Seneca Turnpike. The Carr House was completed by the summer of 1856 and opened to the public on the occasion of a firemen's tournament that summer.

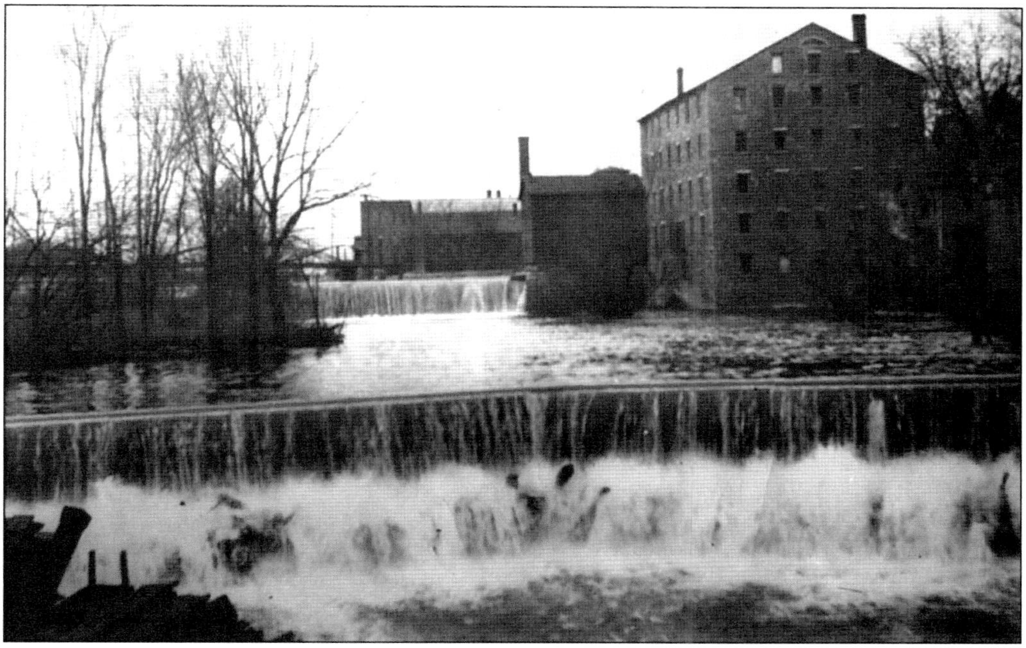

The falls were man-made. The Seneca River runs from Seneca Lake to Cayuga Lake and drops 42 feet. In the early days, they were just a series of rapids. When the village was settled, waterpower became available as dams were built to create mill runs. The falls powered the industries that made Seneca Falls a world leader in pumps and firefighting equipment.

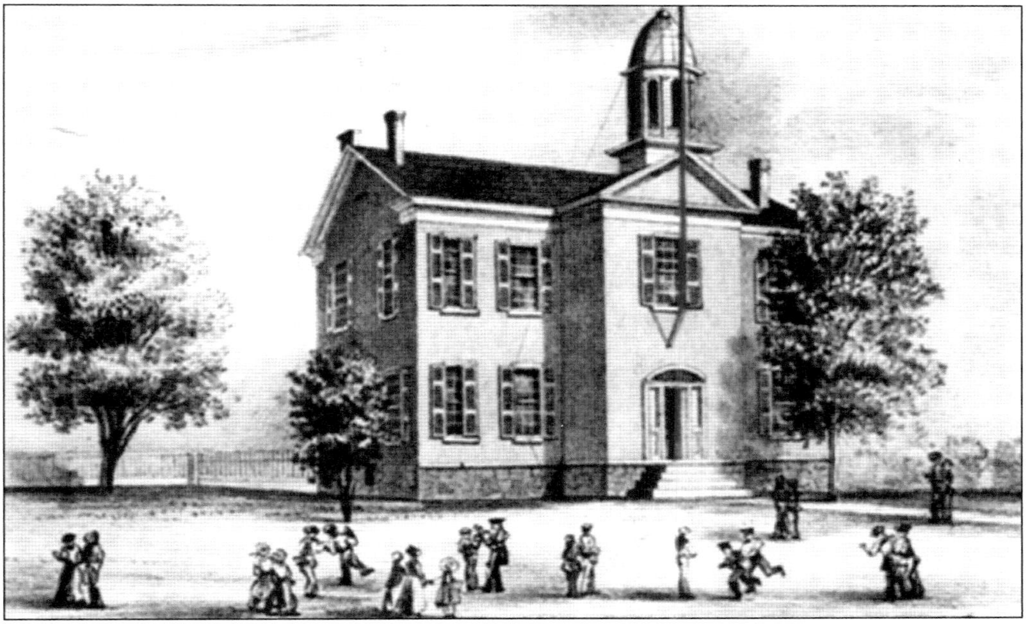

In 1832, Col. Wilhelmus Mynderse donated land for an academy, and a subscription was opened to build a building. Promoting this project were Asher Tyler, Gary V. Sackett, Richard Gay, William King, Abram Payne, M. B. Bellows, Isaac Smith, and D. W. Foreman. The cost was $1,666.32, which did not include the cupola.

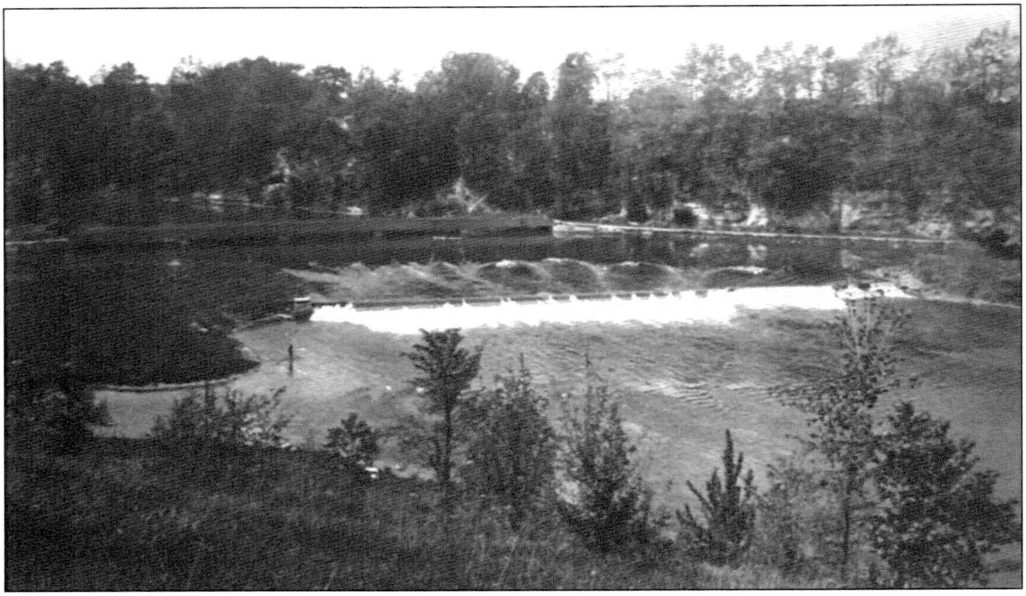

The lower falls on the Seneca River were located east of the village on the flats. The Cayuga-Seneca Canal was located on the south side of the river as it went through the village. Just above the lower falls, the canal crossed over to the north side at Brown's Bridge that can be seen in the background of the photograph. This area of the Seneca River would become Van Cleef Lake.

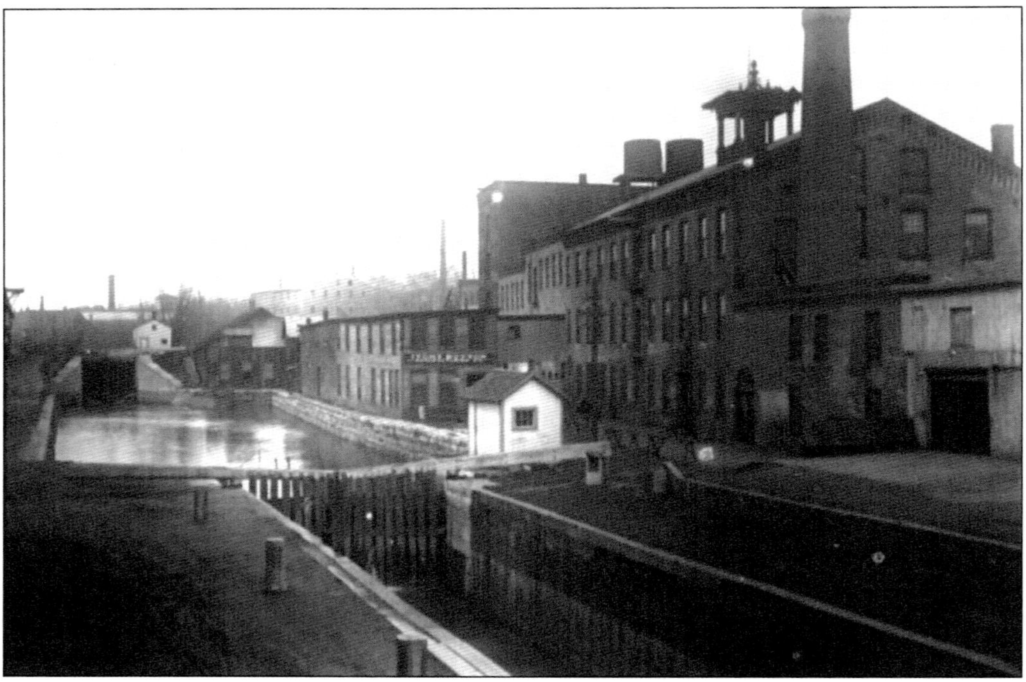

On the old Cayuga-Seneca Canal there were several locks through the village. One was located next to the Seneca Woolen Mill. Notice how the small lock is, one man could operate the lock gate. The white building is the lock keeper's house.

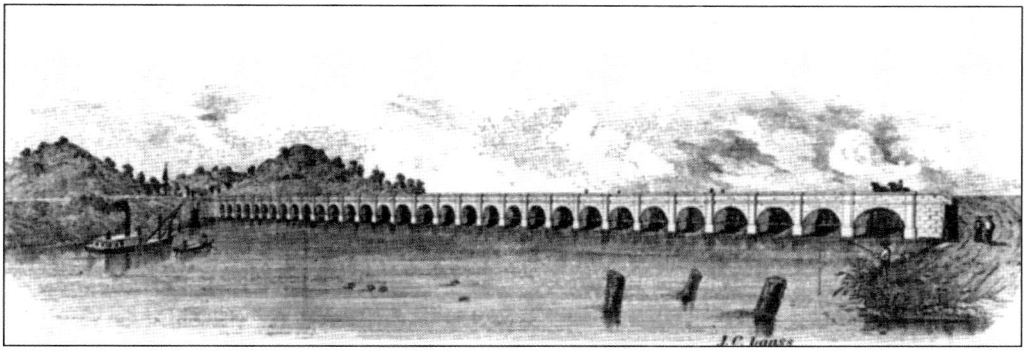

Richmond Aqueduct on the Erie Canal allowed the canal to cross over the swamp at Montezuma. The aqueduct was designed by Van R. Richmond, an engineer for the state who designed the bridges and locks for the Erie Canal.

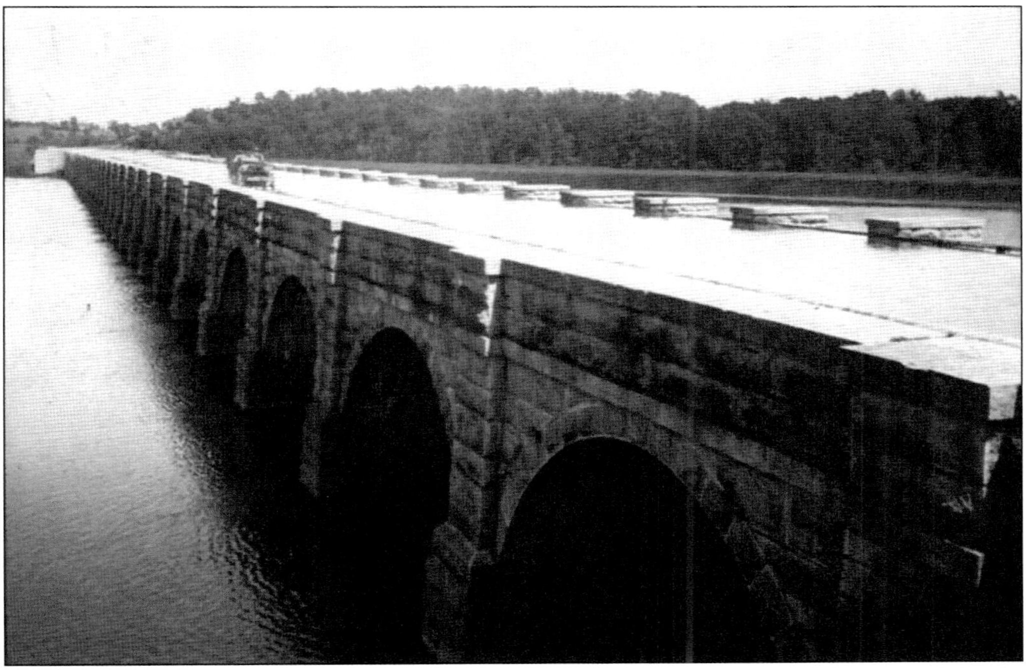

This photograph was taken in the early 20th century and shows that the aqueduct was large enough to accommodate an automobile. This was just one of a few aqueducts built on the Erie. A few of the stone pillars can still be seen at Montezuma Swamp.

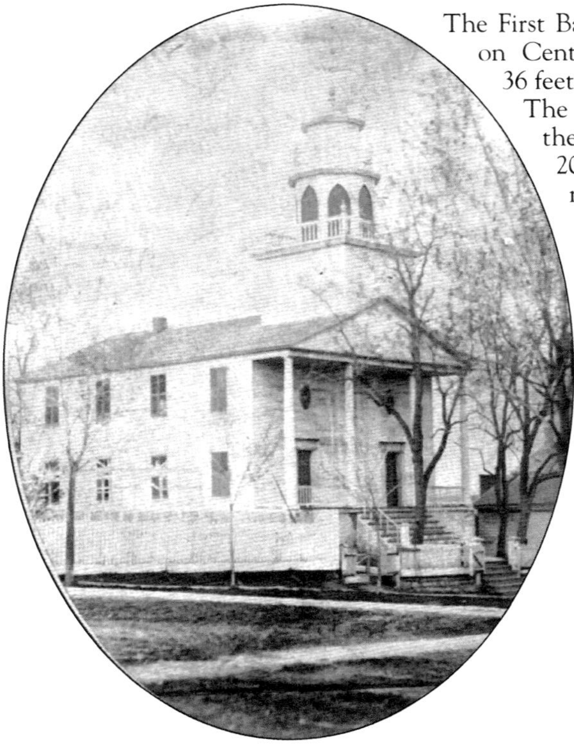

The First Baptist Church founded in 1828 was built on Center Street, a frame building measuring 36 feet by 44 feet with a steeple and a basement. The lot was purchased by Gary V. Sackett, and the building cost about $1,835. In the early 20th century, the Baptists moved to the north side of the canal into the former Wesleyan Methodist Church.

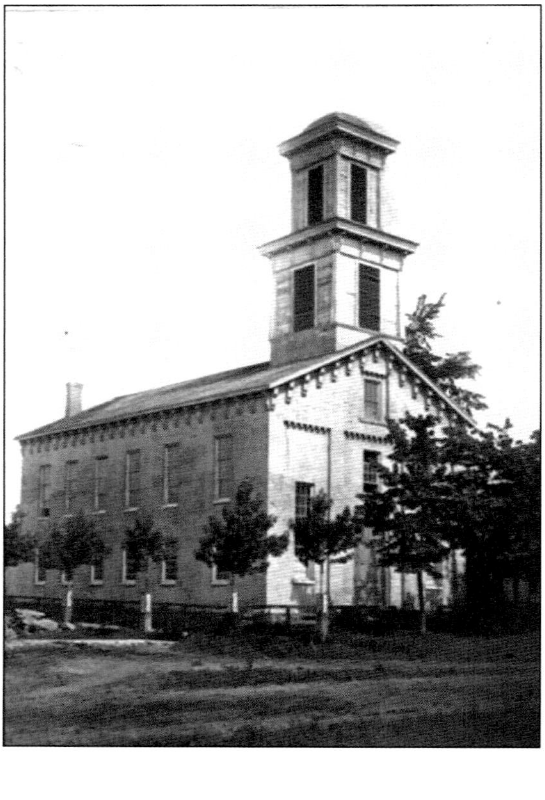

The Methodist Episcopal Church was incorporated on January 6, 1829. A subscription was stared for a building with $200 from Joseph Metcalf. Wilhelmus Mynderse donated a lot on State Street. The building was started in the summer of 1830 and was completed by the spring of 1831 for a cost of $3,000. In 1833, the Seneca Falls Church was detached from the circuit and has ever since been an independent station.

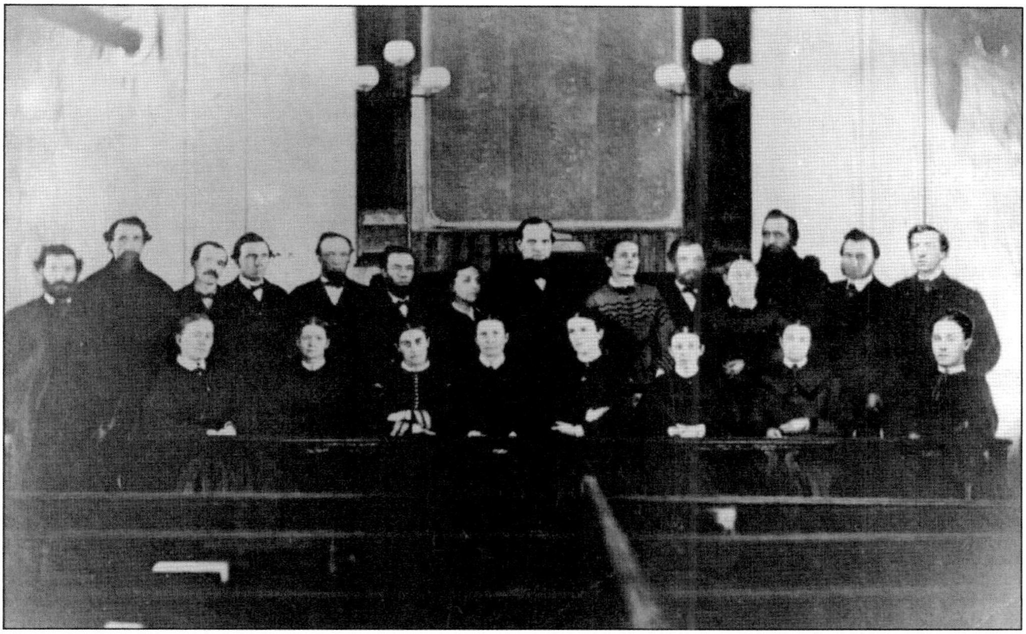

This photograph of the Wesleyan choir is thought to be the only photograph of the church in existence. The simple chapel, which was the site of the 1848 Convention for Women's Rights, has been the subject of an intensive search for an image of its 1840s appearance. A prize of $10,000 was offered for an image of the early building. None was ever found.

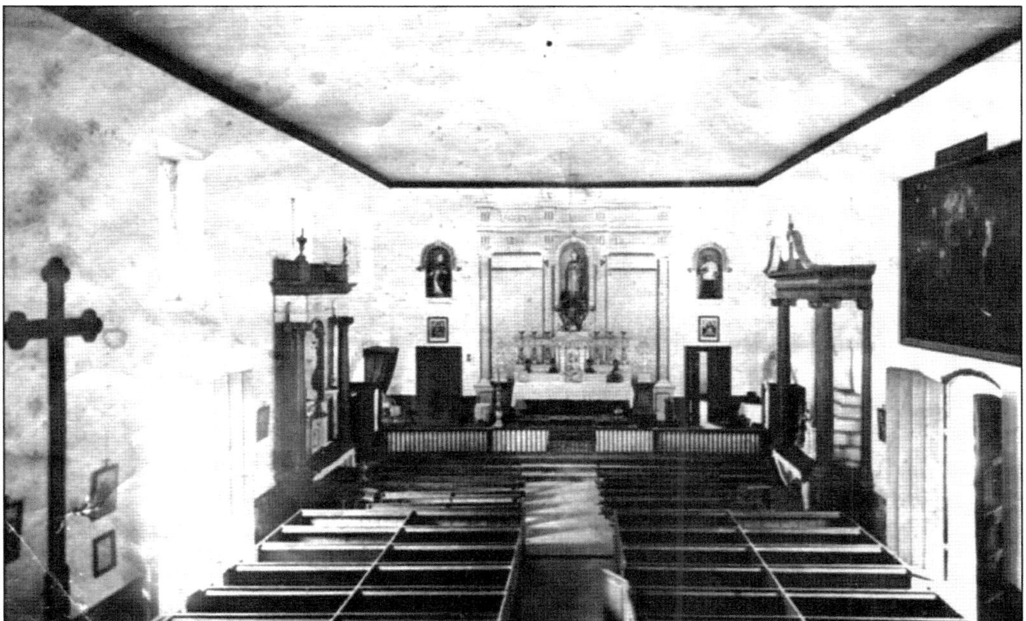

The first Catholic mass was celebrated in 1835 by Fr. Francis O'Donohoe in the home of Henry Graham. The gathering was so large that the floor gave way. That very day a subscription was started, and a small building was purchased on Swaby Street. The new church was dedicated to St. Jerome. In 1864, a new church was built and dedicated to St. Thomas.

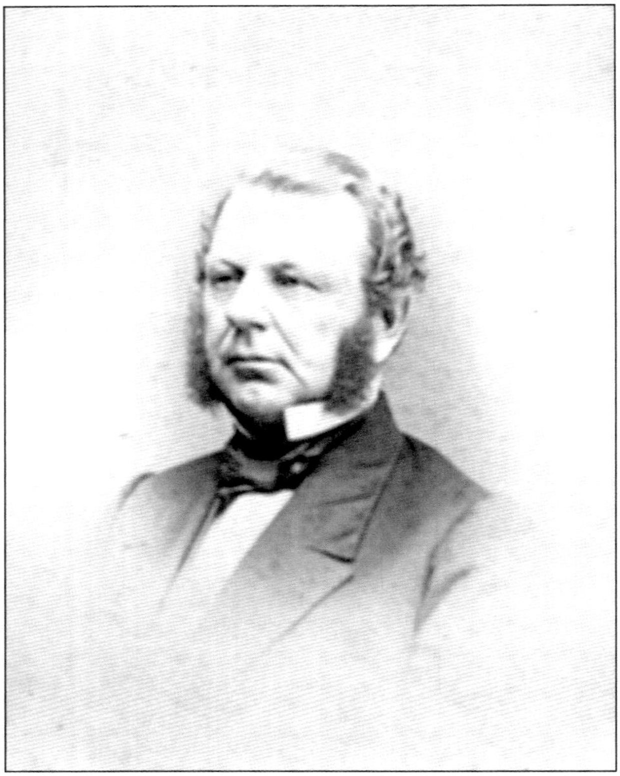

Edward Mynderse, son of Wilhelmus, was born in Seneca Falls in 1816. His mother was the daughter of Lawrence VanCleef and was the first European child born in Seneca Falls. Edward was identified with several firms in the village, including Silsby, Mynderse and Company, Downs, and was a stockholder in the Seneca Falls Woolen Mills.

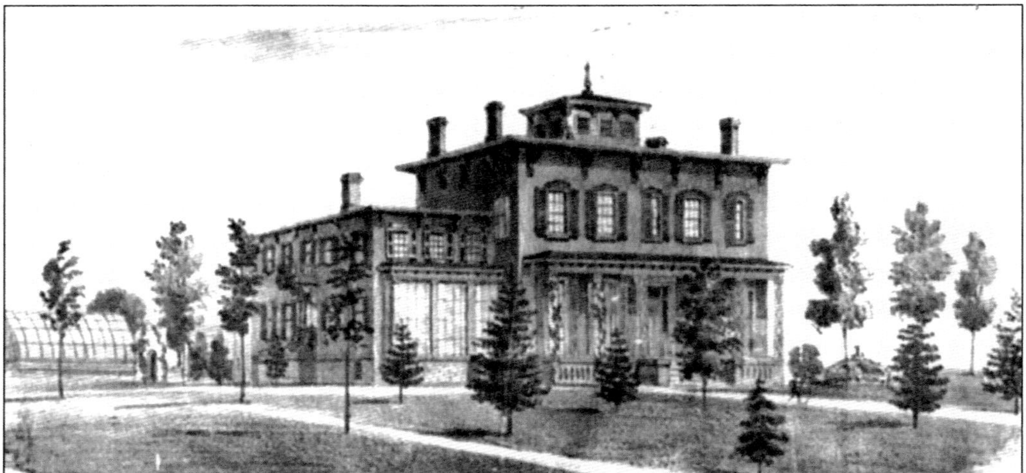

The Italianate-style home of Edward Mynderse located on Cayuga Street was purchased in the 1870s by Ellen Partridge and extensively remodeled in the 1880s by Rochester architect James Cutler. The house was changed to a Queen Anne style and is now the home of the Seneca Falls Historical Society.

Seabury S. Gould, the founder of Gould's Manufacturing Company, came to Seneca Falls in 1834 as a merchant. In 1852, he sold his interest in the mercantile business and engaged in manufacturing pumps at the corner of Ovid and Green Streets with Abel Downs in the firm known as Downs and Company. In 1864, Downs severed his ties with the company, and it became known as Goulds Pumps Manufacturing Company.

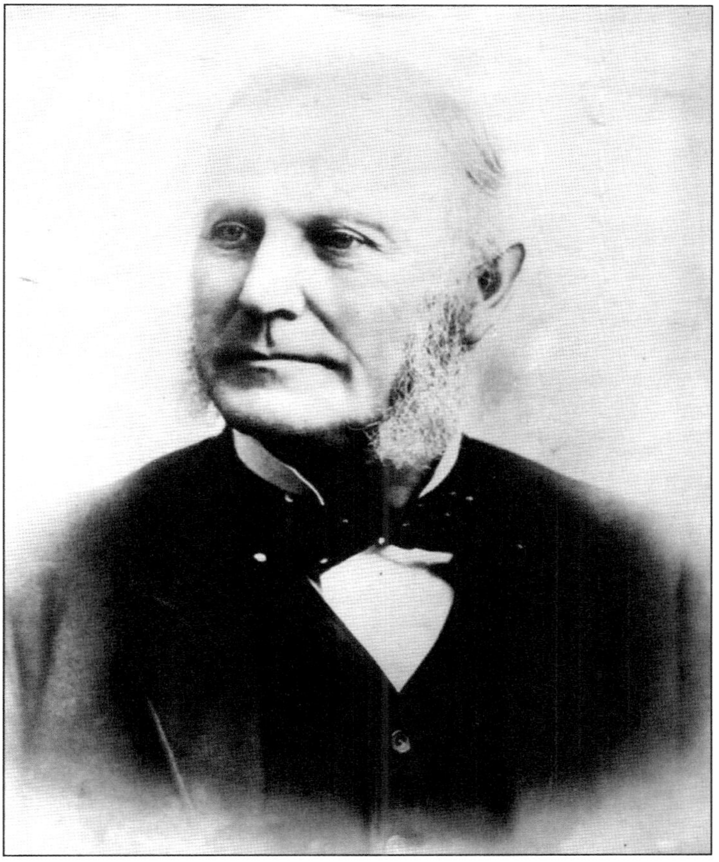

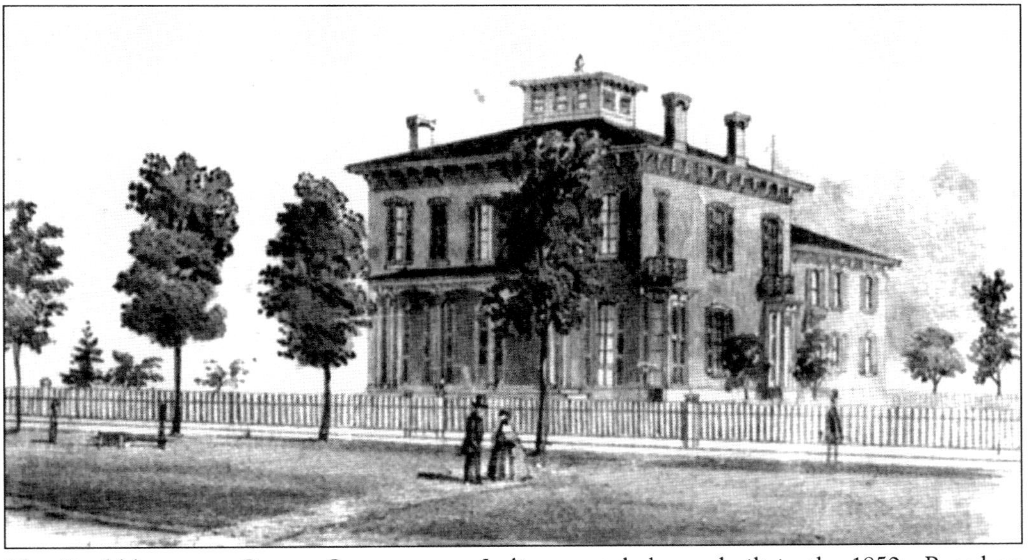

The Gould house on Cayuga Street was an Italianate-style house built in the 1850s. Based on Italian villas, these houses had a central stair that went all the way up to the attic. On the roof, a cupola with windows that could be opened would help cool the house in the summer time.

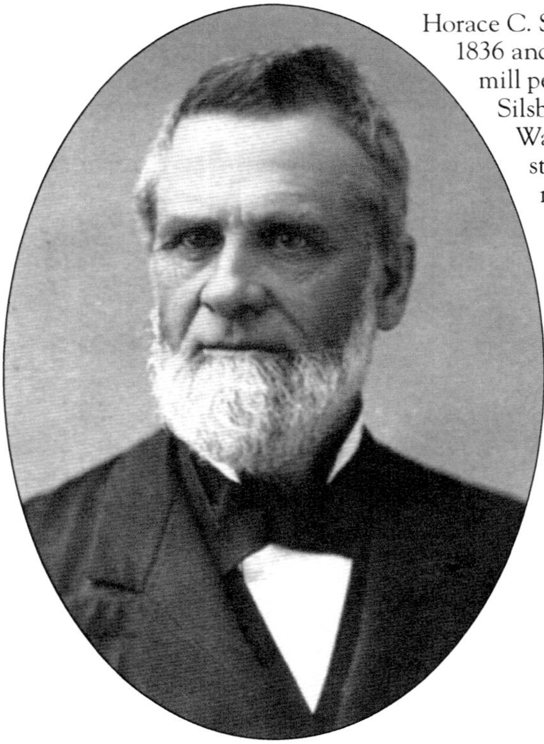

Horace C. Silsby arrived in Seneca Falls in the spring of 1836 and was involved in the manufacturing of axes, mill pecks, and edge tools with his brother William Silsby and William Wheeler. Working with Washburn Race and Birdsall Holly, he made stove regulators, rotary pumps, and finally rotary steam fire engines.

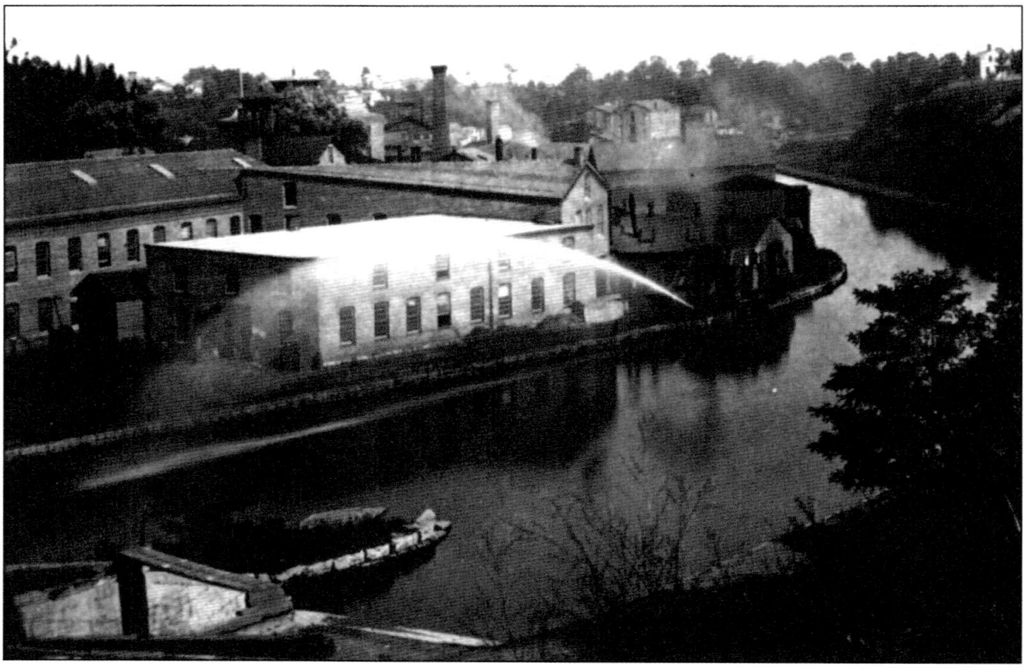

On one of the islands of the Seneca River, the Silsby Company tests one of their pumps. With the invention of a rotary pump, water could be thrown in a steady stream instead of a pulse from reciprocal pumps.

Two

WOMEN AND OTHER RADICALS

With the coming of the railroad in the 1840s, travel was much easier, and as people moved about the country, ideas were also being spread. Seneca Falls was on the main east-west railroad line that carried immigrants to the west for better land and to California during the Gold Rush. It was also easy to go to Rochester and Syracuse for business or pleasure. Some of the ideas that were spreading were abolition, anti-slavery, the free soil movement, women's rights, temperance, and Sunday school reform. In fact, this area was so active in all of these causes and there was such a fervor that it was known as the "Burned Over District."

The many Quakers who were living in Waterloo were very active with the Free Soil Party members of Seneca Falls. There were several abolitionist groups in the village. The Underground Railroad was very active in the Finger Lakes, and there were several freedom seekers living in the area.

Another cause was women's rights, which was championed by Elizabeth Cady Stanton. It was partly her frustration with having to live in this small village away from the stimulating intellectual life that she had known in Boston and Albany that caused her to call the first women's rights convention in 1848.

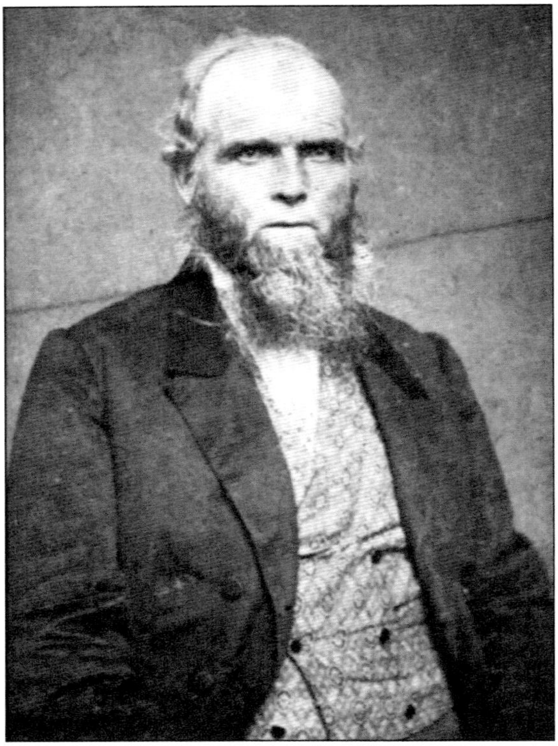

Ansel Bascom was the first president of Seneca Falls. With David Dudley Field, he was largely instrumental in the legislation giving women of New York State the right to own property in their own name. Bascom attended the first women's rights convention.

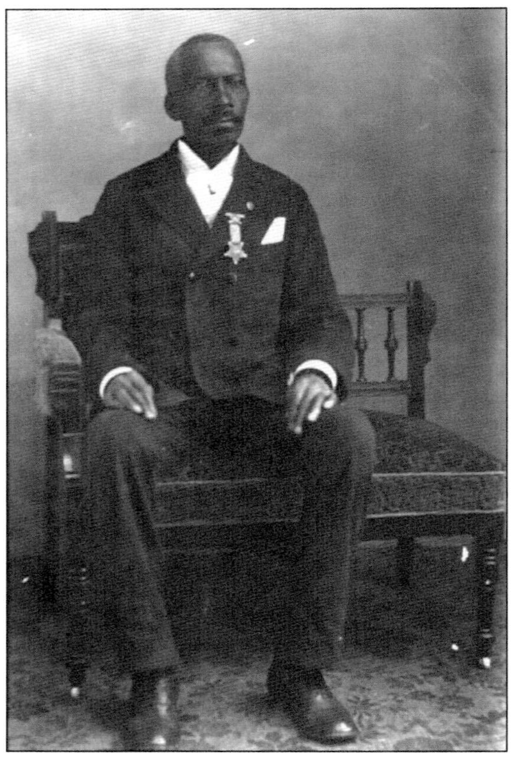

William Freeman, a freedom seeker who came to Seneca Falls on the Underground Railroad, was a hairdresser. He joined the Grand Army of the Republic and was attached to the Heavy Artillery Company G, Second Battalion, where he served with honor.

Jacob P. Chamberlain was president of the Seneca Woolen Mills which manufactured plain and fancy men's wear. Chamberlain also owned the upper Red Mills and the lower Red Mills. He farmed roughly 200 acres in Seneca Falls and was fairly successful at all his endeavors. Chamberlain was also a signer of the Declaration of Sentiments at the first women's rights convention in 1848.

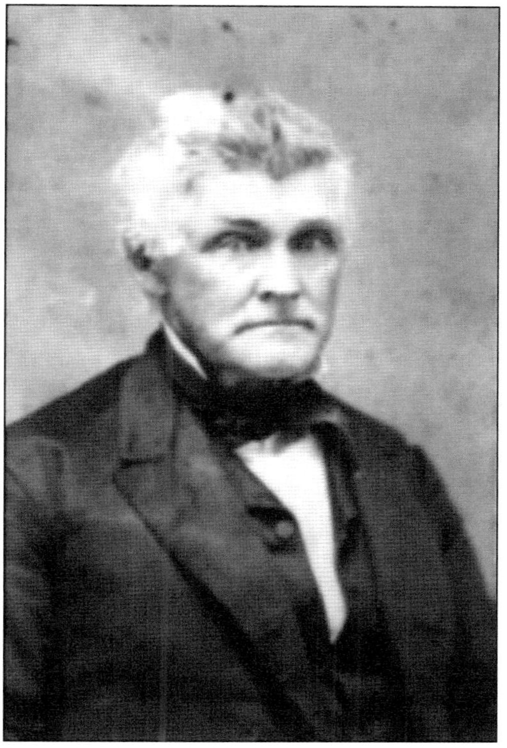

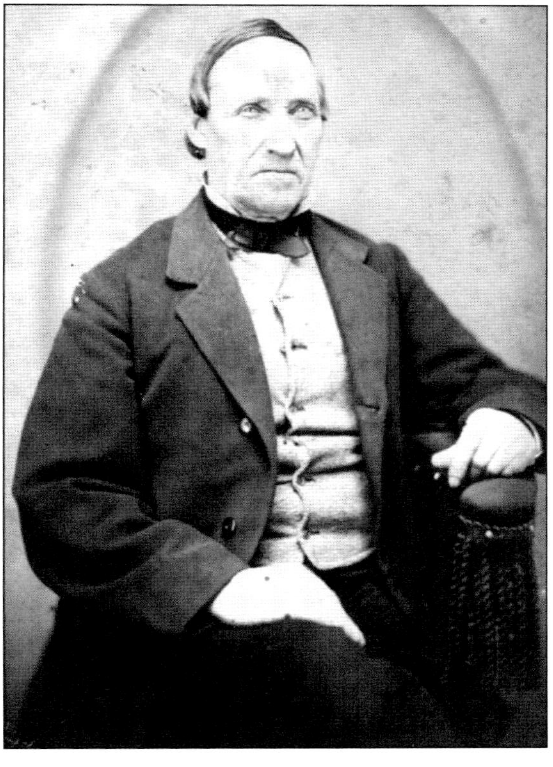

Henry Seymour, from 1840 to 1847, engaged with John P. Cowing in the manufacturing of pumps. Seymour continued to produce pumps for another four years after Cowing left the business. Seymour organized and planned the National Yeast Company of Seneca Falls. Seymour also attended the women's rights convention in 1848 and signed the Declaration of Sentiments.

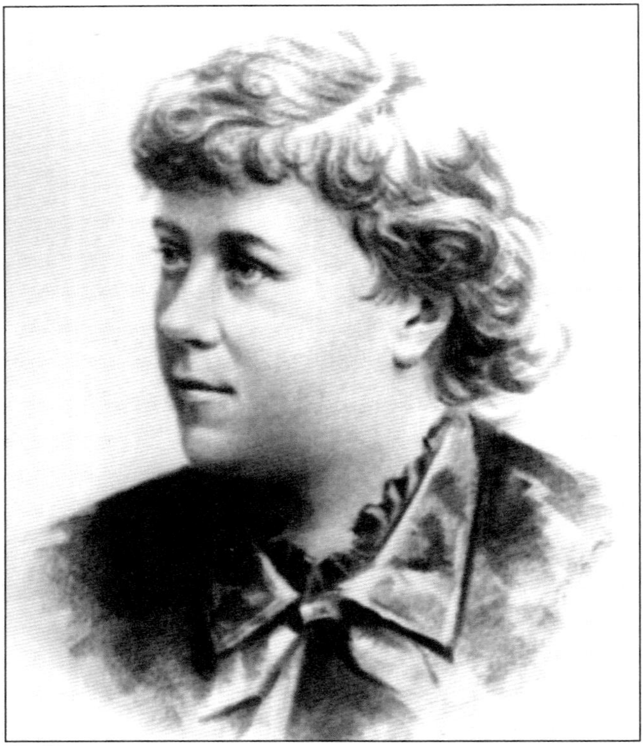

This drawing is of a young Elizabeth Cady Stanton, daughter of Judge Daniel Cady in Johnstown, who learned about the inequality that faced women as she listened to women ask for help in her father's law office. As a spirited young woman, she was determined to find a way to change the laws.

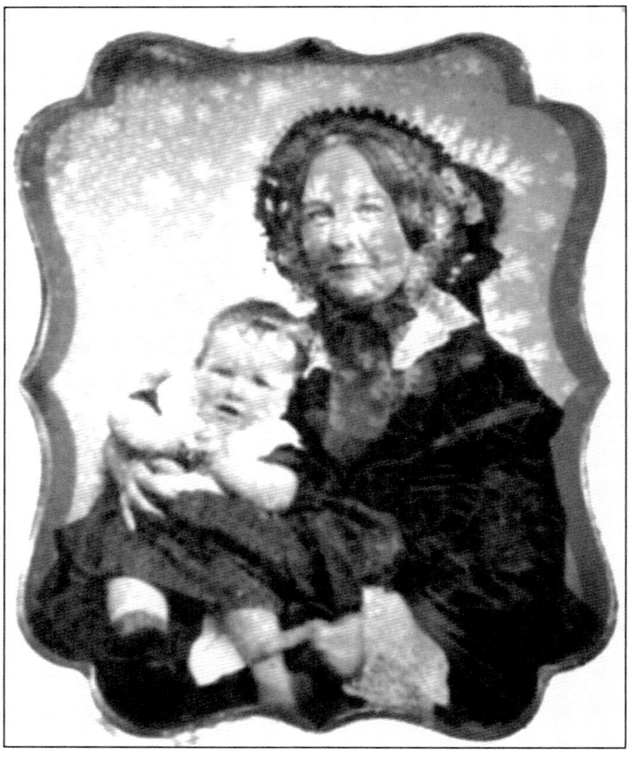

This ambrotype of Elizabeth Cady Stanton and her daughter Harriot was taken about 1856. Stanton was very happy to finally have a second daughter after four sons. While raising seven children, Elizabeth also made time to write articles and speeches demanding equal rights for women, especially the right to vote.

Lucretia Mott was a Quaker that Stanton had met while in England at an international abolition convention. Mott was an elected delegate but was refused admission to the convention floor and was only able to listen to the proceedings. Stanton and Mott became life-long friends and proponents of women's rights at this convention.

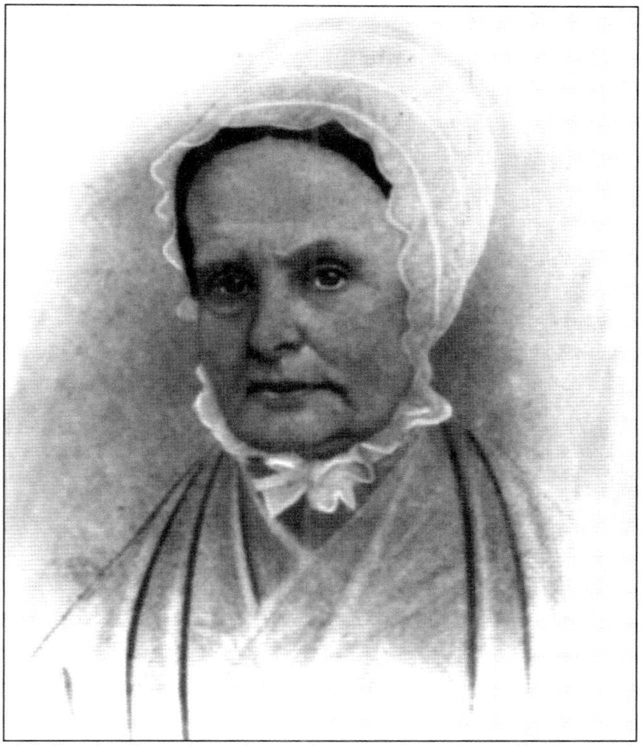

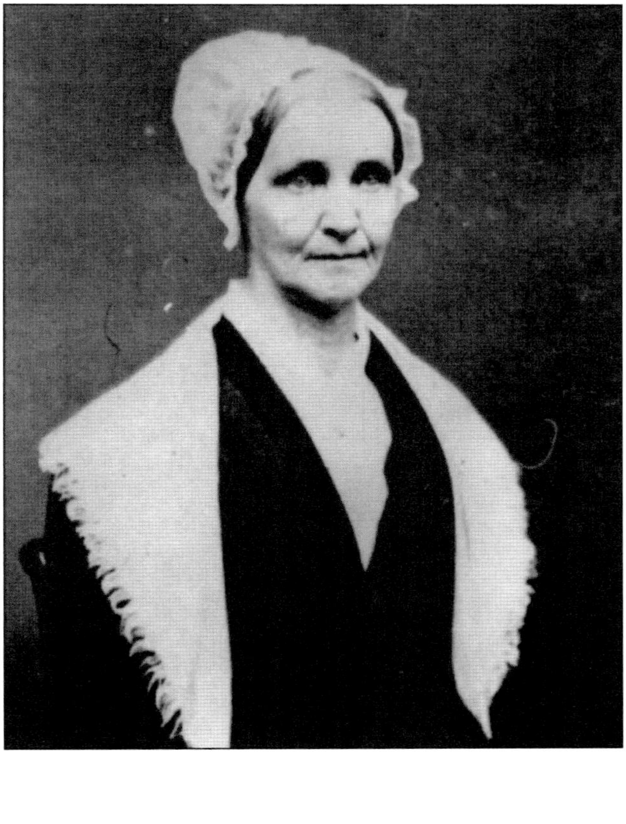

Mary Ann M'Clintock was a Quaker in Waterloo who met with Stanton, Mott, Jane Hunt, and Martha Coffin Wright in early July 1848 for tea. At this gathering, Stanton voiced her frustration with the status of women and the first women's rights convention was planned.

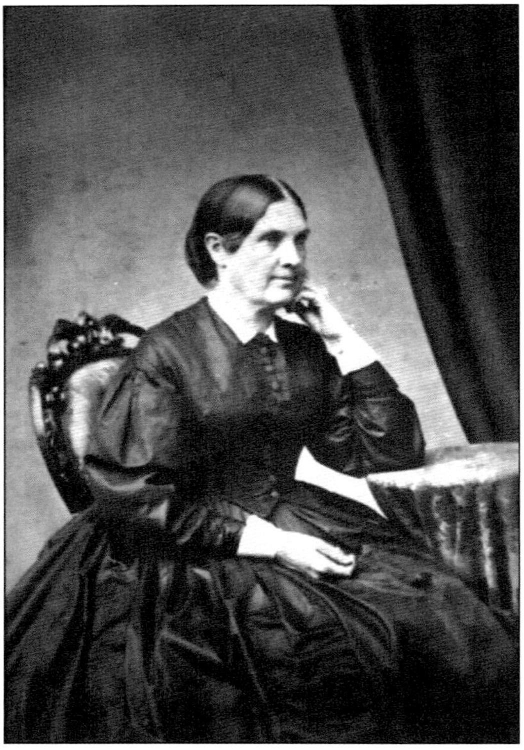

Jane Hunt was the wife of abolitionist Robert Hunt of Waterloo and also interested in Women's Rights. She was the hostess of the tea where the women's rights convention was conceived.

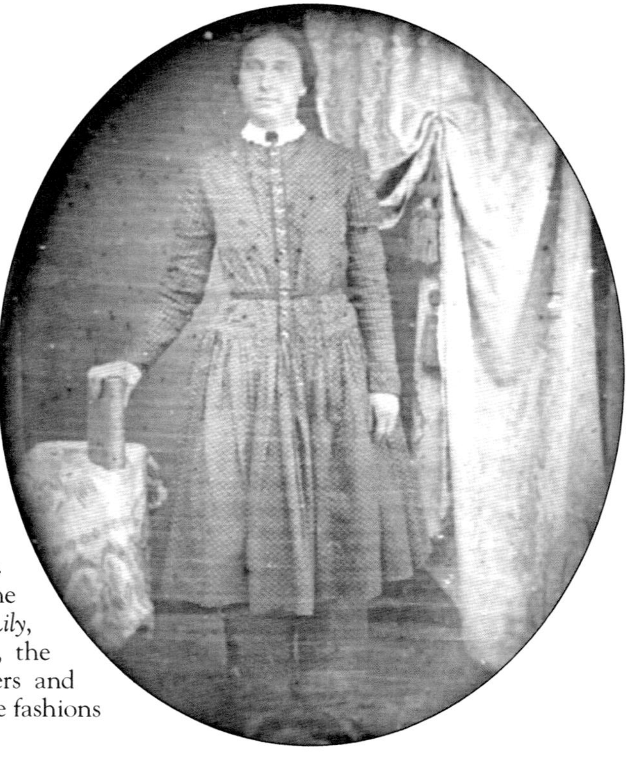

This is a daguerreotype of Elizabeth Smith Miller, cousin of Elizabeth Cady Stanton in a bloomer costume. Miller had been to Europe and was quite taken with the Turkish trousers that some of the progressive women were wearing. Bringing the idea to Stanton, the reform dress was touted in the *Lily*, Amelia Bloomer's newspaper. Thus, the costume became known as bloomers and was much more comfortable than the fashions of the time.

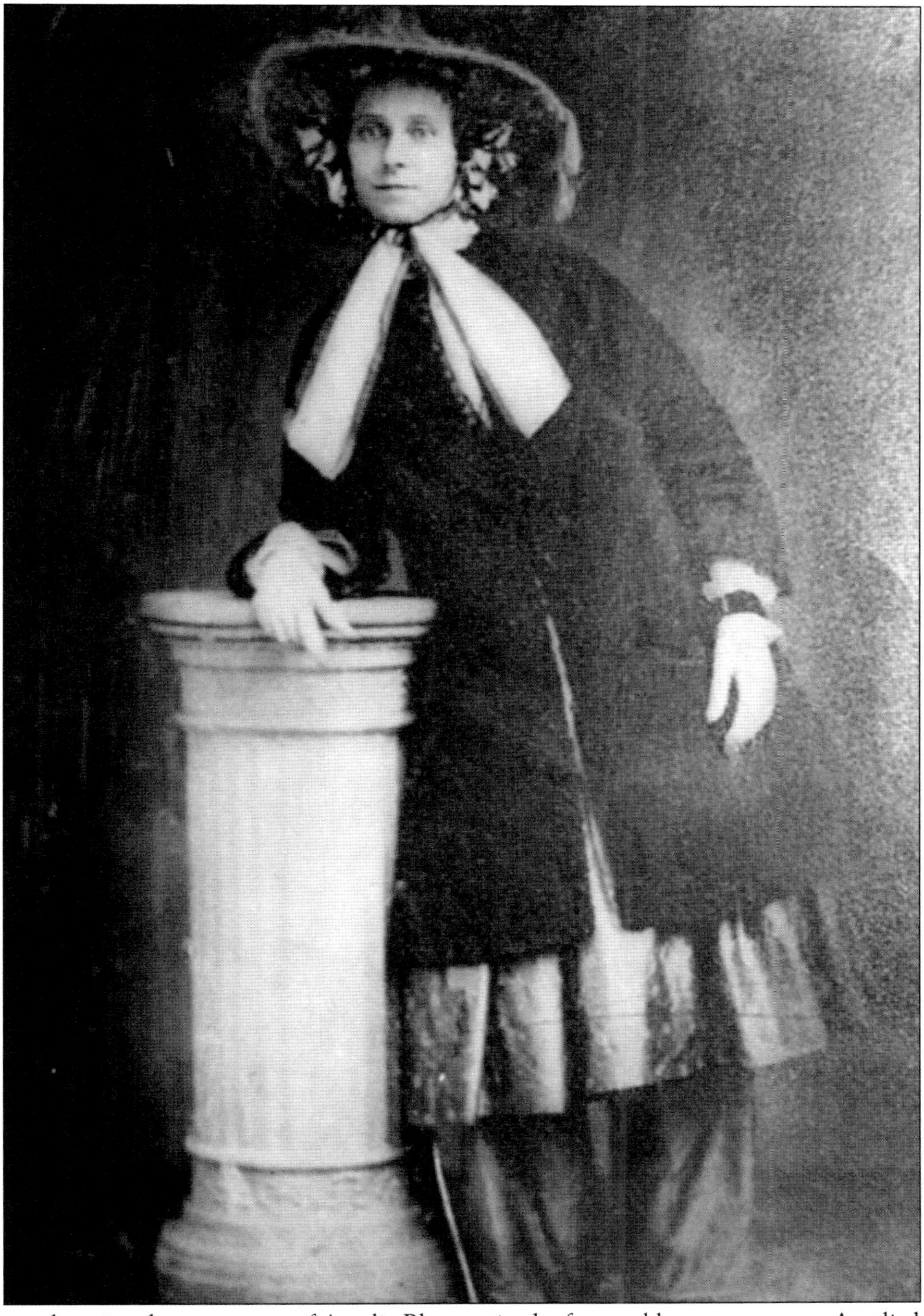

Shown here is a daguerreotype of Amelia Bloomer in the famous bloomer costume. Amelia had been a governess when she married Dexter Bloomer, a local lawyer. When Dexter became the postmaster of Seneca Falls, Amelia became his assistant, which was very unusual for the time. It was Amelia who introduced Stanton to Susan B. Anthony in front of Trinity Episcopal Church one afternoon.

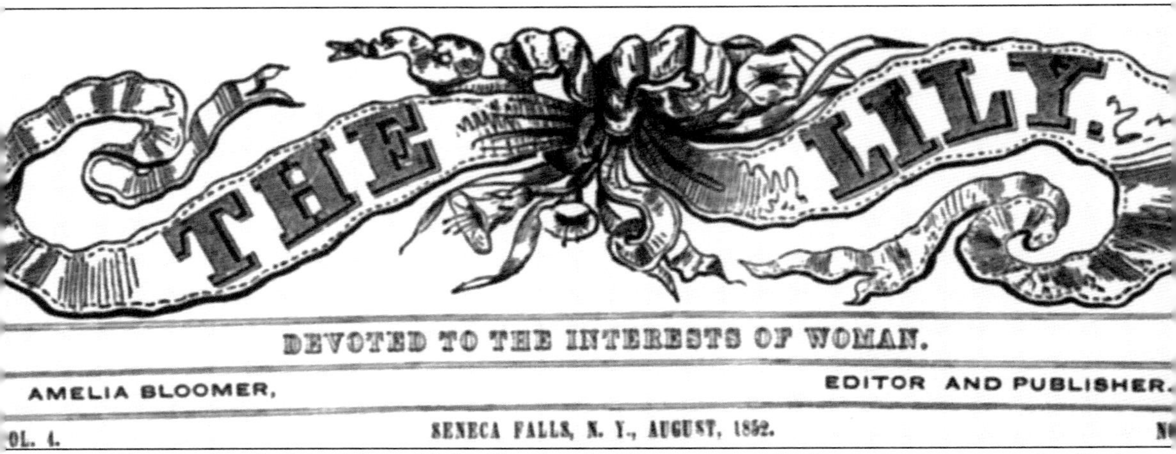
THE LILY.

DEVOTED TO THE INTERESTS OF WOMAN.

AMELIA BLOOMER, EDITOR AND PUBLISHER.

OL. 4. SENECA FALLS, N. Y., AUGUST, 1852. N

The masthead of the *Lily*, published by Amelia Bloomer, was the first newspaper owned, edited, and published by a woman for women. Many subjects were discussed such as temperance, dress reform, and women's rights.

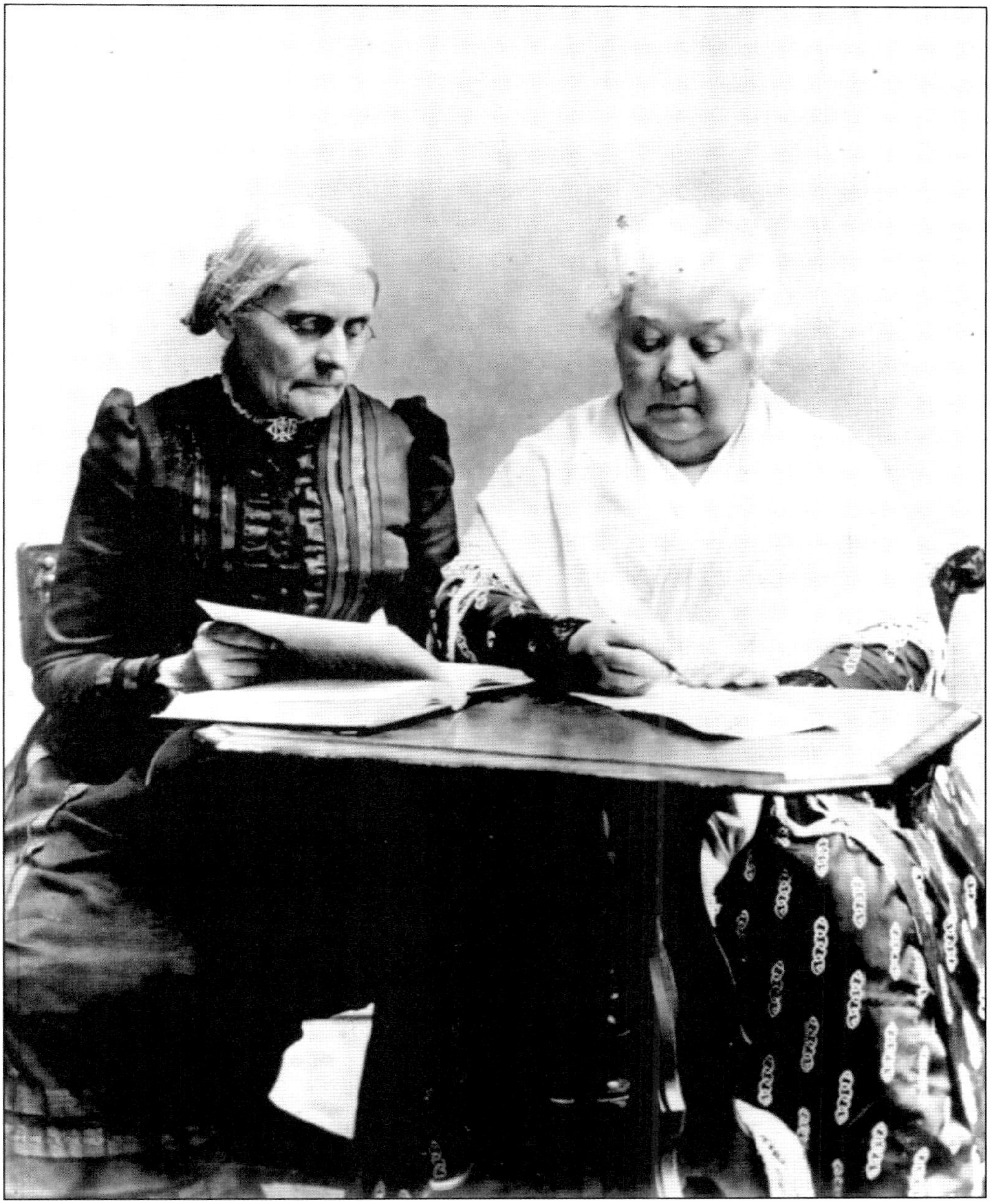

Susan B. Anthony (left) and Elizabeth Cady Stanton were the primary leaders of the women's rights movement. Both women were strong supporters of the right to vote and pressed the issue. Stanton wrote the speeches while Anthony traveled across the country to deliver them.

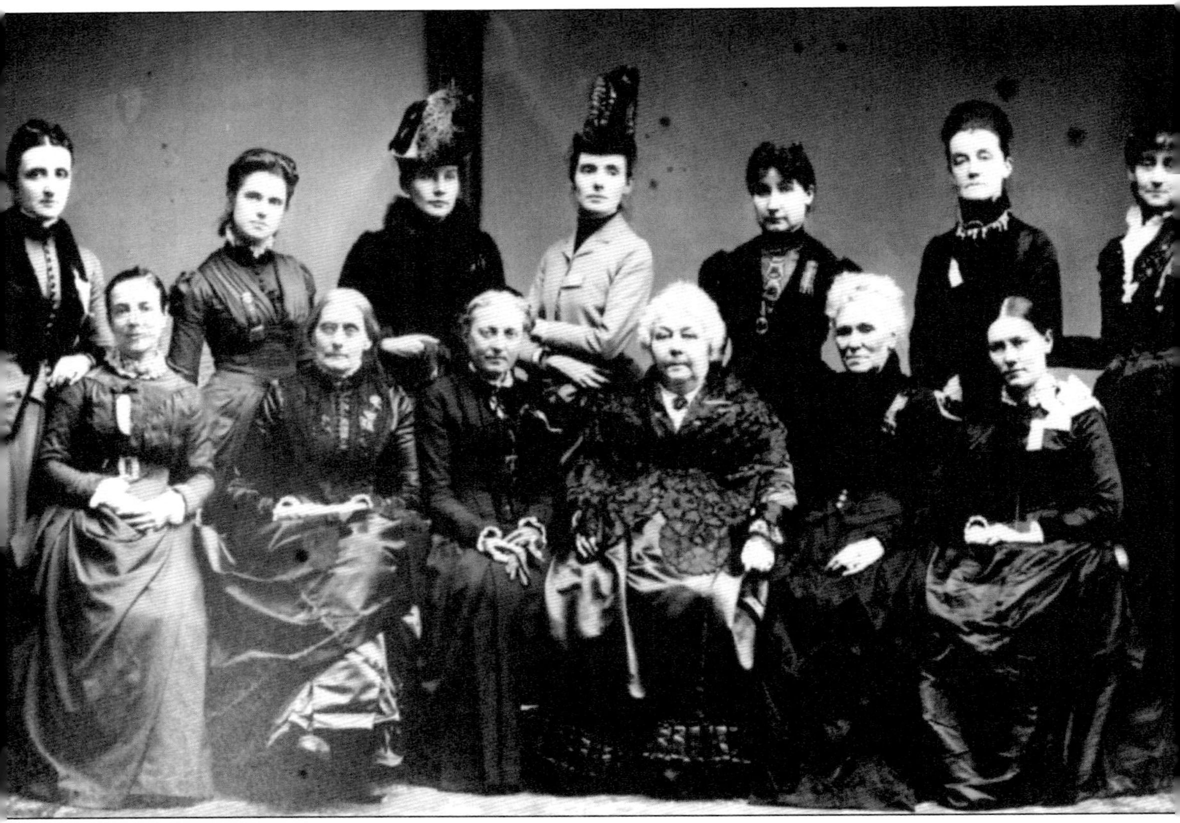

This is an International Women's Congress meeting held in Washington, D.C., March 25 to April 1, 1888. Seen here are, from left to right, (first row) Laura Chant (Scotland), Susan B. Anthony (Rochester, New York), Isabelle Bogelot (France), Elizabeth Cady Stanton (New York), Matilda Joslyn Gage (Fayetteville, New York), and Baroness Alexandra Gripenberg (Finland); (second row) Bessie Starr Keefer (Canada), May Wright Sewell (Philadelphia), Rachel Foster (Philadelphia), Alice Scatched (England), Sophia Groth (Norway), Margaret Moore (Ireland), and Margaret Dilke (England).

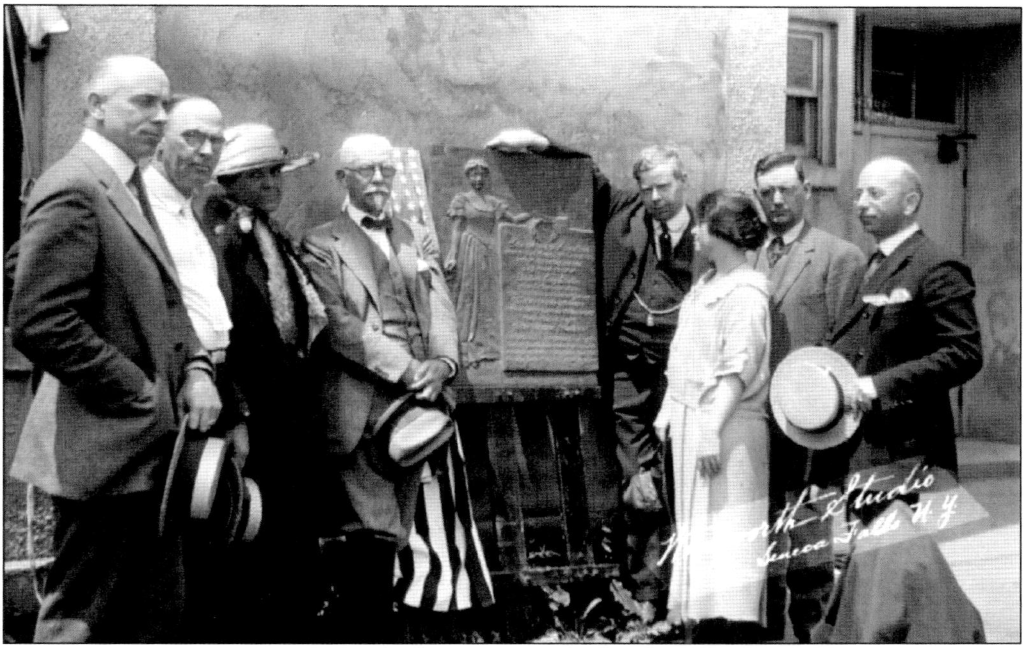

Seen here is the dedication of the plaque commemorating the 1848 women's rights convention in 1923. The owner of the building refused to have the plaque placed on his building. From left to right are Carl Rogers, Bert Mackey, Theodosia Moran, Dr. William Follette (mayor of Seneca Falls), Devillo Pollard, Anita Politzer, Earl Clark, and L. D. Stafford.

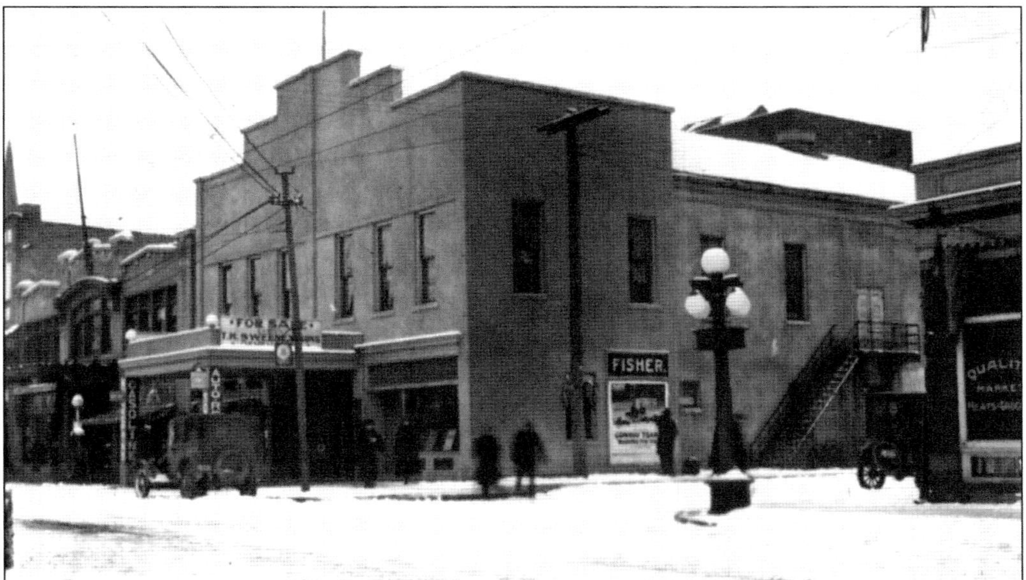

The Wesleyan Chapel was located on the corner of Falls Street and Mynderse Street when the women's rights convention was held. The congregation was very active in the abolition movement. The original building was remodeled several times, and the structure was buried in additions. The National Park Service has removed the additions and has kept only what is known to have been the 1848 building.

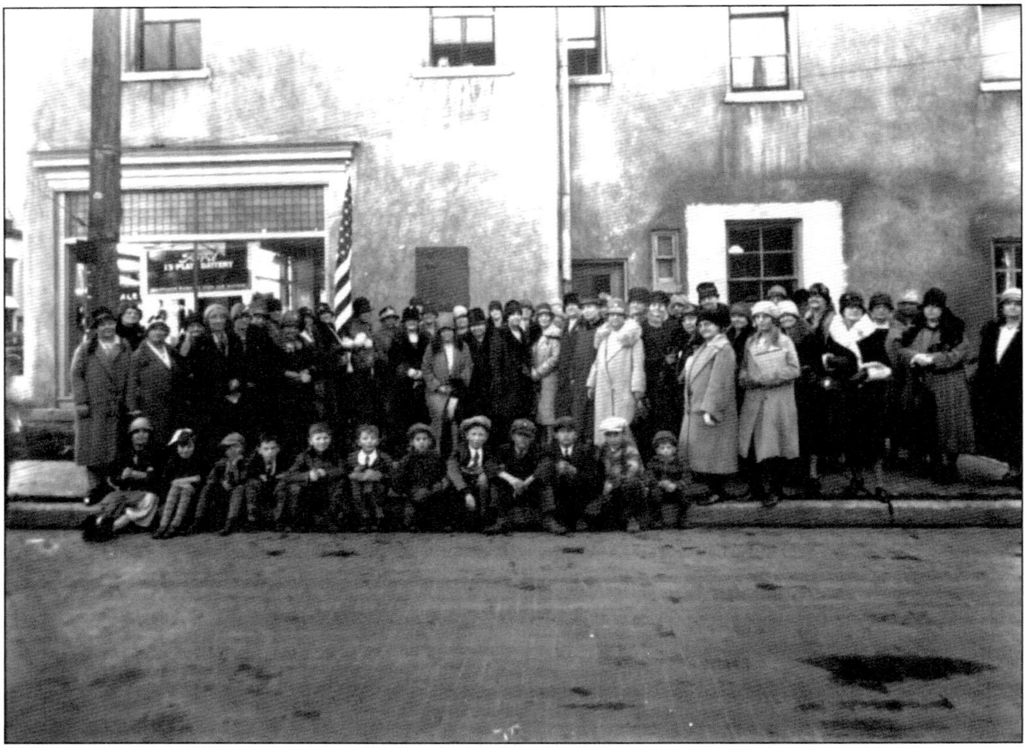

In 1928, the League of Women Voters stands on the corner of Mynderse Street and Fall Street, the site of the first women's rights convention. The Wesleyan Chapel had been a theater, a car dealership, and finally a laundromat.

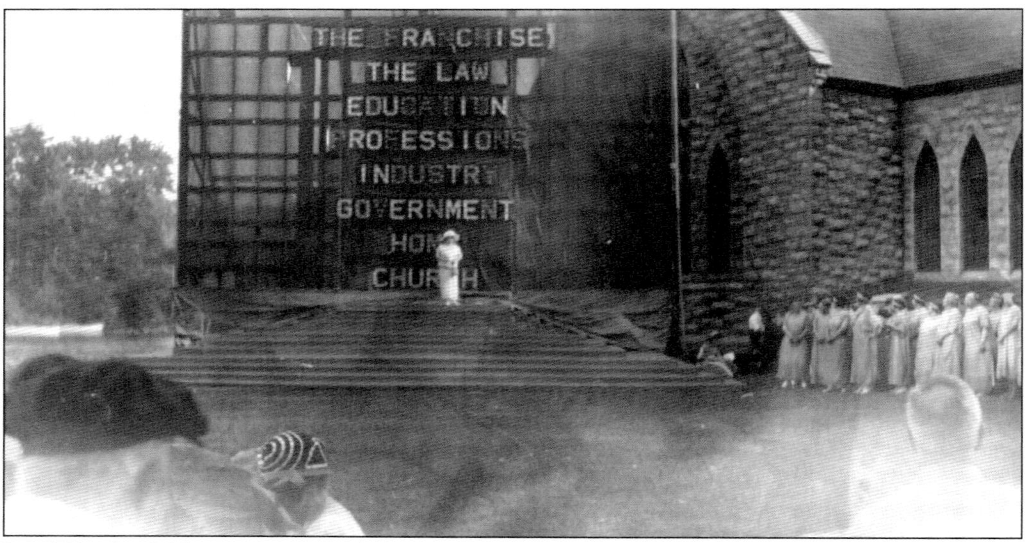

In 1923, the 75th anniversary of the convention was celebrated throughout the village with pageants and displays. One of these displays was on the lawn of Trinity Episcopal Church featuring a Greek maiden and this lighted sign.

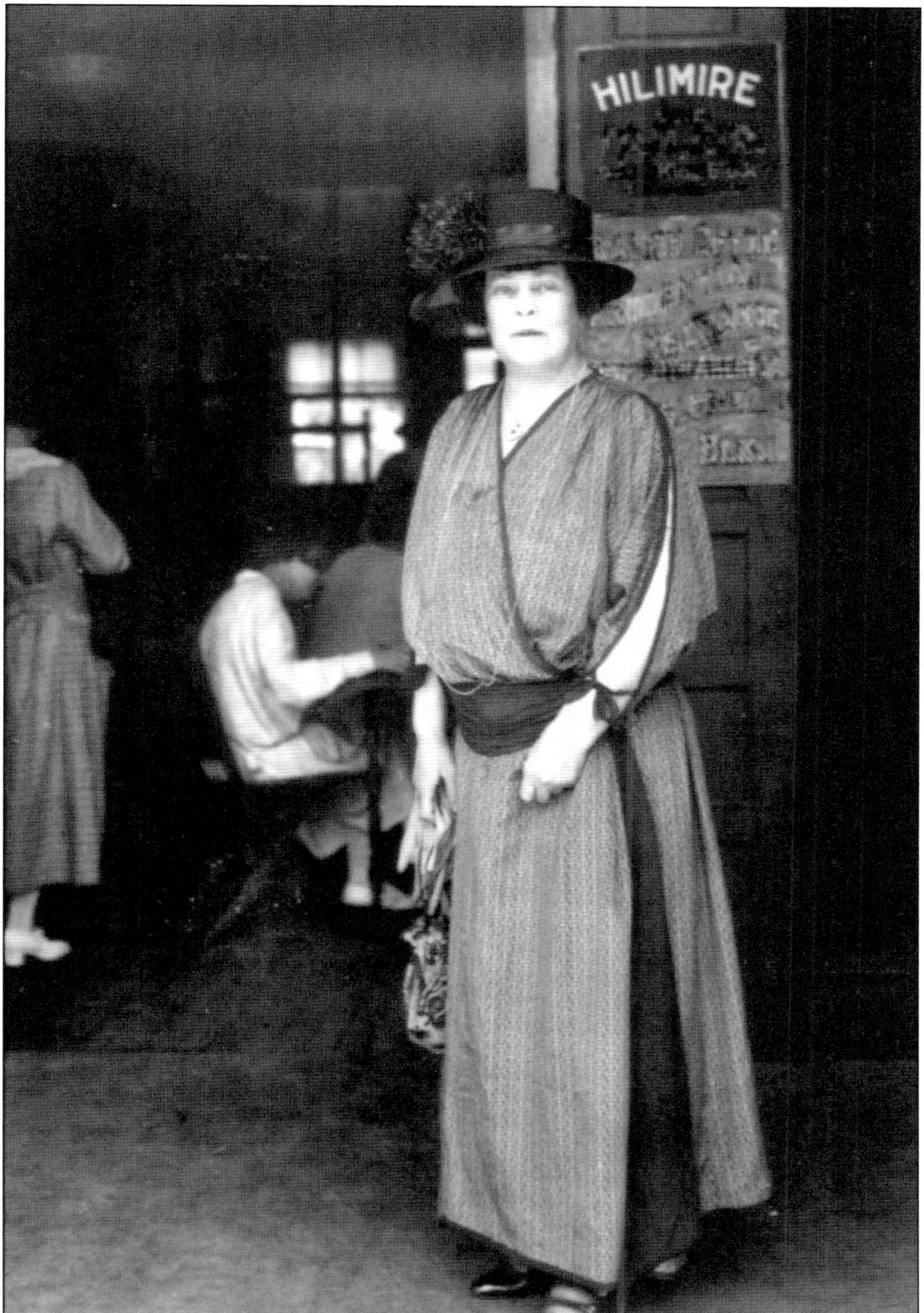

Alva Belmont, the former wife of William Kissam Vanderbilt, was very active in the suffrage movement in the 20th century. This photograph was taken in Seneca Falls for the 1923 commemoration. Belmont hosted a suffrage lunch in Newport, Rhode Island, and had plates, cups, and saucers made that said "Votes for Women" on the rim.

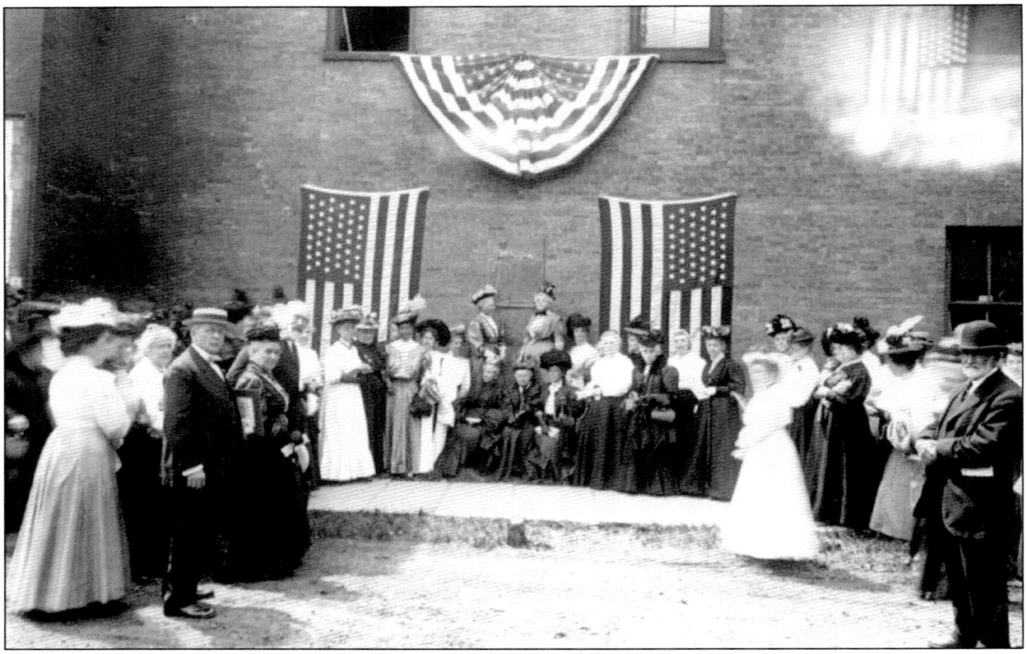

Seen here is the 60th anniversary of the 1848 convention, next to the former Wesleyan Chapel in Seneca Falls.

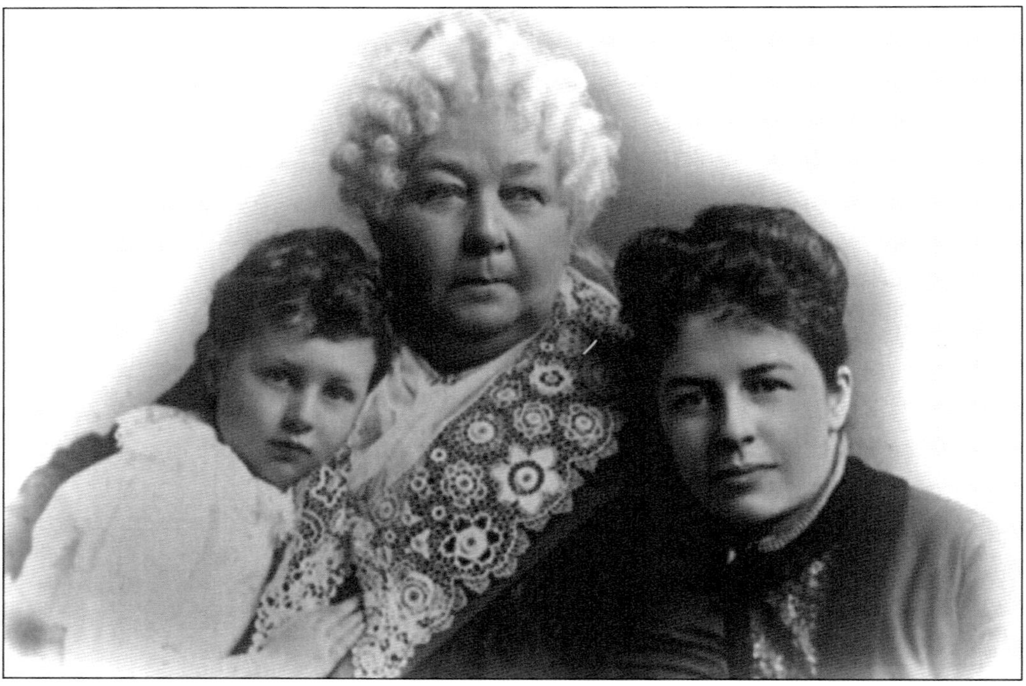

Elizabeth Cady Stanton is shown here with her daughter Harriot Stanton Blatch and granddaughter Nora. Harriot carried on the fight for suffrage and lived to see the 19th Amendment passed, and she kept her mother's spirit alive for future generations. Nora would graduate from Cornell University in 1905 as the first woman civil engineer in the United States.

Three

NOT JUST THE WOMEN MADE SENECA FALLS FAMOUS

After the commotion caused by the women's rights convention, Seneca Falls stayed in the forefront of the national scene with manufacturing and farm produce during the Civil War. Locally produced pumps were known worldwide and fire engines made in the area have been found in just about every state in the union. Several industrial patents were filed by inventors in Seneca Falls and the mills produced more socks for the Union army than any other city except New York City. Not only did Seneca Falls make several types of hand pumps for extinguishing fires, but Birdsall Holly patented a rotary steam engine that made the hand pumps obsolete. Soon Seneca Falls Silsby Steam Fire Engines were in use all over the United States. Goulds Pumps sold pumps, bells, and cast items in France, Russia, Spain, and South America.

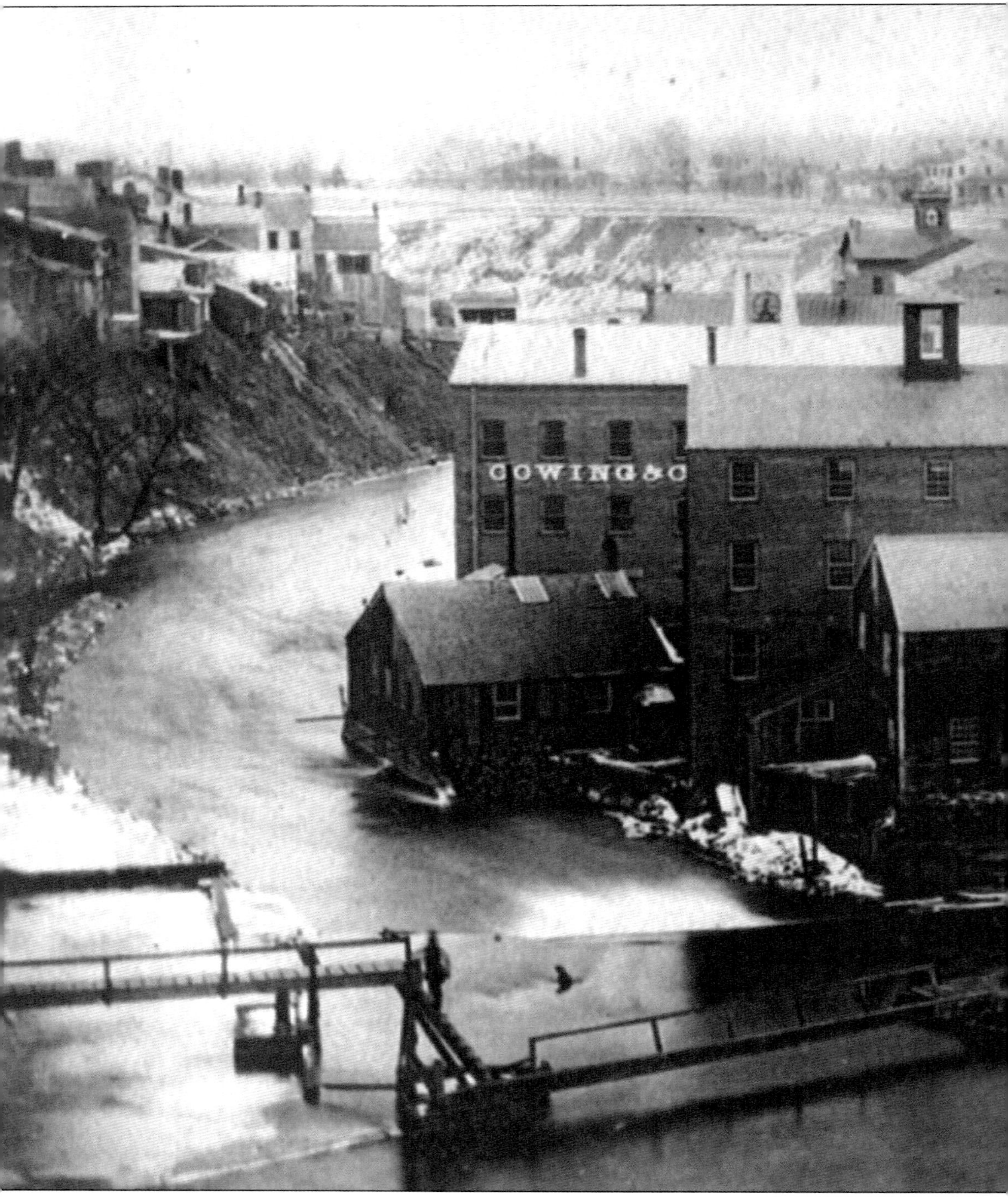

Cowing and Company was located on the flats of Seneca Falls. Manufacturing wooden pumps then cast-iron pumps, the company grew and kept adding buildings to the site. Eventually a large six-story building housed the company. Catwalks allowed the workers easy access from the village, but it was most likely very slippery in the winter. Unfortunately there were many

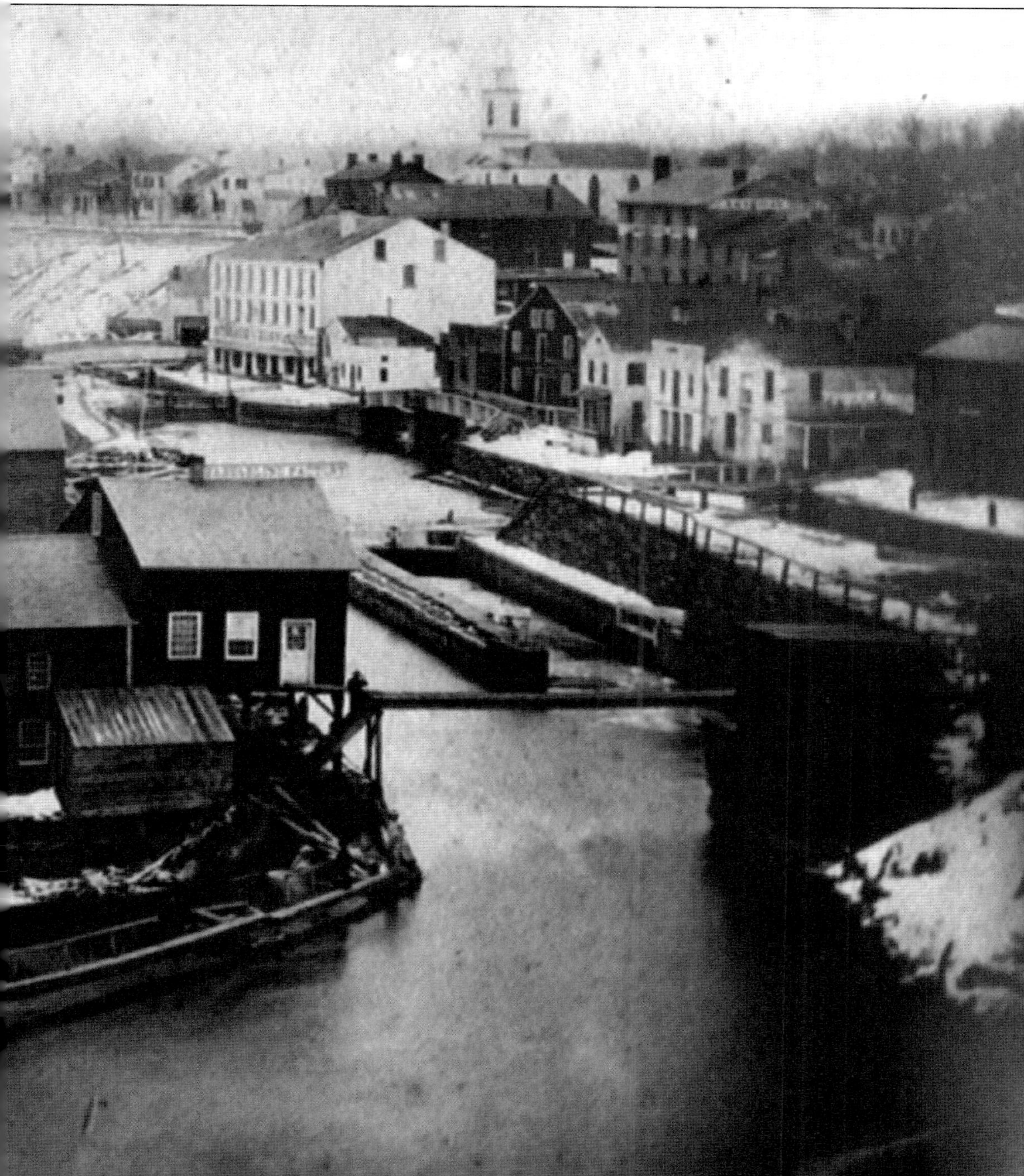

set backs for John P. Cowing, but it was through an indomitable will and honesty of purpose that he was able to recover and rebuild. It was said that he never took advantage of his creditors to save himself from financial ruin.

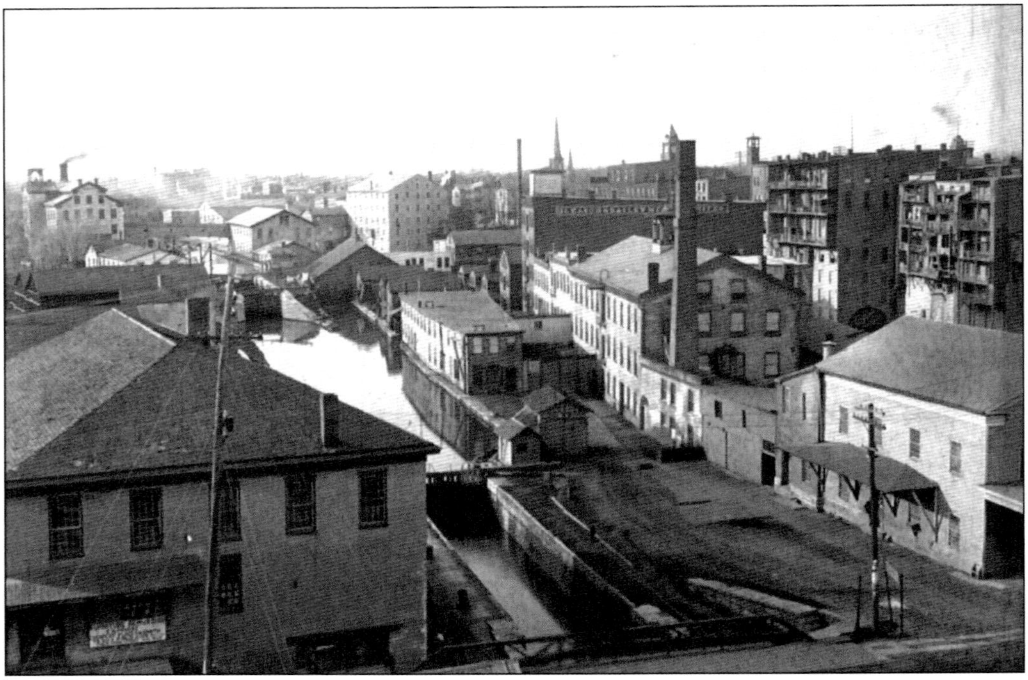

Seneca Falls became a bustling mill town with factories and mills located on islands formed by the Seneca River and the Cayuga-Seneca Canal. This view is overlooking the flats with the roof of Mechanics Hall in the foreground on the left. The locks can be seen near the Seneca Woolen Mill to the left. The backs of the buildings on Fall Street can be seen on the right.

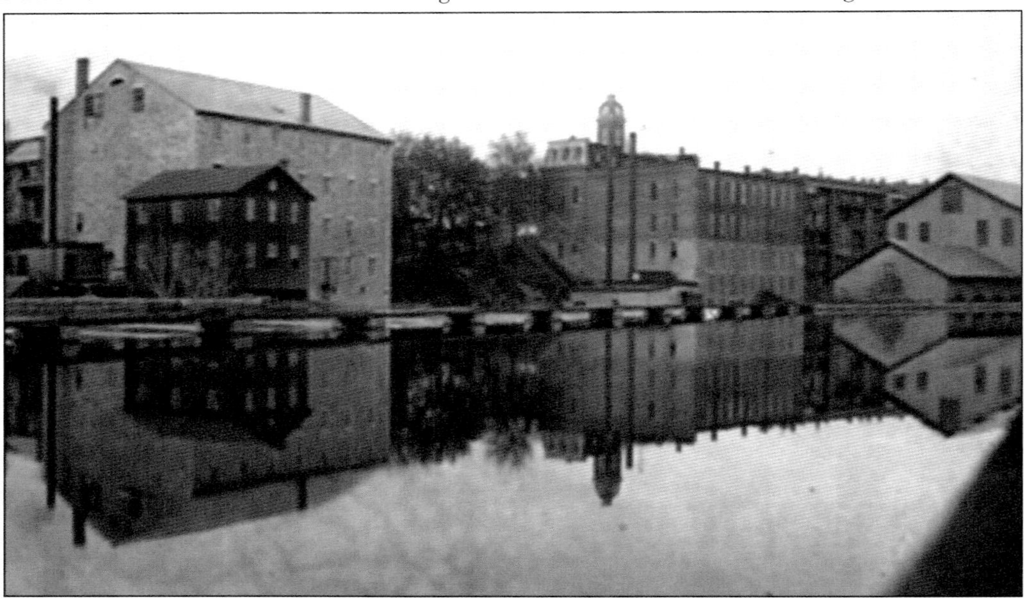

The canal could be a quiet place as seen in this view with the reflections on the water. Looking northeast from the Bridge Street bridge the City Mill building can be seen on the left. The clock tower on the Partridge building is seen in the center. The upper falls were located near the corner of the City Mill building.

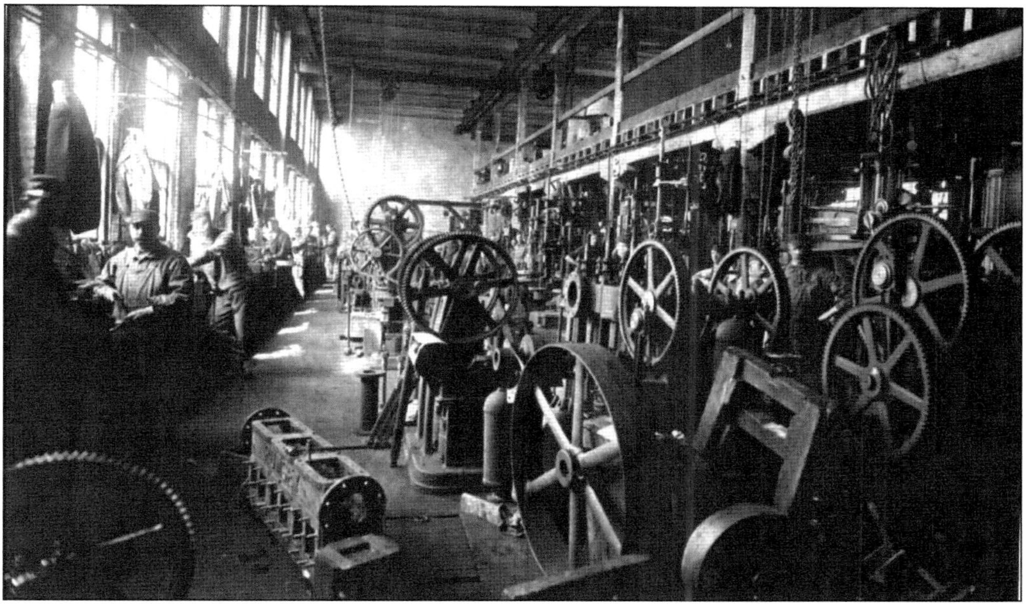

This is the assembly floor of Rumsey Pump Company. These were some of the pumps that were used worldwide to move water, oil, and sewage. The foundry made sad irons, shelf brackets, and bells. These items were good training for the young foundry men; once they could make clean castings of the simple items, they could move on to more complex castings.

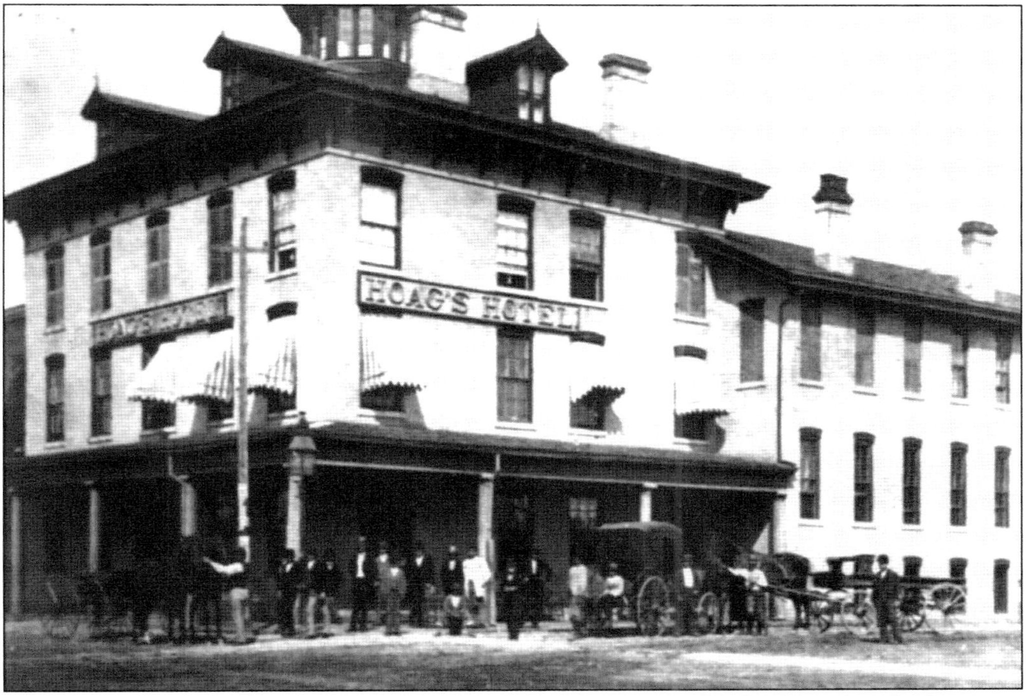

The Hoag Hotel on the corner of Fall Street and State Street was the third hotel in this location. The very earliest was the Clinton House followed by Carr's Hotel. To the right of the hotel is a livery stable.

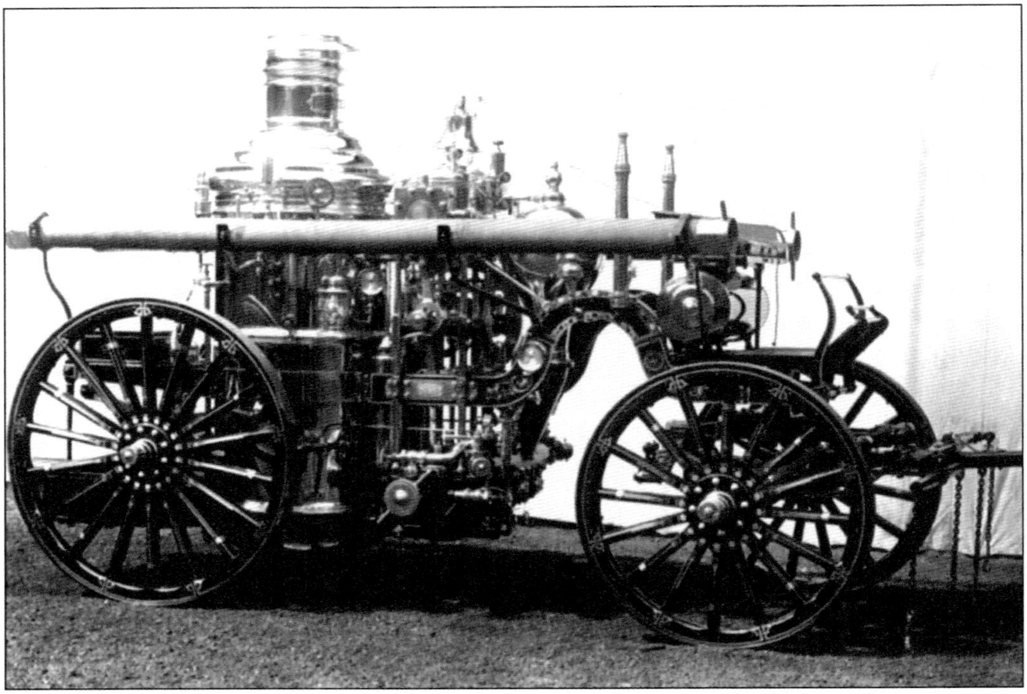

The Silsby steam fire engine was an engineering marvel. A steam boiler provided power to a rotary pump that would throw a stream of water over 200 feet high. All of this apparatus was on a frame that could be drawn by horses or men. The large engines had a pre-boiler that would keep the boiler ready to go at a moments notice, and it also heated the firehouse.

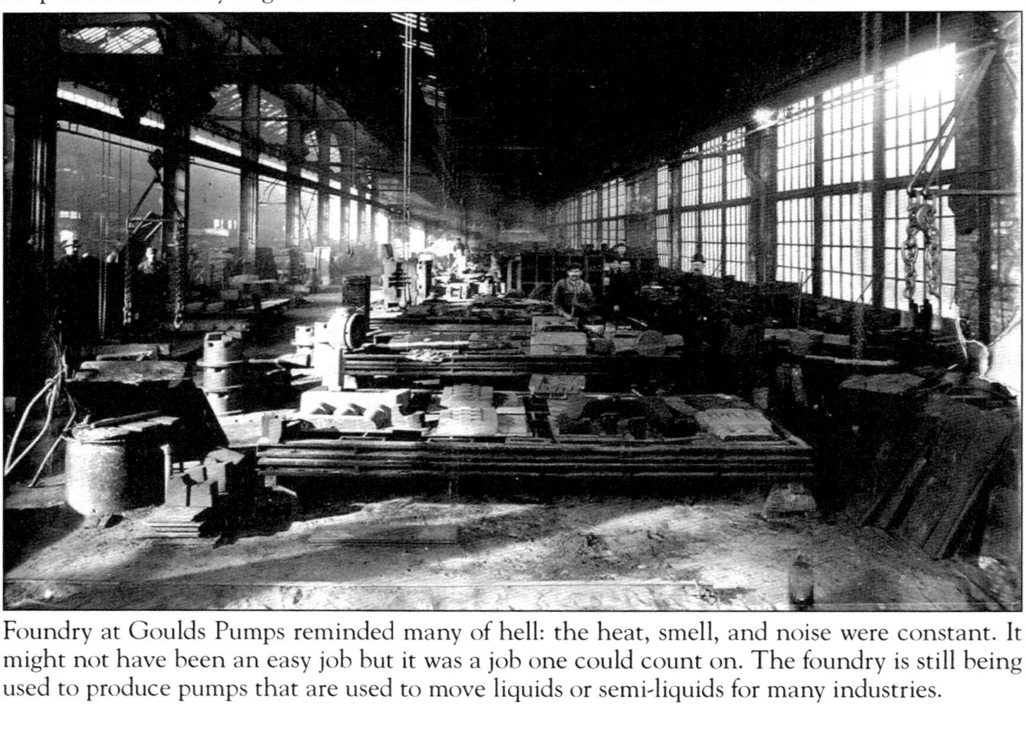

Foundry at Goulds Pumps reminded many of hell: the heat, smell, and noise were constant. It might not have been an easy job but it was a job one could count on. The foundry is still being used to produce pumps that are used to move liquids or semi-liquids for many industries.

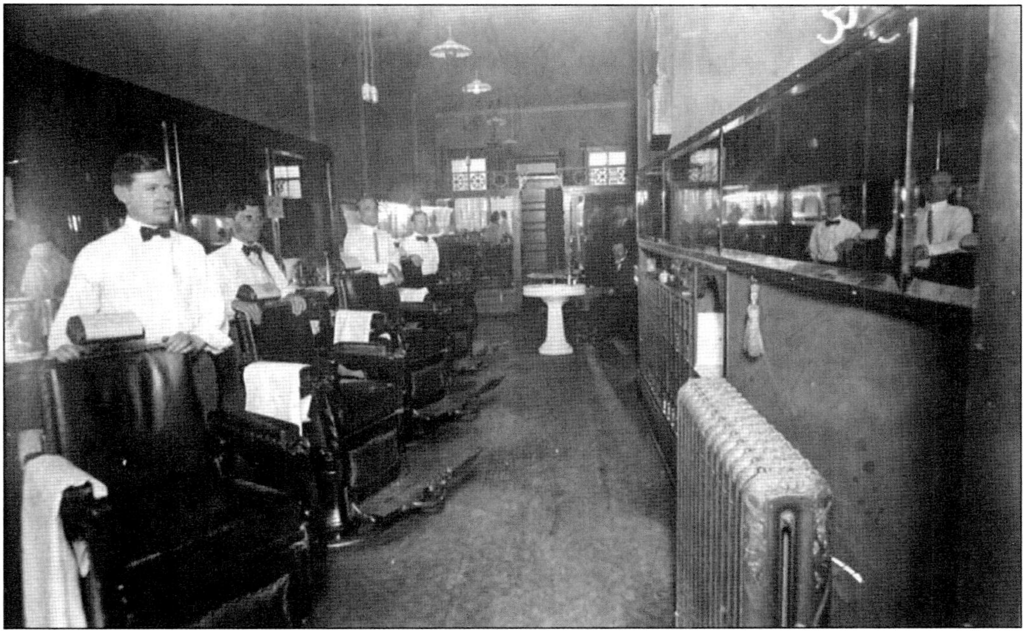

The Van Tine barbershop was located in the Johnson Opera Block. Arthur Van Tine is the barber standing in the front; the others have not been identified. For a small village, Seneca Falls had several barbers, hairdressers, and beauty salons. The economy seemed to support several businesses of the same type.

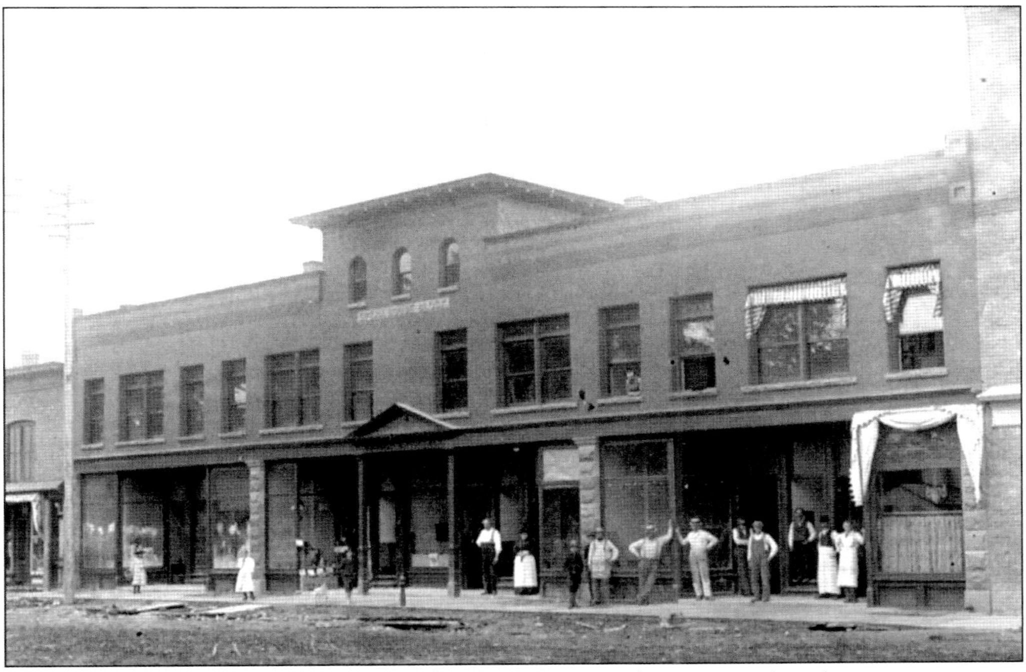

The Johnson Opera block was supposed to have an opera house in it, but that part was never built. Only retail spaces were completed. This building, opened in the early 1900s, was a state-of-the-art commercial space.

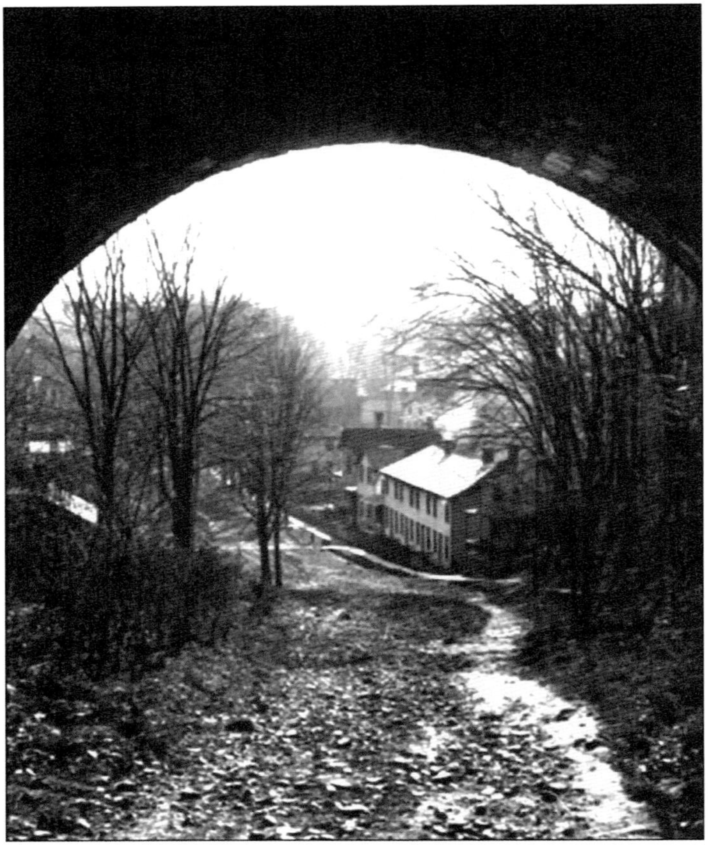

Dey Street ran from Cayuga Street to the flats of Seneca Falls. The railroad bridge frames the view. The houses on Dey Street belonged to working class families. Many schoolchildren who lived on the south side of town would walk up the hill to attend school. Today most of Dey Street is under Van Cleef Lake.

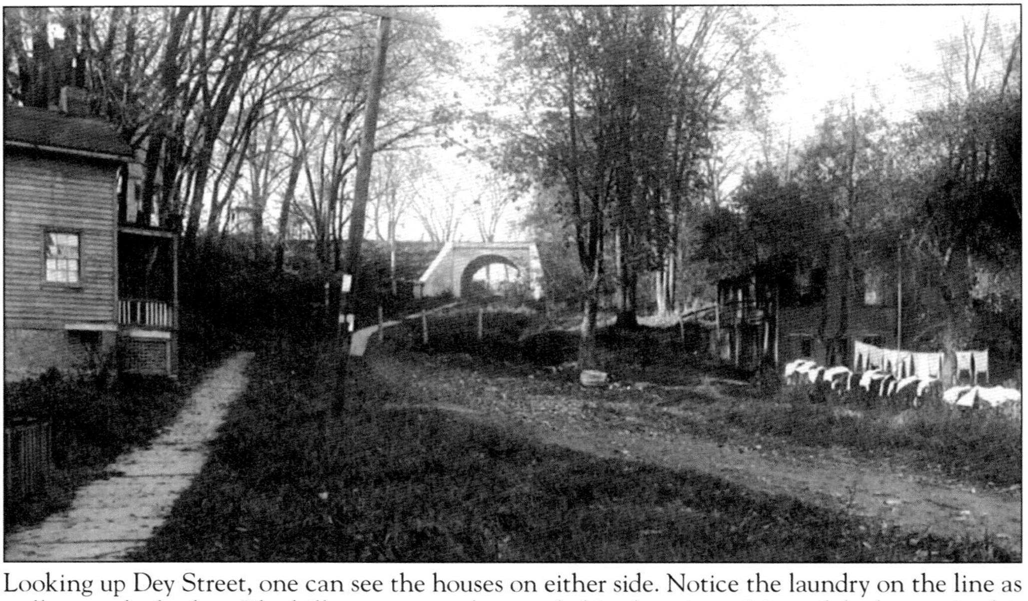

Looking up Dey Street, one can see the houses on either side. Notice the laundry on the line as well as on the bushes. The hill was a great place to sled in the winter. Most of the houses in this area were lost when the Cayuga-Seneca Canal was enlarged.

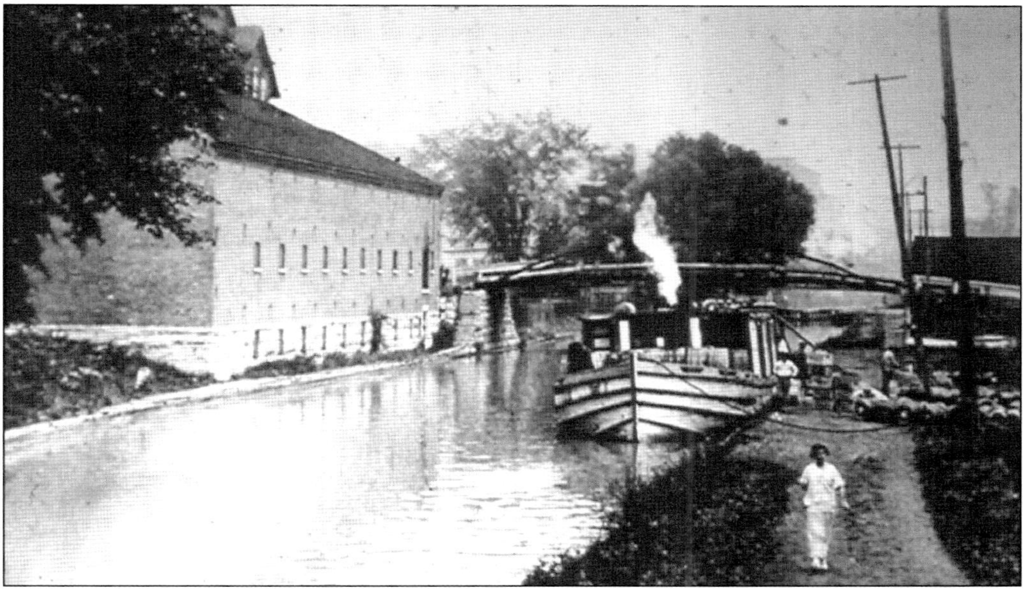

The towpath of the canal was on the south side of the Seneca River. The canal and river were separated by a wooden bulkhead. The canal boats could tie up on either side of the canal as there was a small catwalk on top of the bulkhead. In the background the Bridge Street bridge can be seen. It was a small, arched bridge.

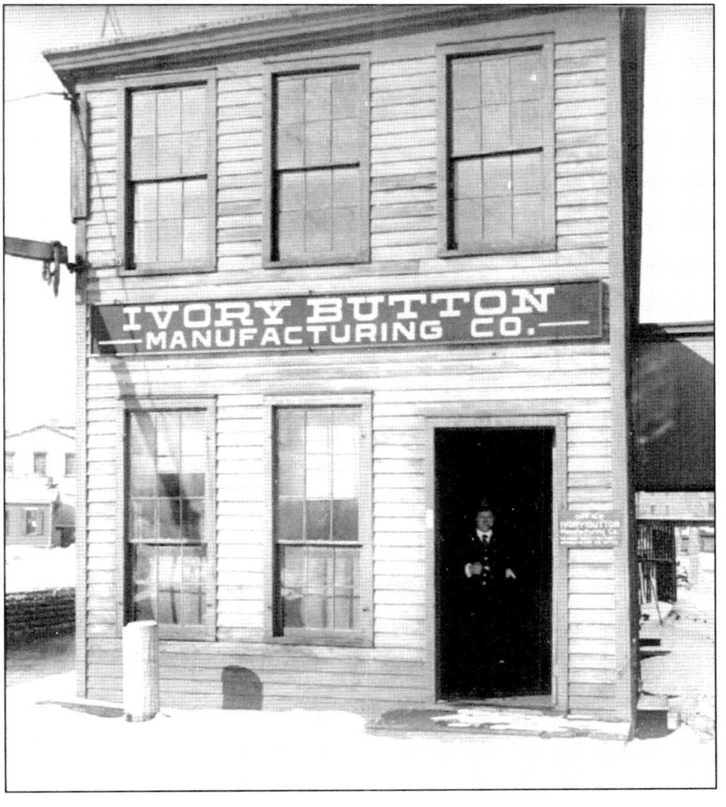

This is the Ivory Button factory of Seneca Falls, one of three button factories (the American and Eagle being the other two) that produced buttons from an "ivory" nut. This nut is from a palm tree and when sliced, buttons could be punched out and polished to look like ivory. These buttons were made here until about 1912.

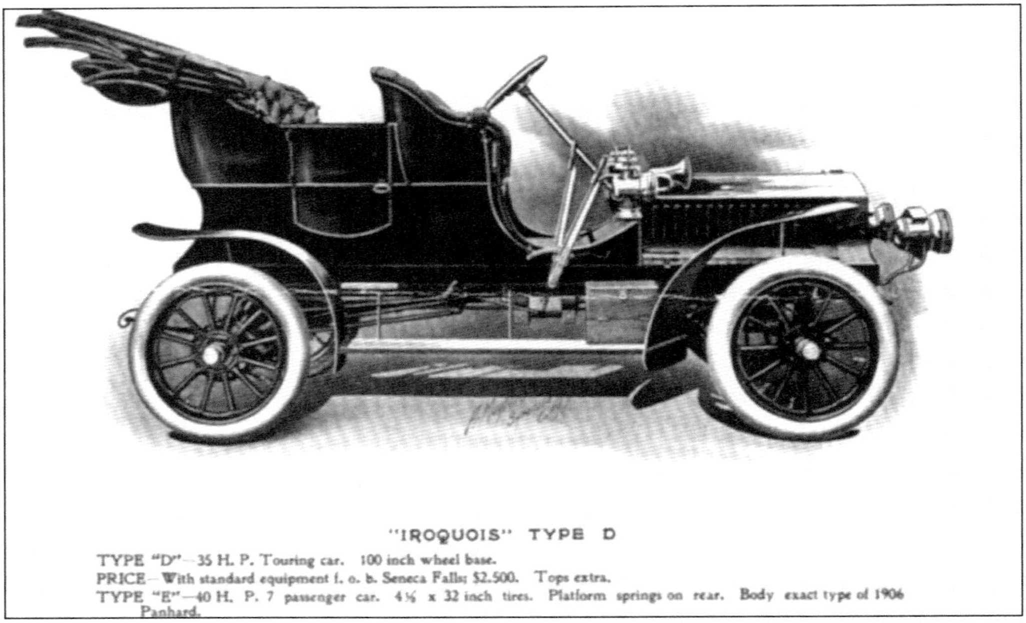

The Iroquois Automobile Company was located in Seneca Falls for a short time. Only a few of the automobiles were ever made; it is thought there were only six. The company then moved to Syracuse and made just a few more before it failed. As of the 1970s, it was thought that there was only one left, a delivery truck.

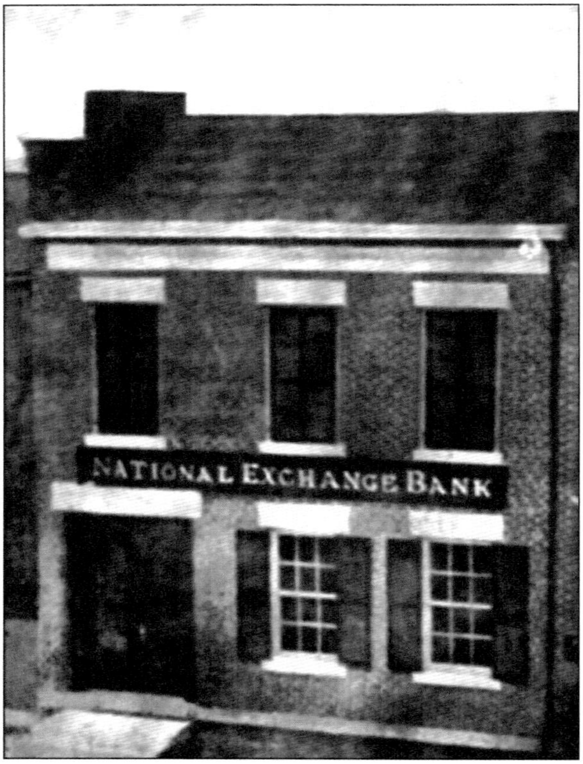

The National Exchange Bank was located on Fall Street just east of the Ovid Street bridge. Chartered in 1865 with capital of $1 million and a circulation of $90,000, Justus B. Johnson was the first and only president of the bank. At that time, banks issued their own currency, with the engravings of local landmarks. It was not until later that the federal government printed all of the currency.

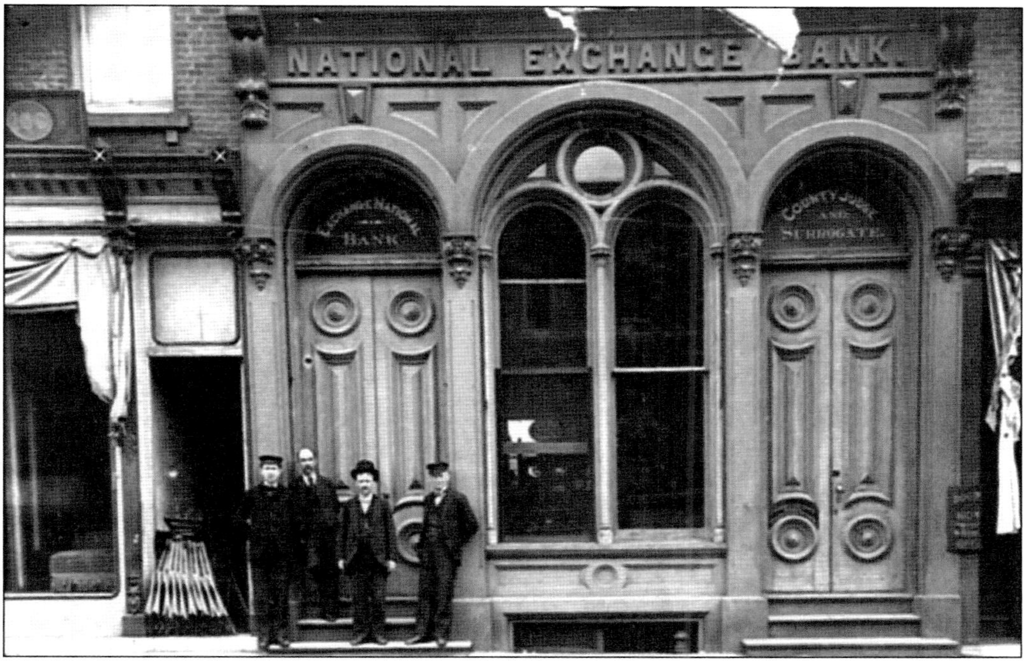

In the 1880s, the National Exchange Bank moved to the other side of Fall Street in the middle of the block. Notice how much more substantial the building looks. The head cashier was Norman H. Becker.

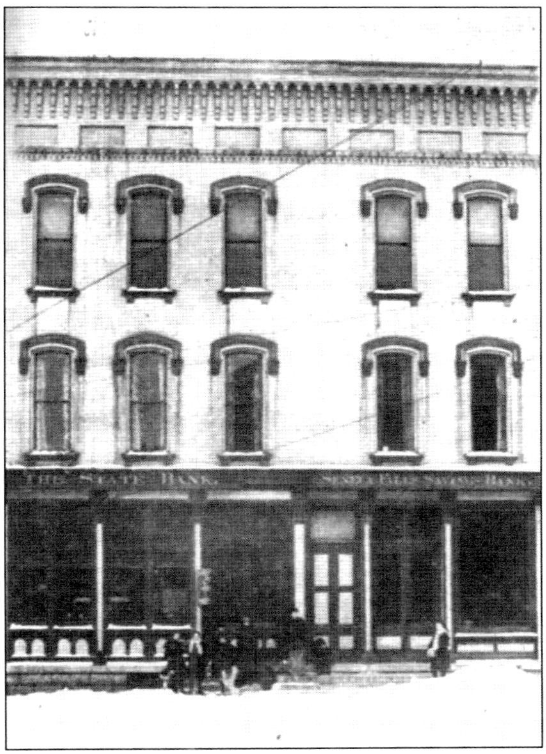

The names of the banks are hard to read, but the State Bank is on the left and the Seneca Falls Savings Bank is next door on the right. The State Bank later moved to a refurbished building on the corner of Fall and Cayuga Streets, and the Seneca Falls Savings Bank has a new building a block away from the original building.

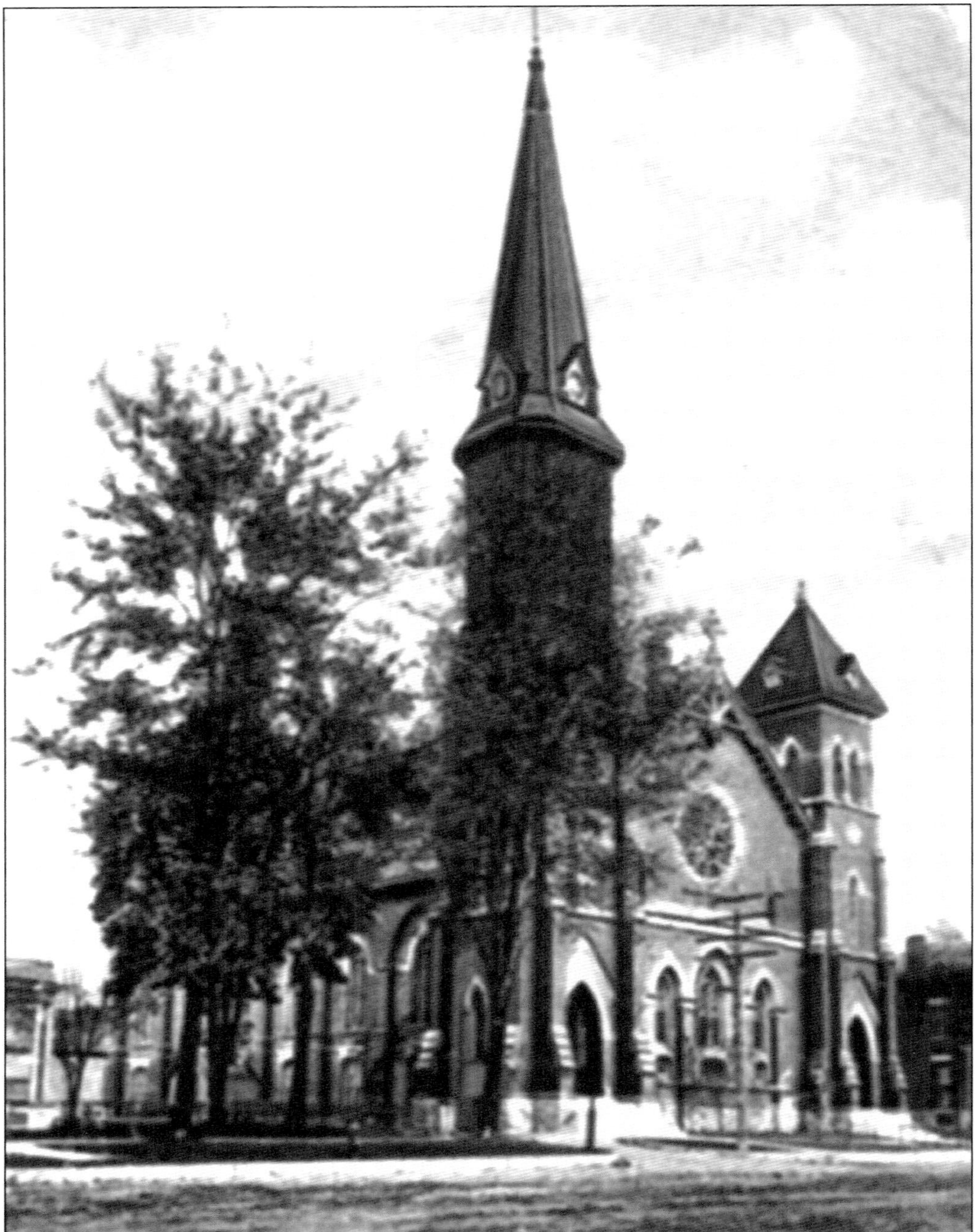

This First Presbyterian Church is actually the third building on the site. The original frame building was moved to State Street and became a meeting hall. A brick structure was built in 1842 and used until 1871. The cornerstone for this building was laid on September 12, 1878, and the final cost was $60,000. The style is English Gothic, with a large tower that is 166 feet tall and a smaller tower being 90 feet tall.

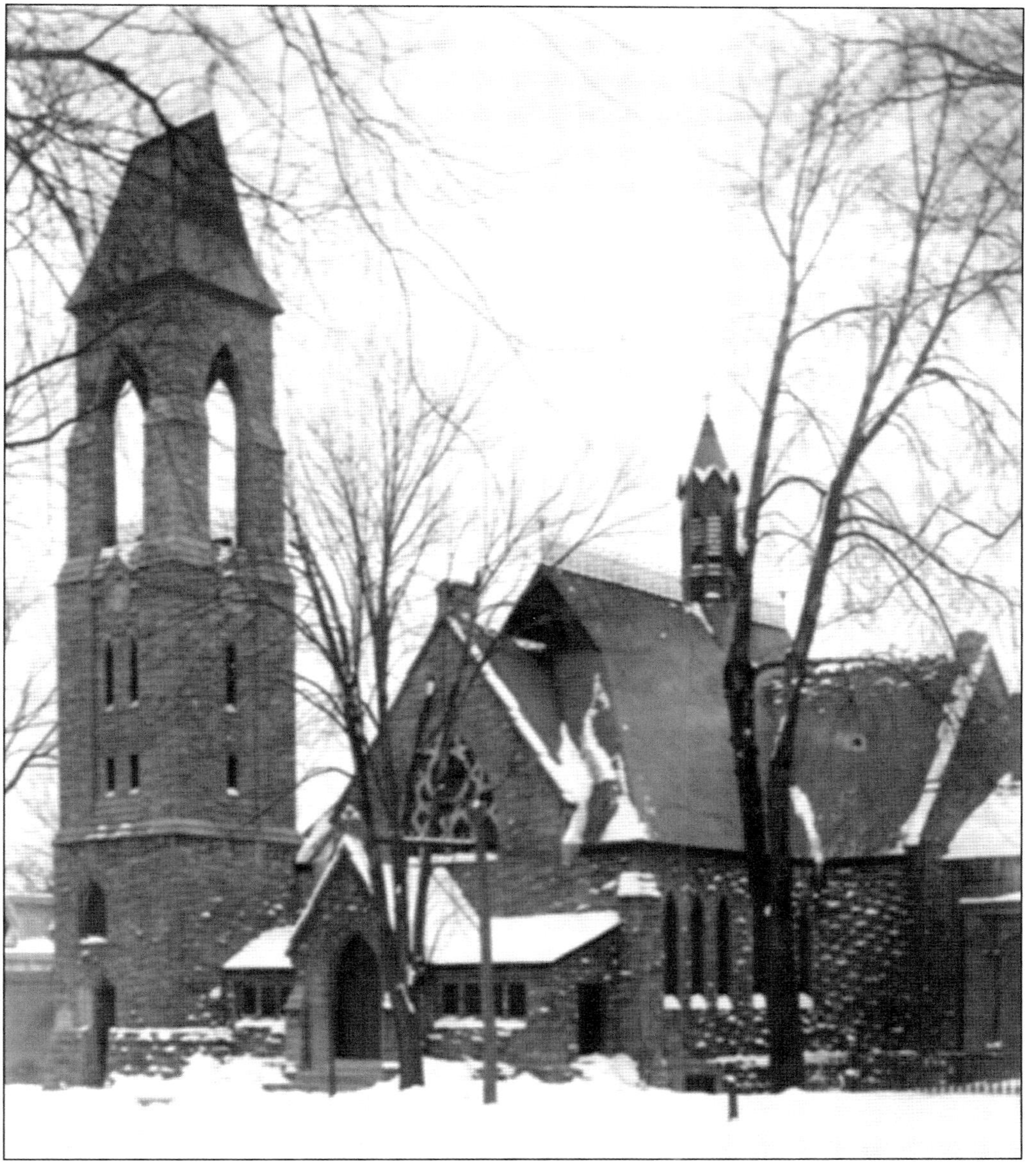

Built in 1885 when the original building on Bayard Street was considered too small, Trinity Episcopal Church is now one of the most photographed buildings in New York. The tower was originally much taller than the existing tower today. Safety issues caused it to be lowered. When the Cayuga-Seneca Canal was being enlarged in 1912, the engineers felt that the church would have to be razed, as it would be too close to the water. Luckily the congregation was able to prevail and save their building.

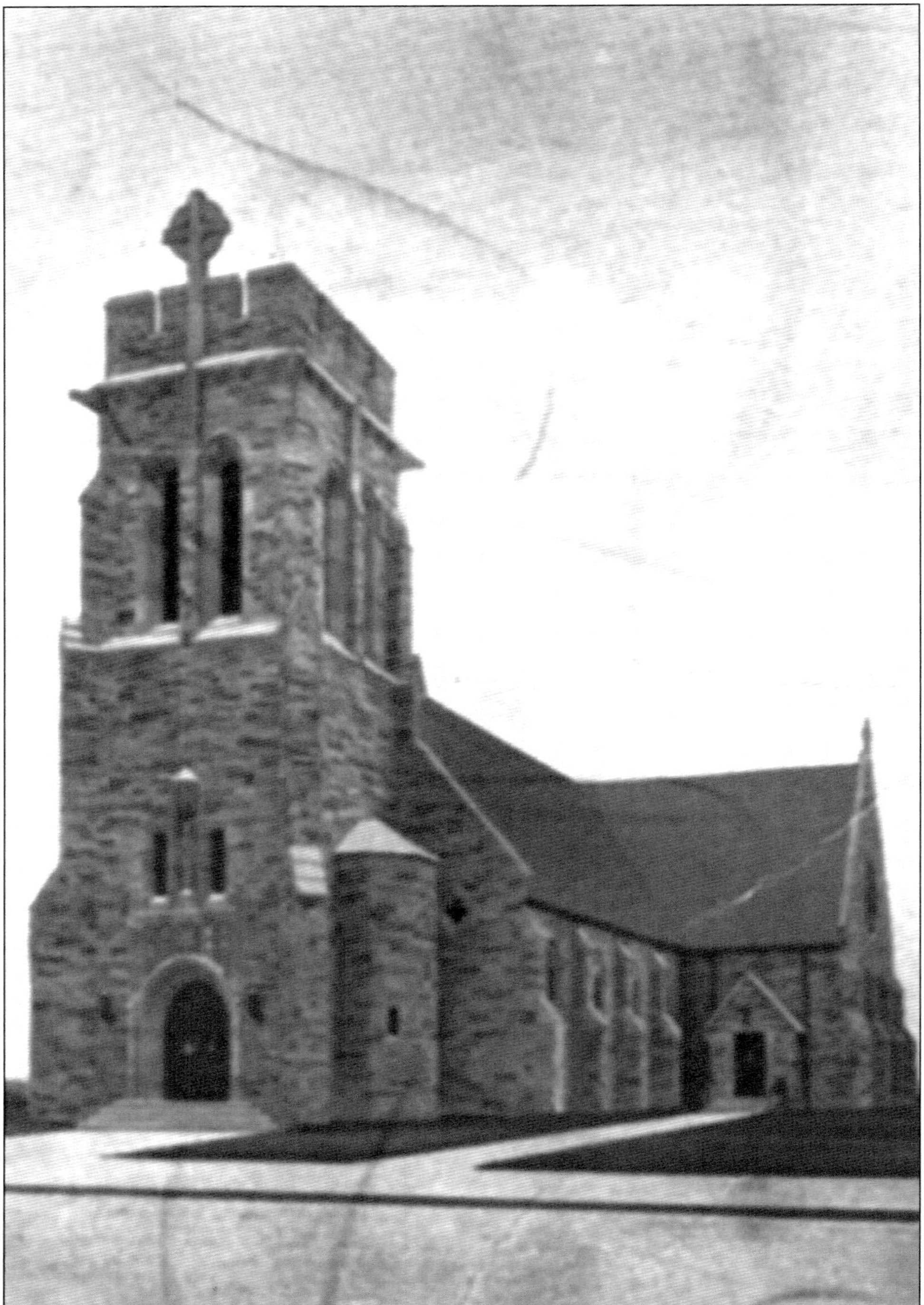

As Seneca Falls was growing, there were several churches on the south side of the village. The first Catholic church was St. Jerome's, which served until 1841. Father O'Flaherty proposed a new church, St. Thomas. By 1851, a larger building was needed, and St. Patrick's was built. The present edifice was dedicated in 1931.

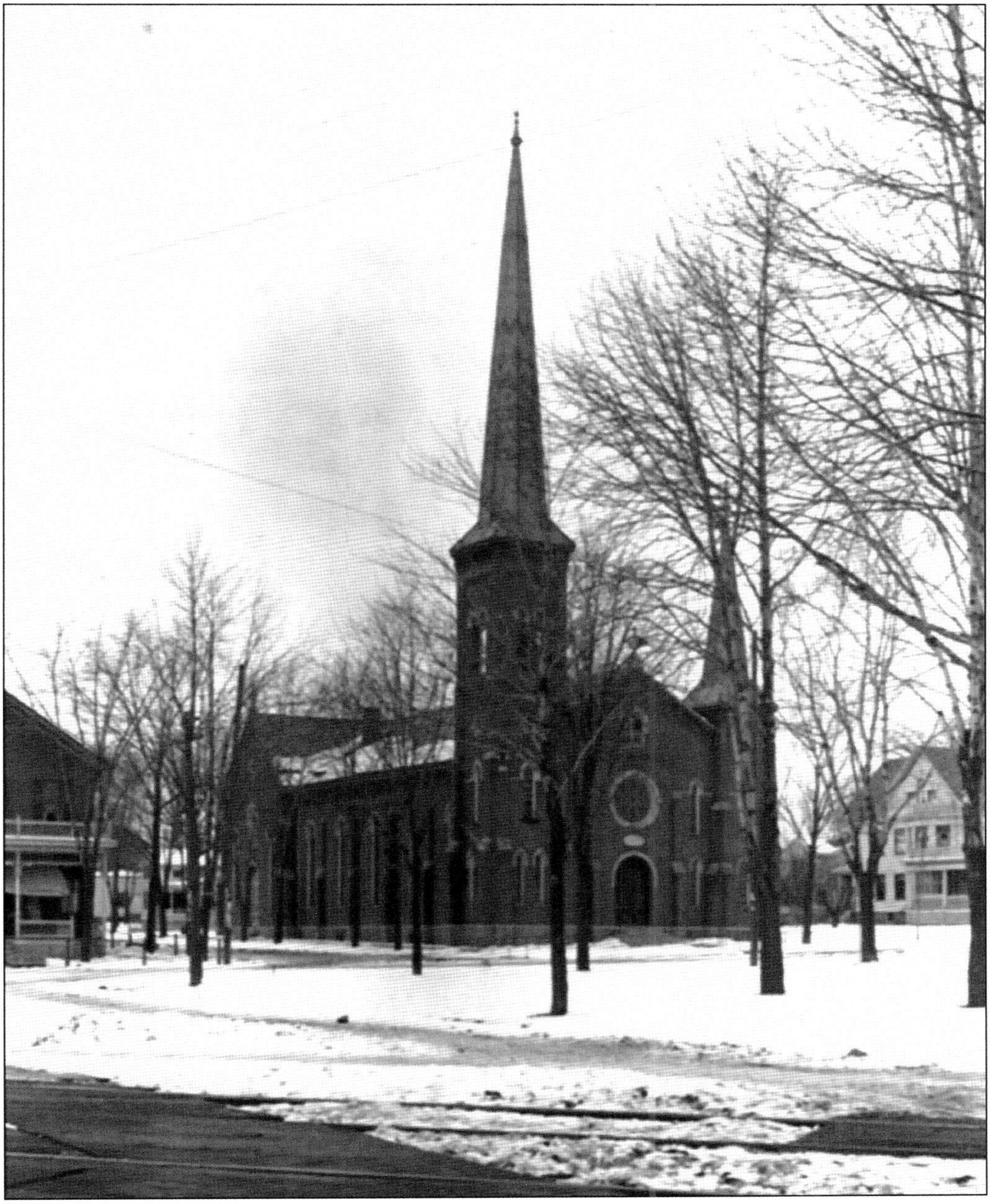

The present First Methodist Episcopal Church is on the site of the original church overlooking the village park on State Street on land that was donated by Wilhelmus Mynderse. On the right is the present manse, and on the left is a neighborhood grocery store. Many in the congregation were active abolitionists.

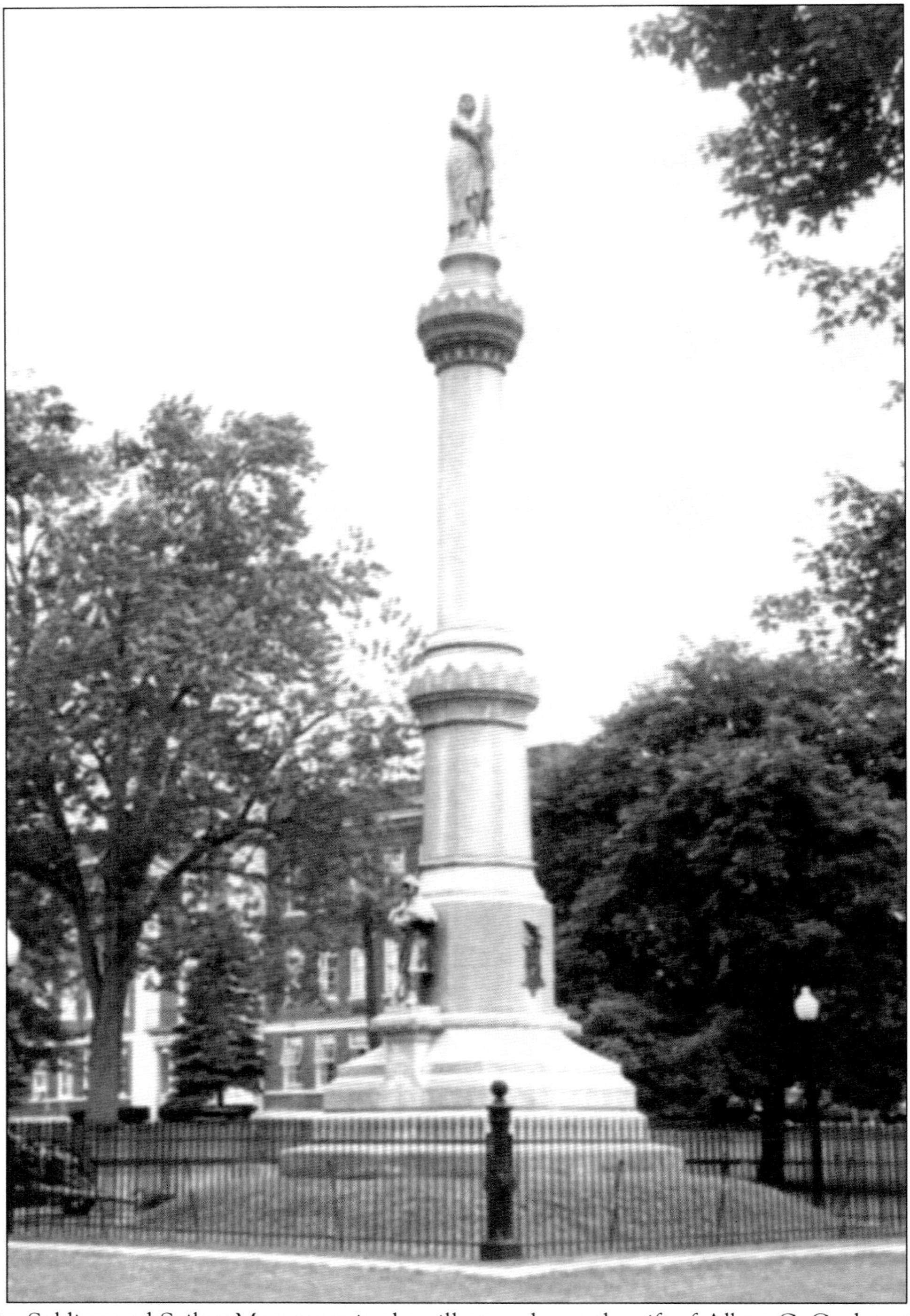

The Soldiers and Sailors Monument in the village park was the gift of Albert G. Cook to the community. Cook, the president of the First National Bank, wanted to leave something that would be a monument to the brave soldiers and sailors who gave their lives for their country. Caroline Cook and her daughter carried out Albert's wishes after his death in 1885.

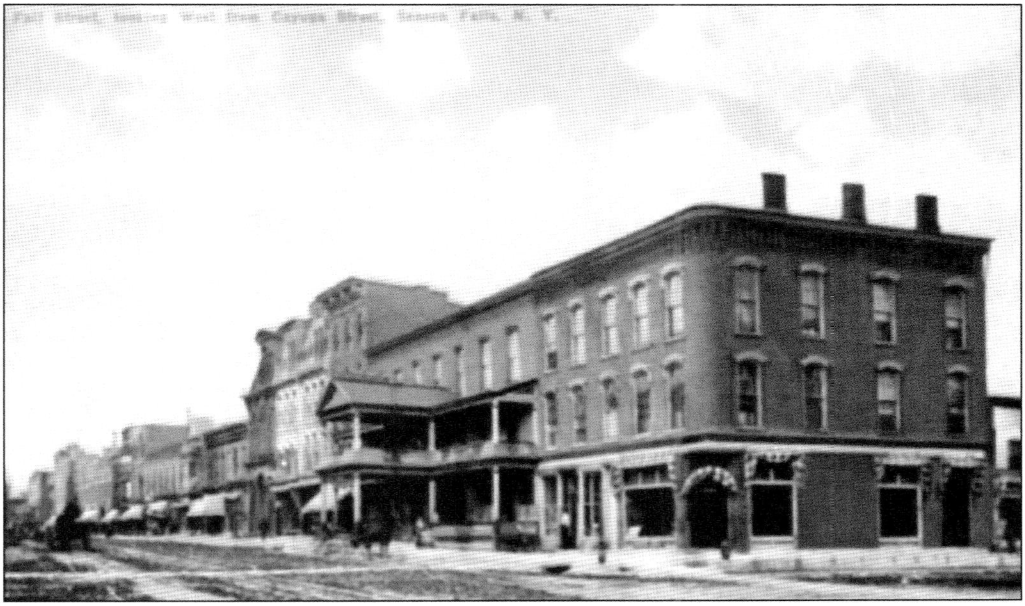

Thomas James was a freedom seeker who settled in Seneca Falls in the 1850s. He was a barber by trade and had a good clientele; Elizabeth Cady Stanton noted in a letter after having her hair bobbed "You should see the curls and locks on the floor of Thomas James Barber Shop." James also had a house near the train station and other properties in town. When he died in 1868, he was worth $16,000.

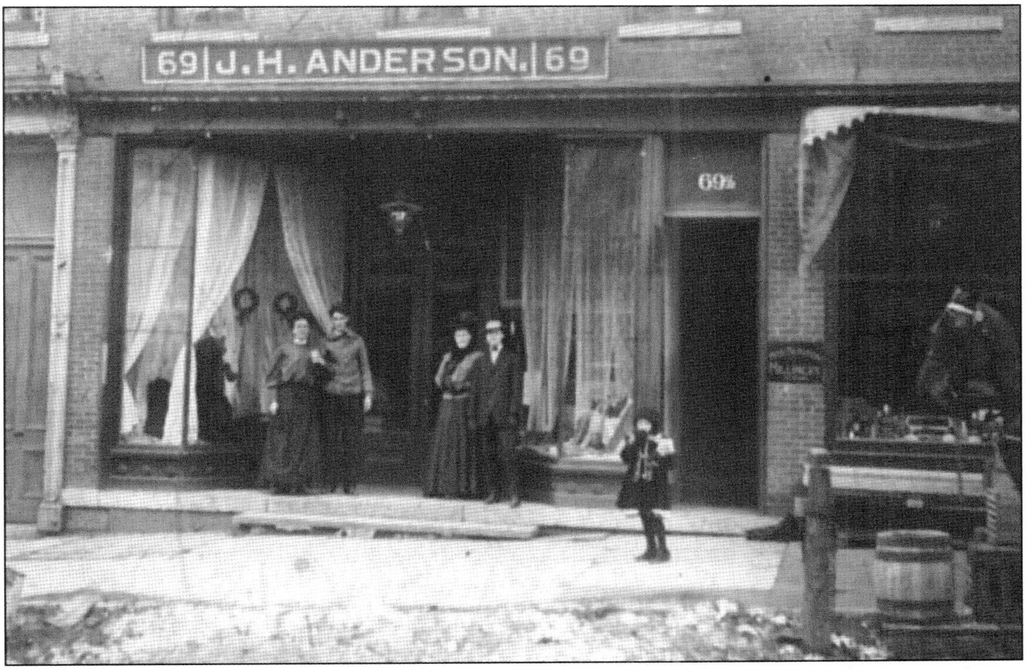

This is the J. H. Anderson Dry Goods, a typical dry goods store of the late 19th century. James Anderson carried an assortment of dry goods, notions, carpets, cloaks, and sundries. Anderson was a retail merchant for 64 years and was well respected by his friends and competitors.

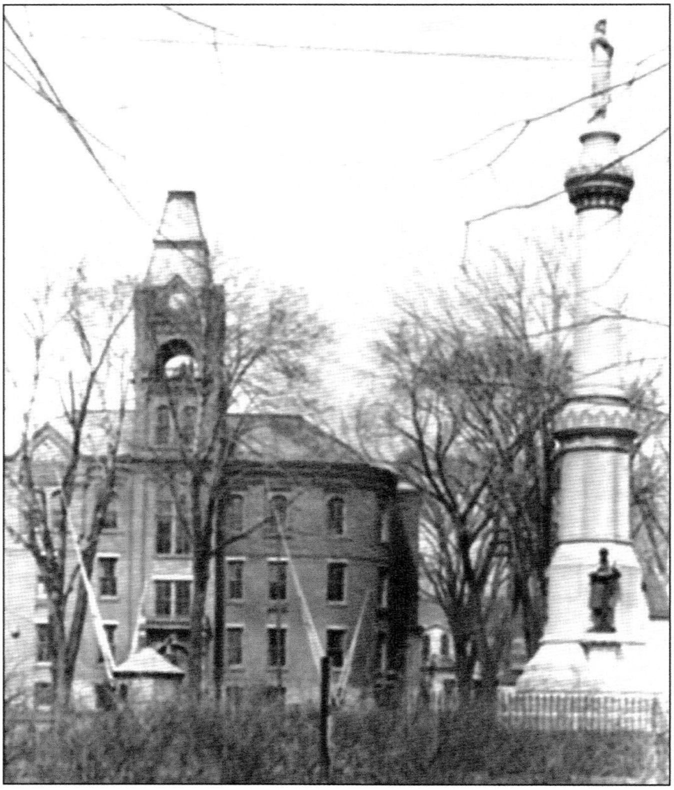

Mynderse Academy was built in 1886 for a cost of $30,000. The original school on this site was the Seneca Falls Academy. At this time, the schools of Seneca Falls consisted of primary schools in each ward and the secondary school just north of the village. The title "academy" was given because Greek and Latin were part of the curriculum.

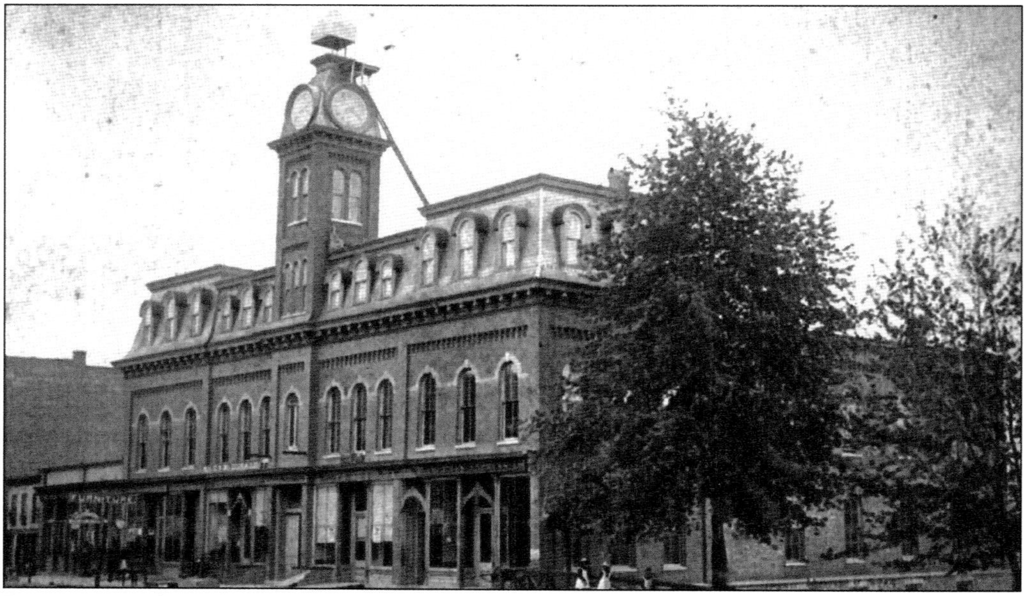

Erastus Partridge, a businessman and banker, built the Partridge building on Fall Street at the top of Water Street. Several different businesses were located in this building, including the post office and the office for the *Seneca County Courier* the county newspaper. Notice the large clock on the tower atop the building.

Partridge was born near Norwich, Connecticut, on May 9, 1798. Of scanty means, Partridge used industry and perseverance to reach success. In 1824, he opened a store in Seneca Falls. After many prosperous years, Partridge commenced private banking in 1848 and by January 1854, he established the Bank Of Seneca Falls, the first bank in the village. At the time of his death in 1873, he was an honored and respected member of the community.

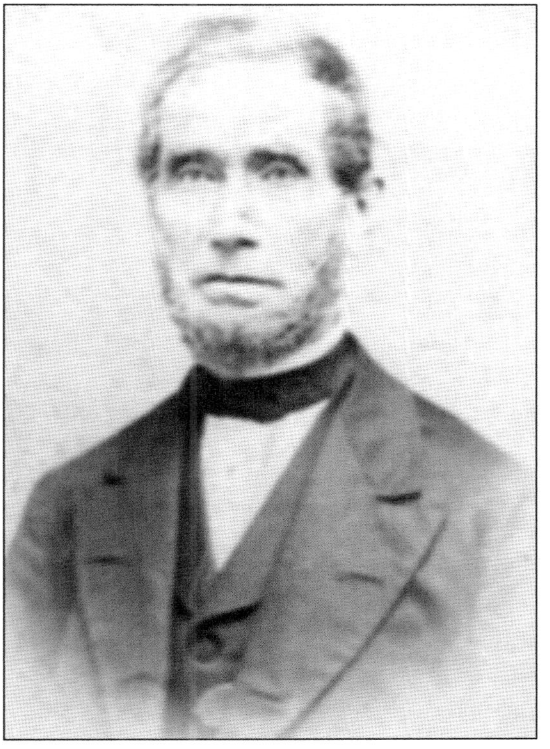

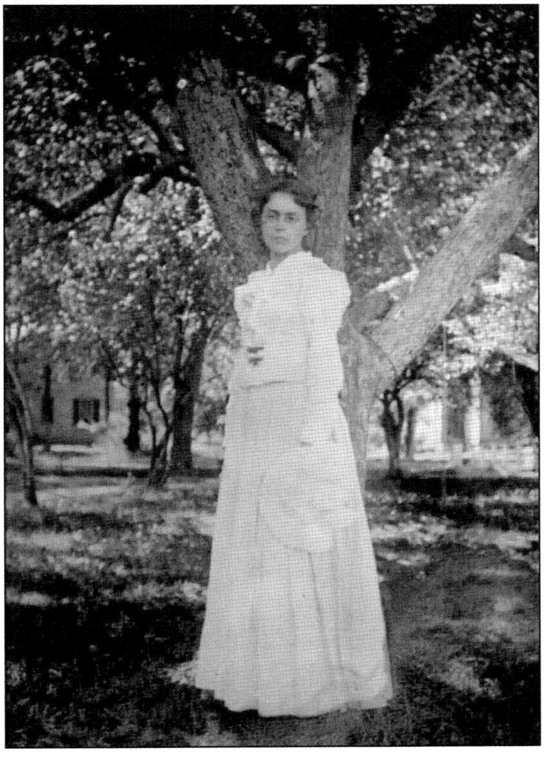

Photography grew rapidly in the years after the Civil War, and one of the more unusual photographers in Seneca Falls was Grace Woodworth, seen here. Returning to Seneca Falls from Rochester, Woodworth enjoyed taking photographs of the fields, rivers, and factories. She also did portraits of Susan B. Anthony and her sister Mary. Many of her glass plates have been preserved at the Seneca Falls Historical Society.

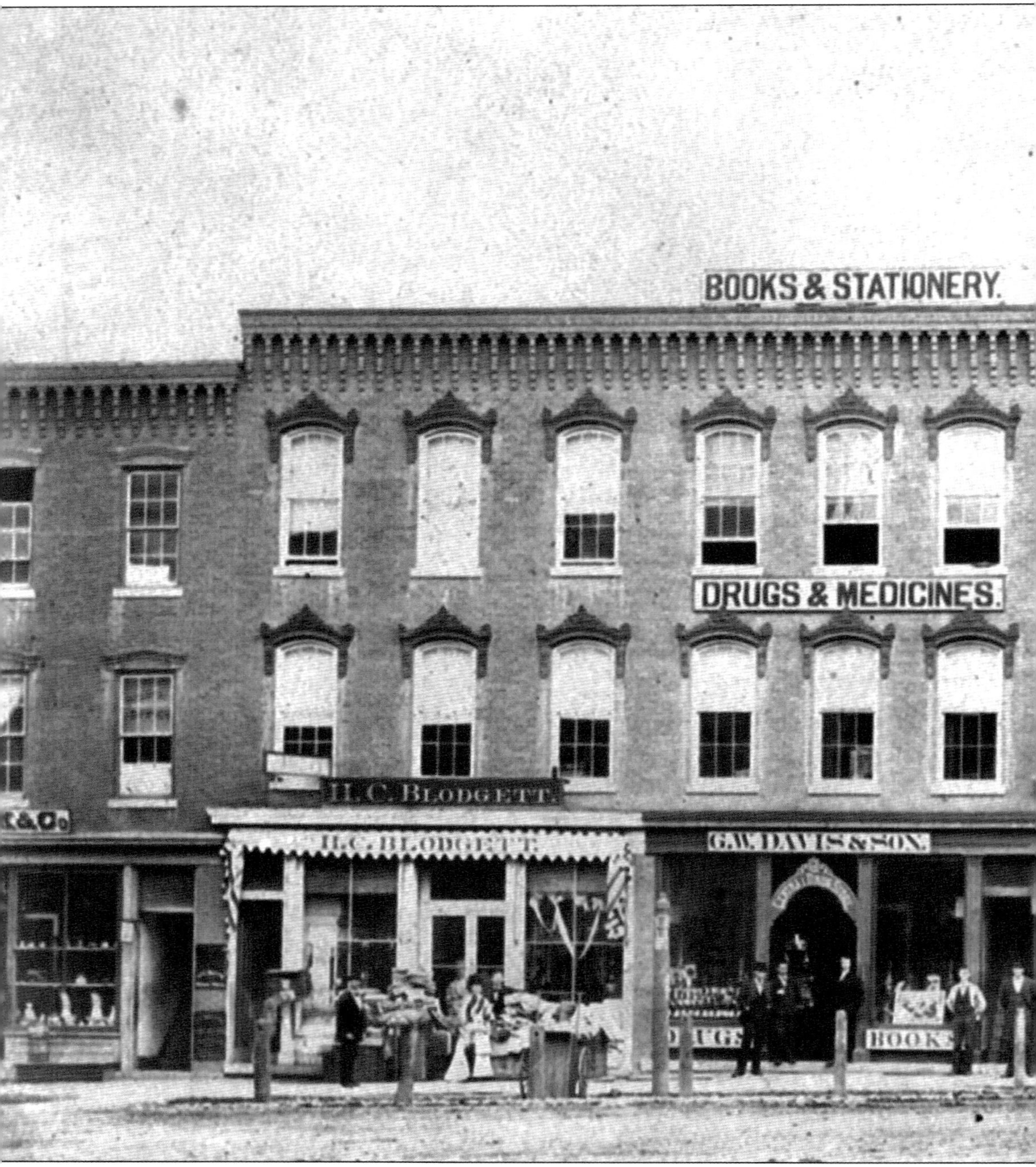

The south side of Fall Street shows many of the various businesses that were thriving in Seneca Falls. George B. Davis, a druggist, was born in Dansville in 1849 but soon moved to Seneca Falls with his family. Davis's father was a physician, and the two opened a drug store in 1866 in the

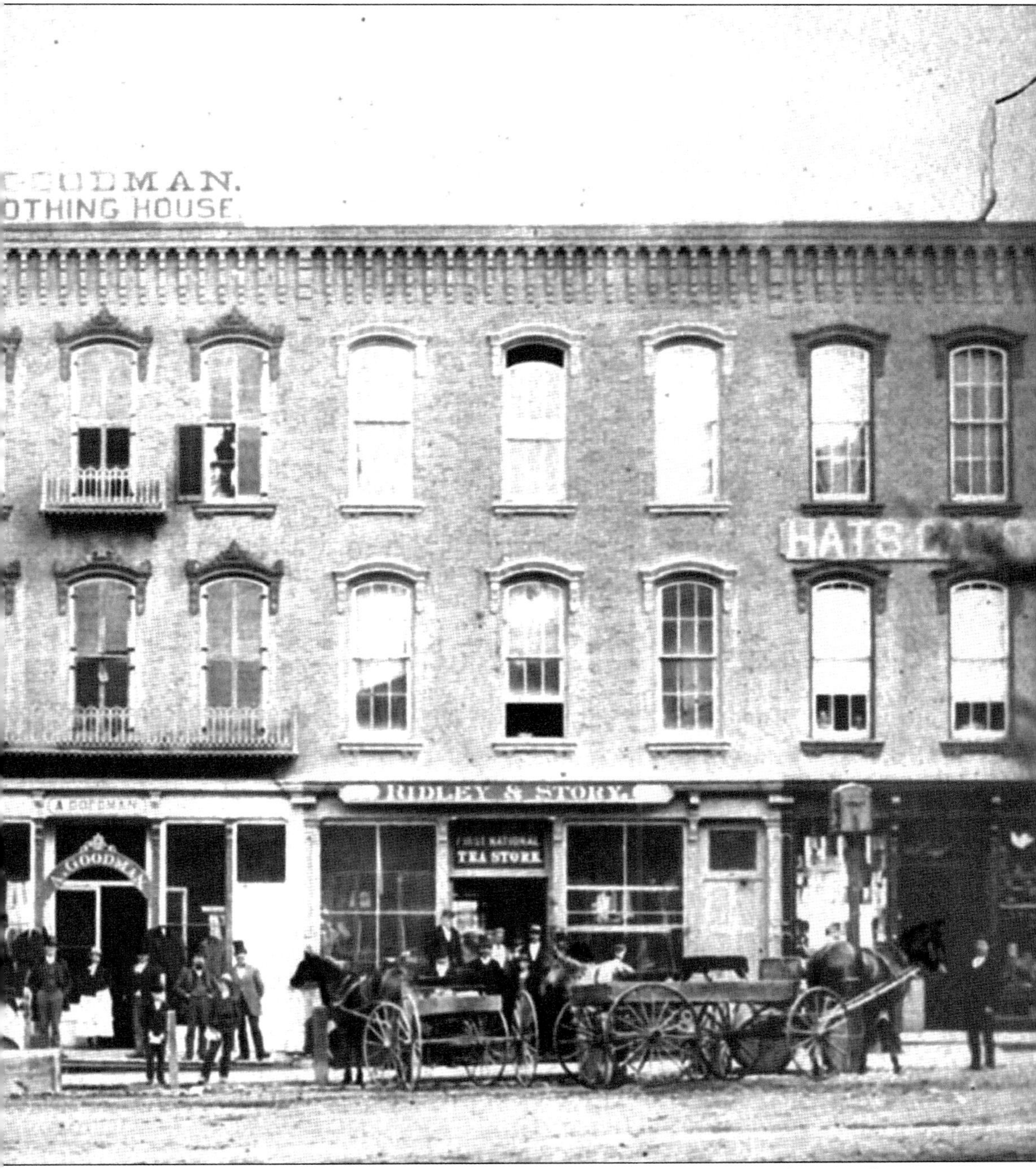

village. The business remained in the Davis family until 1908 when Maynard Harpst became a partner.

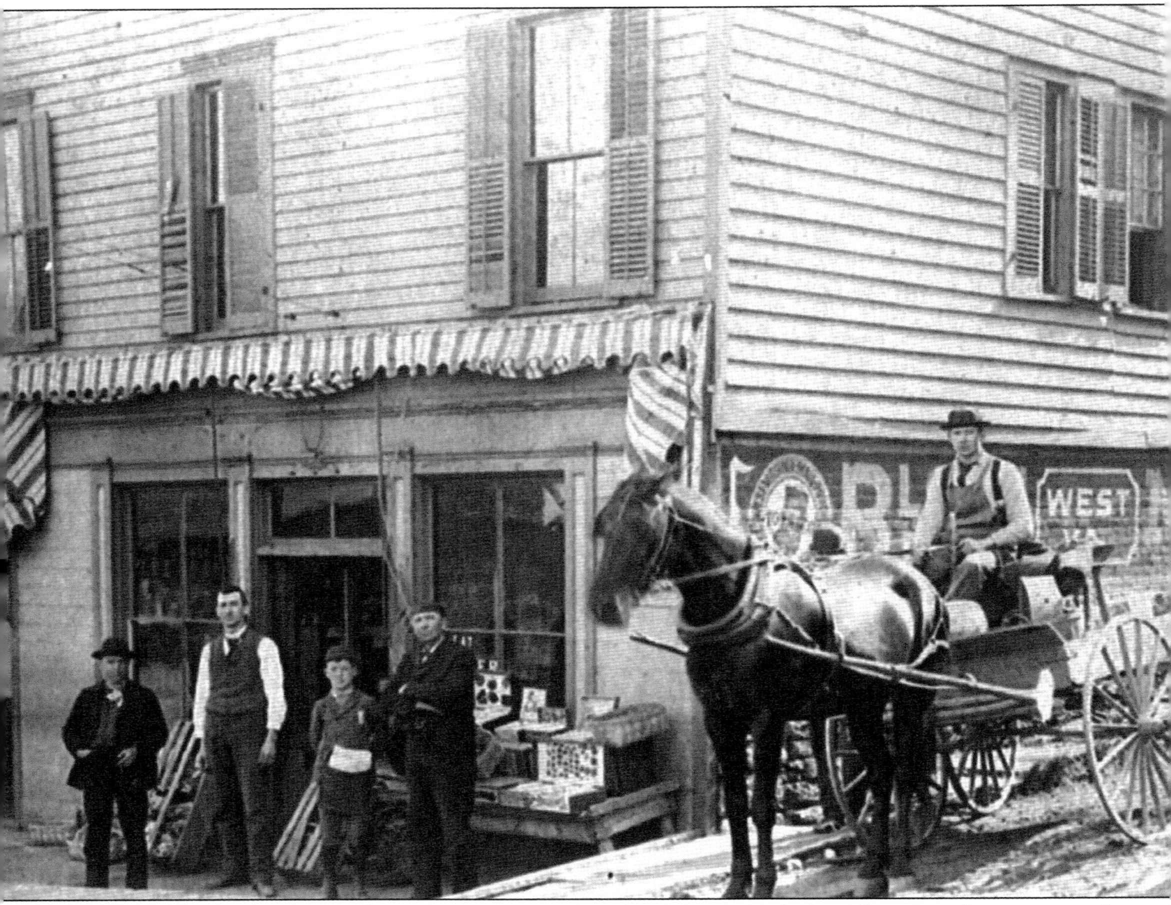

This exterior photograph of a general mercantile gives one a feeling for what shopping might have been like. With goods and products stocked in front of the store, a shopper had a good idea of what the merchant carried. Often, if the order was very large, it might even be delivered and the bill sent. There were several dry goods and mercantiles in Seneca Falls, often just a few doors apart, but they all seemed to thrive.

Four

Fire and Renewal

Fires can start for no known reason, but in Seneca Falls in 1890, there were wooden buildings, gas lights, and some questionable electrical wiring. Some time during the night of July 30, a fire started in one of the buildings on Fall Street. The alarm was sounded, and the fire companies sprang into action. It was a warm night, and there was a breeze. The local fire companies were unable to control the blaze. Waterloo fire companies were called to lend a hand. The fire roared on unstopped. Telegrams were sent to Geneva and Auburn for help. Due to the great distance, about 12 to 15 miles from either town, it was decided that the fire equipment, horses, and men would be loaded on flatbed railroad cars. This saved a great deal of time and kept the horses from becoming exhausted before they arrived at the fire.

After three days, the fire was finally extinguished. Most of the south side of Fall Street was gone, about two thirds of the north side was destroyed, and a block of State Street was gone.

Luckily there were no deaths or serious injuries. The cause of the fire was never discovered, but the village was determined to rebuild. Within just a few short years, Seneca Falls was a bustling village again; this time most of the buildings were brick.

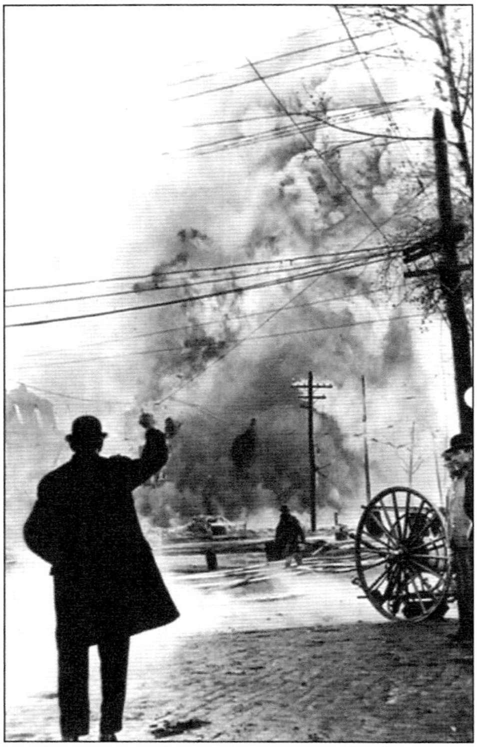

As fire devastates Seneca Falls, a man is silhouetted against the smoke. A hose cart, on the right—probably made right in Seneca Falls at Goulds, Rumsey, or Silsby—is being put to use. Old construction, no fire code enforcement, and some unusual electrical work caused many fires, but it also created a need for the hand pumps, hose carts, and rotary steam fire engines that were produced in town.

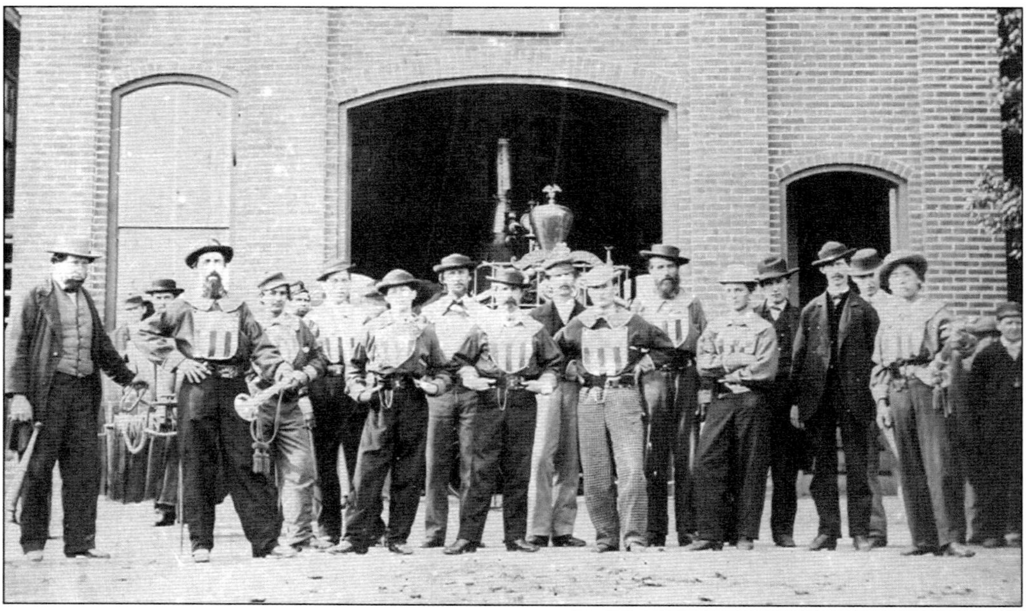

Ready for a parade, the Silsby Steam Engine Company poses in front of the Station on Fall Street. The steam engine can be seen in the background. When the fire companies were not putting out fires they enjoyed competing with other fire companies in things like distance pumping, skill with the hose nozzles, and races pulling the hose carts. In fact, special lightweight racing carts were made as well as very decorative carts for parades.

Young boys watch as a Silsby Steam fire engine rolls by. The early engines were small enough to be pulled by several men, but during a yellow fever outbreak, it was very difficult to find enough men so horses were put to use. Special rigs dropped the harness on the horses, saving time.

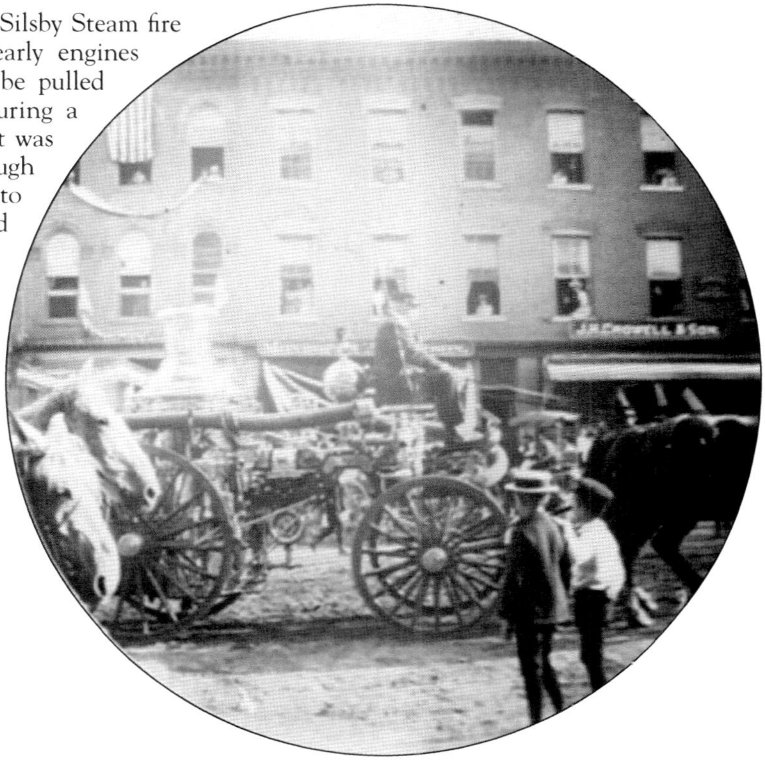

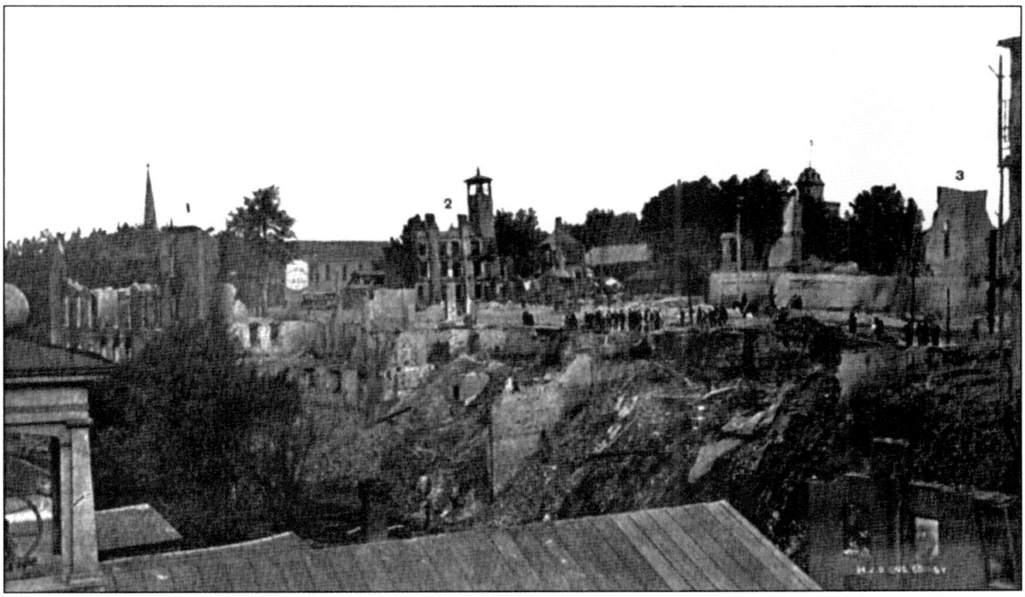

The fire and the ruins can be seen from the top of the Gleason and Bailey building. One can see (1) ruins of the Phoenix Block, (2) the remains of the Hoag House and Steamer Company No. 1, and (3) the Daniels Opera House. This photograph was taken by the Seneca County Courier and presented to firemen at the firemen's parade of July 30, 1891, the one-year anniversary of the fire.

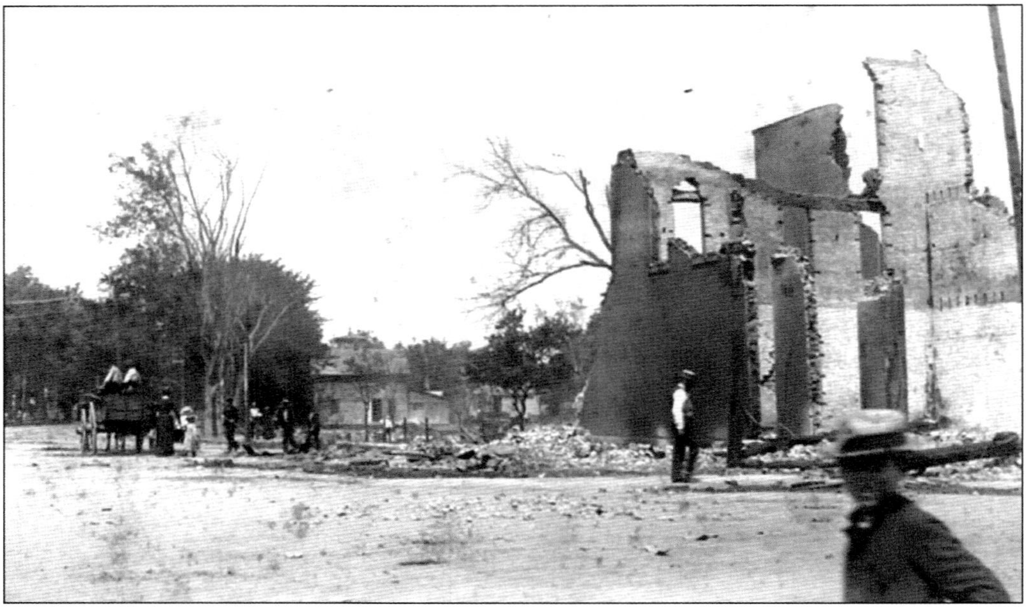

This is all that was left of the corner of Fall Street and State Street after the fire of 1890. The Hoag House would be rebuilt in a short time; the east side of State Street would soon have the Johnson Opera House.

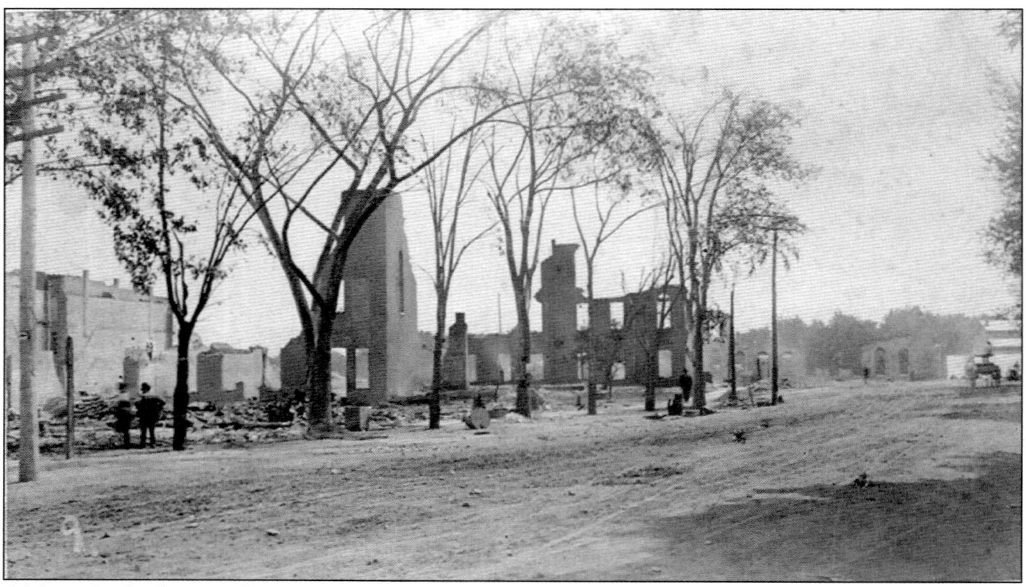

Although the heart of Seneca Falls was destroyed by flames, there were still men of enterprise and capital who were ready to rebuild. Most of the factories and mills on the river were not burned, so they were able to continue to employ the men and produce goods that could be used or exported. As the businesses and merchants could, they started to rebuild.

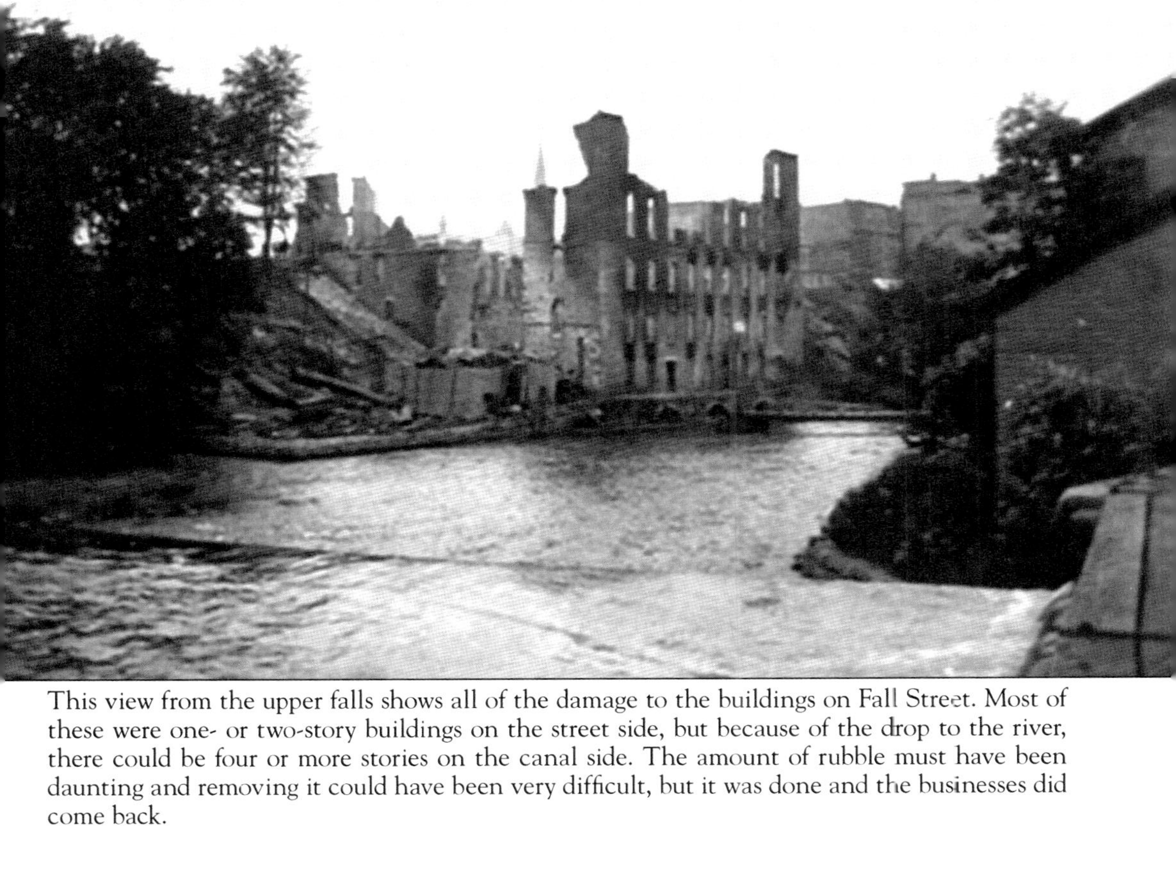

This view from the upper falls shows all of the damage to the buildings on Fall Street. Most of these were one- or two-story buildings on the street side, but because of the drop to the river, there could be four or more stories on the canal side. The amount of rubble must have been daunting and removing it could have been very difficult, but it was done and the businesses did come back.

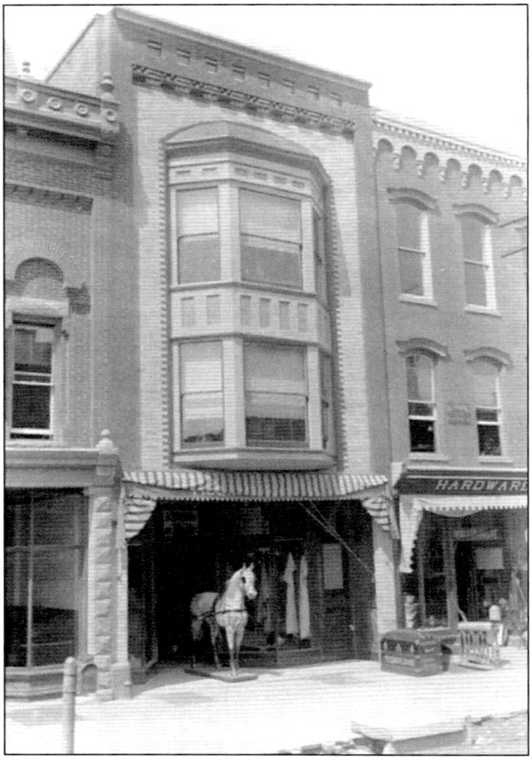

As Fall Street recovered, there were new shops that opened. Dobson Harness Shop carried all types of leather goods from harnesses to suitcases. In a promotional movie made in Seneca Falls in 1915, customers can be seen streaming out of Dobson Harness Shop carrying all sorts of merchandise. There is an unending supply of customers in the few minutes the camera is on the entrance; about 50 people are seen leaving, sometimes twice.

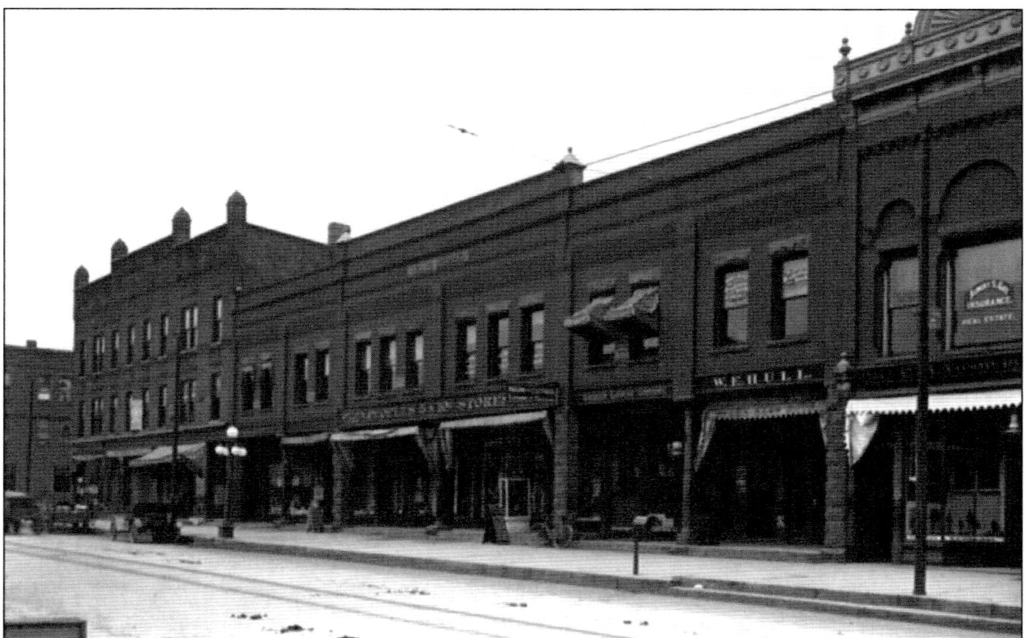

Just west of Dobson Harness Shop, the King block was built, once the location of the Daniels Opera block. This building was used for offices and shops. The American Express office was located here. Some of the original cut stone pillars can still be seen today.

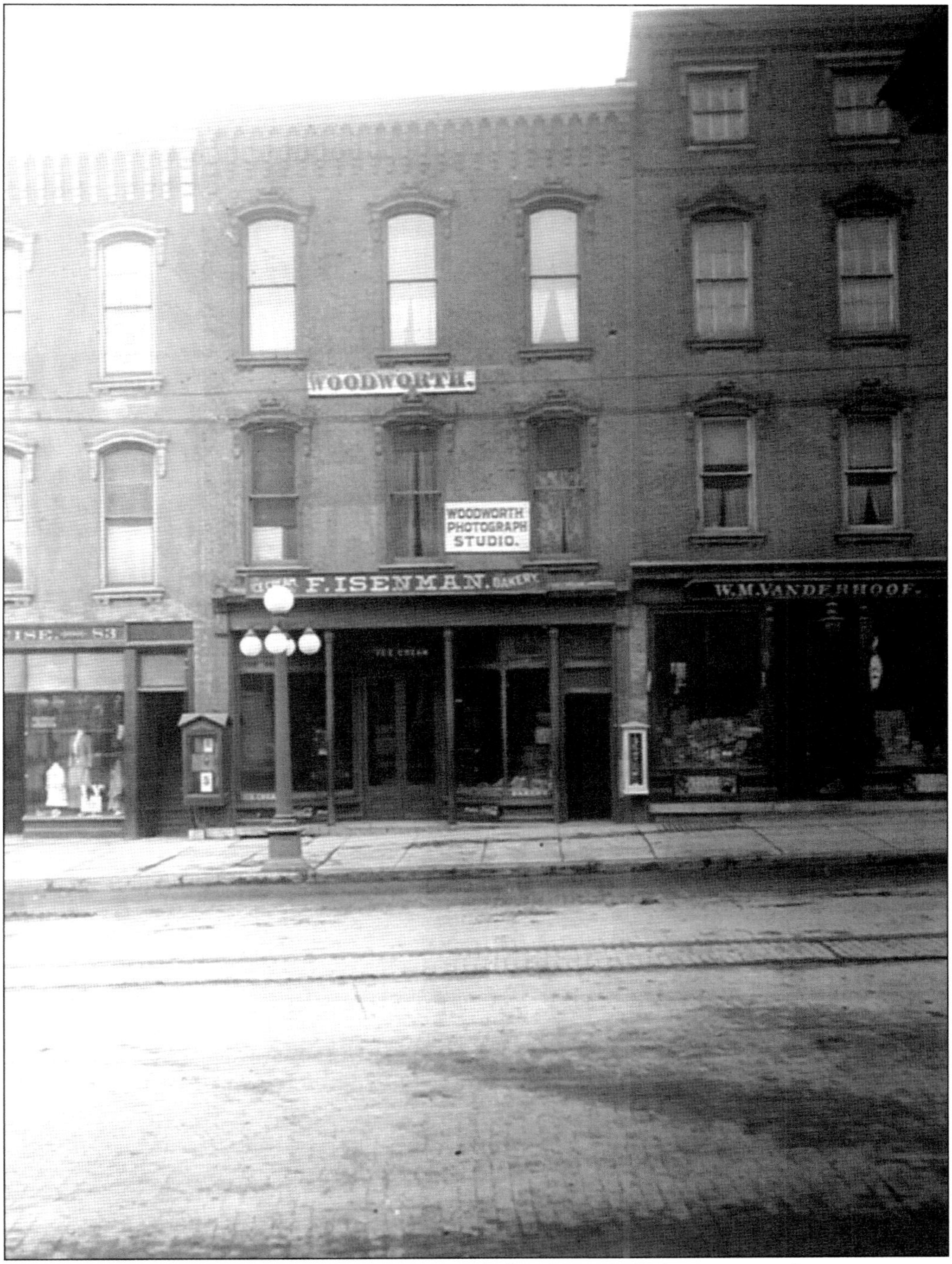

This is Fall Street as seen from Cayuga Street, before New York department of transportation bent Cayuga Street to the east to make it easier for traffic going over the canal. The sign for Grace Woodworth's studio can be seen in the center. Her studio had a skylight to allow for natural lighting. The structure of the skylight can still be seen, but the glass has been removed or covered up.

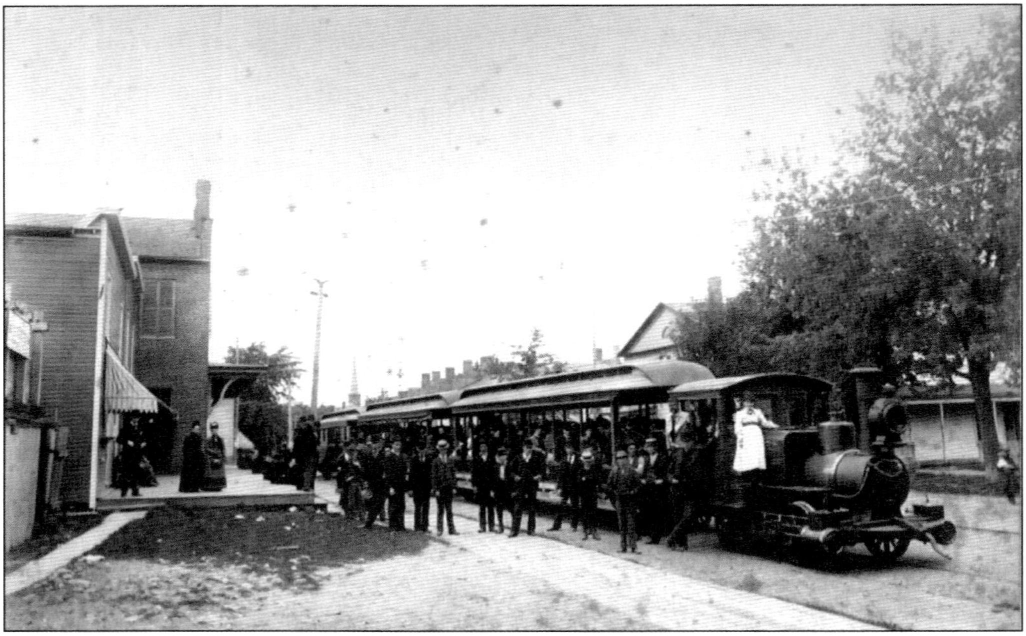

With prosperity came leisure time, and a great way to spend this time was taking the trolley to Cayuga Lake Park. A private company built the trolley line and the park as a destination. The line went from Geneva, to Waterloo, to Seneca Falls, and then to the park. All day at the lake could be had for a small price.

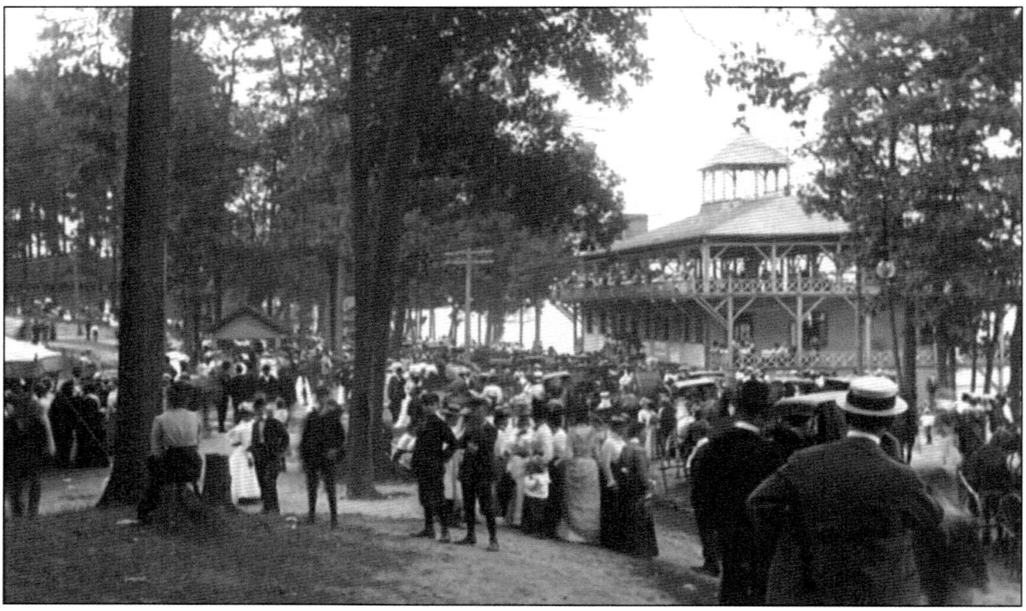

Arriving at Cayuga Lake Park, the excitement could be felt and delicious food, rides, boating, and dancing were offered. This business thrived for several years until the automobile became more popular and no one needed the trolley. The park was abandoned for a short time until it became a state park in the 1920s. Many of the buildings were repaired by the Civilian Conservation Corps (CCC).

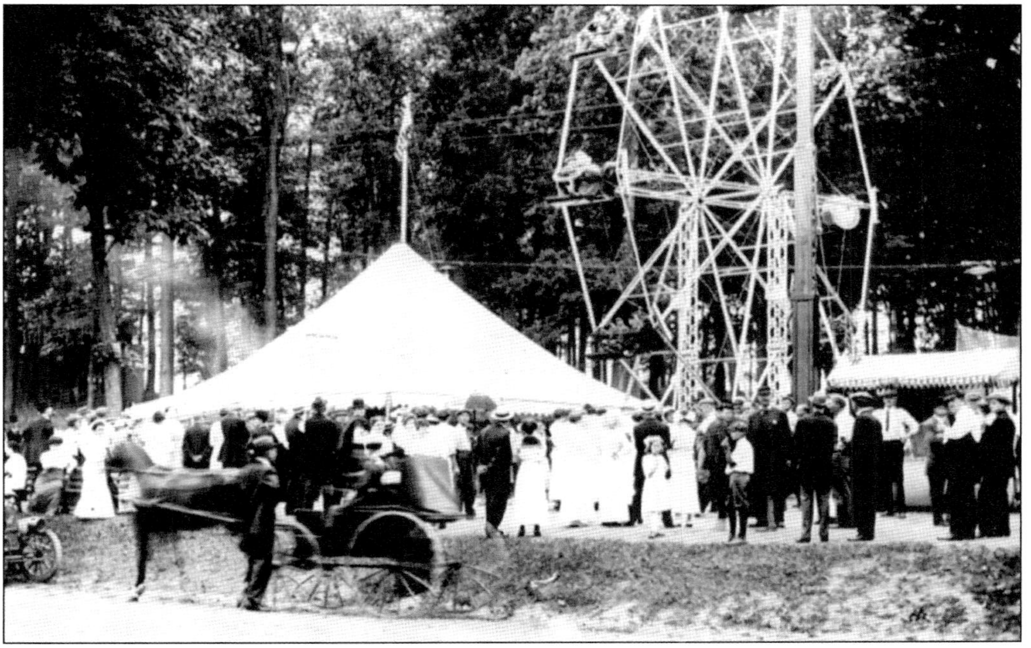

The Ferris wheel was a very popular ride, and from the top, one could see across Cayuga Lake. The motion going around and around was exciting. One also never knew when one might get stuck up there.

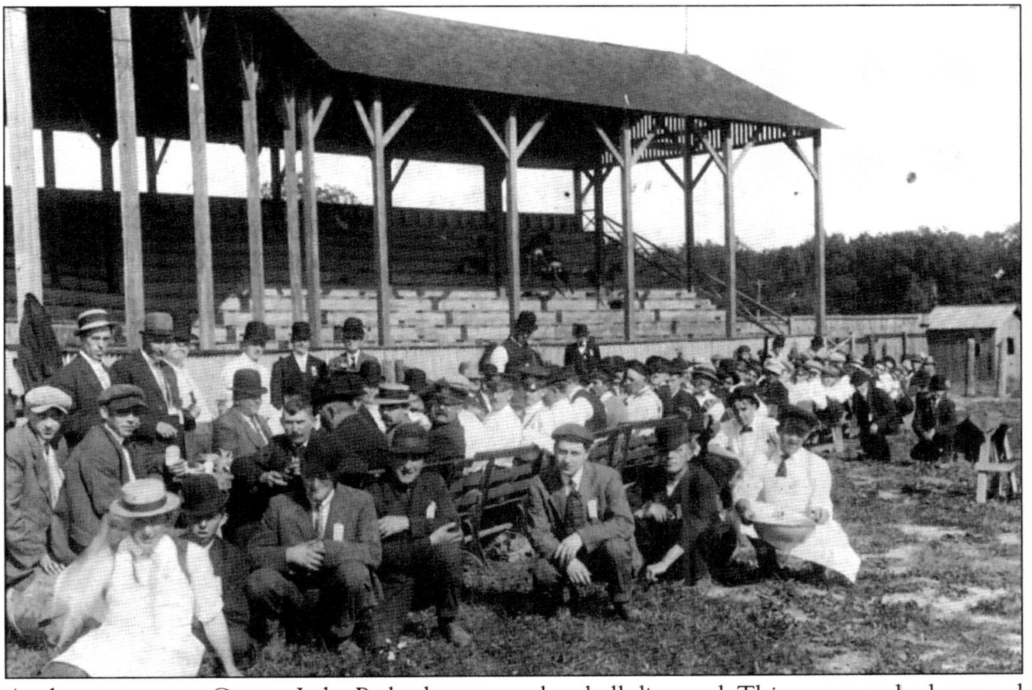

At the entrance to Cayuga Lake Park, there was a baseball diamond. This one even had covered stands. Many local teams played at this field, and some semi-professional and even professional teams would play games here. Baseball was a very popular sport, but it was not played on Sundays.

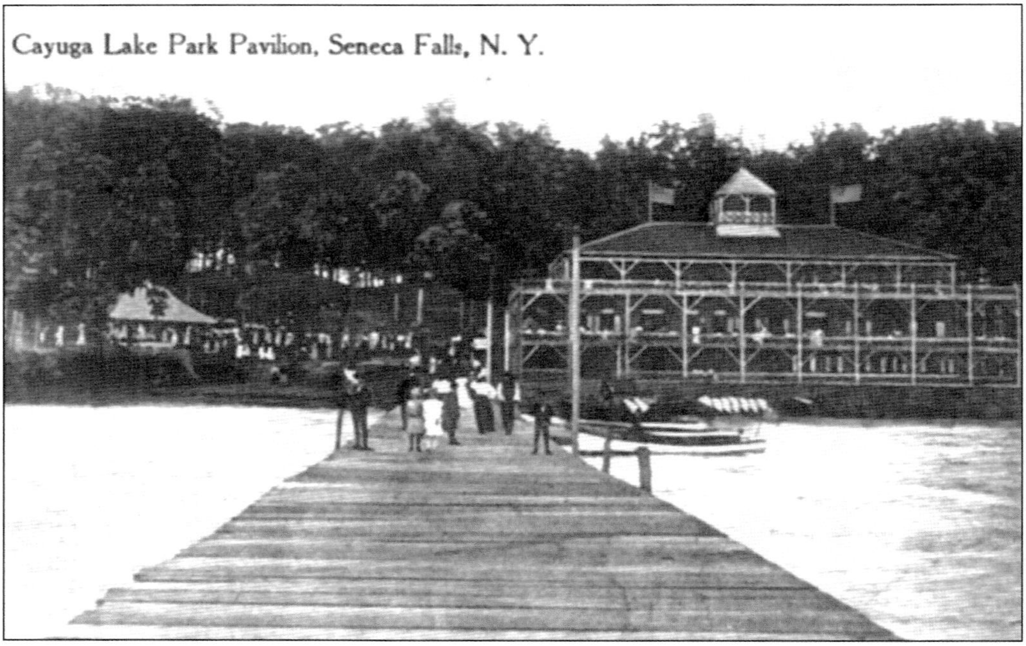

The dock at Cayuga Lake offered several kinds of boats. The *Frontanac* and *Iroquois* were lake steamers that would go all the way to Ithaca and across the lake to Union Springs or Aurora. Anyone who wanted to pilot themselves could rent a rowboat or small sailboat. For true luxury, a small steam launch was available. This was a great place to take a sweetheart.

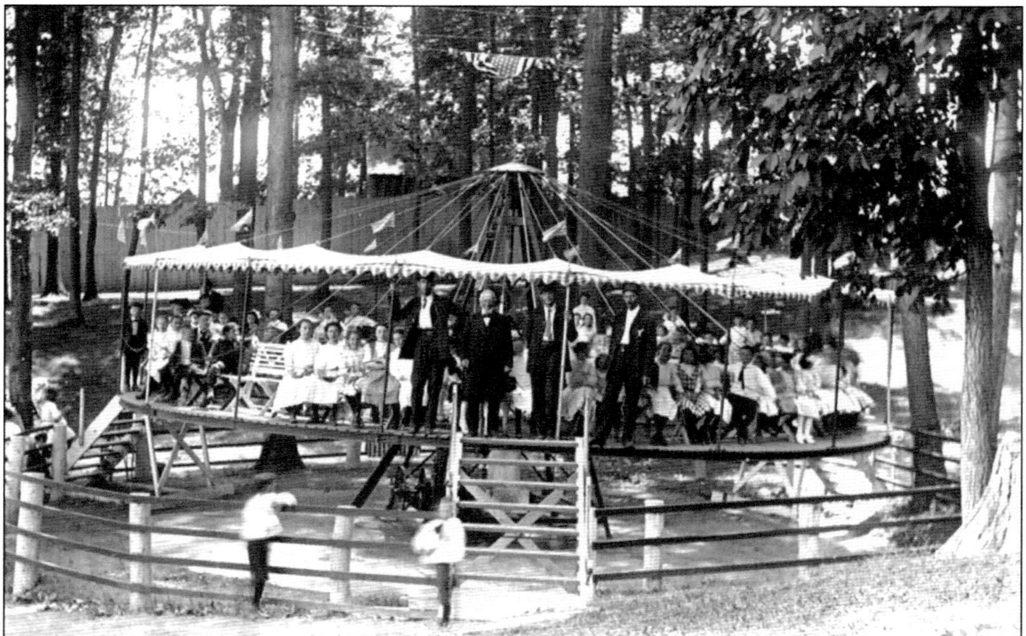

A group of children from St. Patrick's Church are enjoying the merry-go-round at Cayuga Lake Park. This merry-go-round has benches instead of horses. This photograph was taken in July 1906.

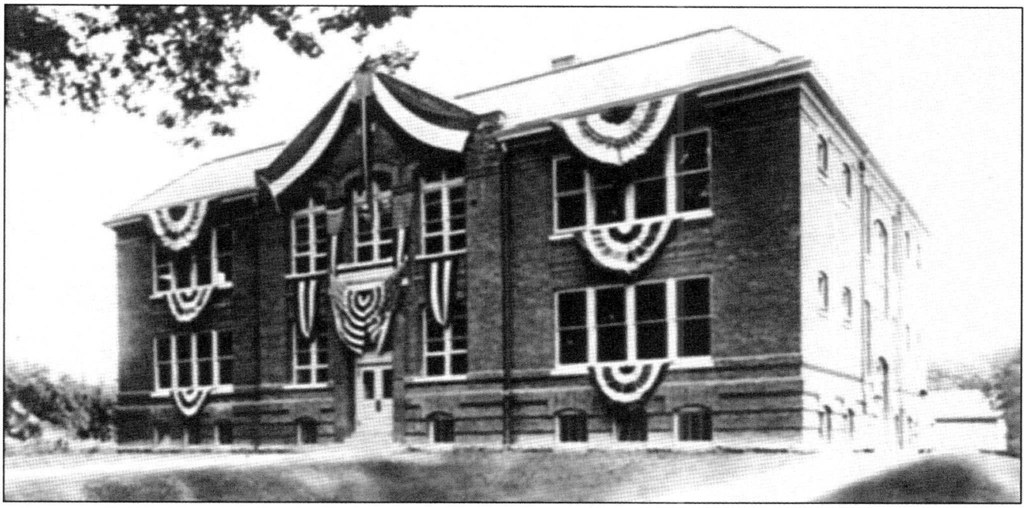

First Ward School was built near Mynderse Academy and was decorated for "Old Home" week. Seneca County residents who had moved away were invited to return for a visit in August 1906. Each town had special activities during the week, and a guest book was available to sign.

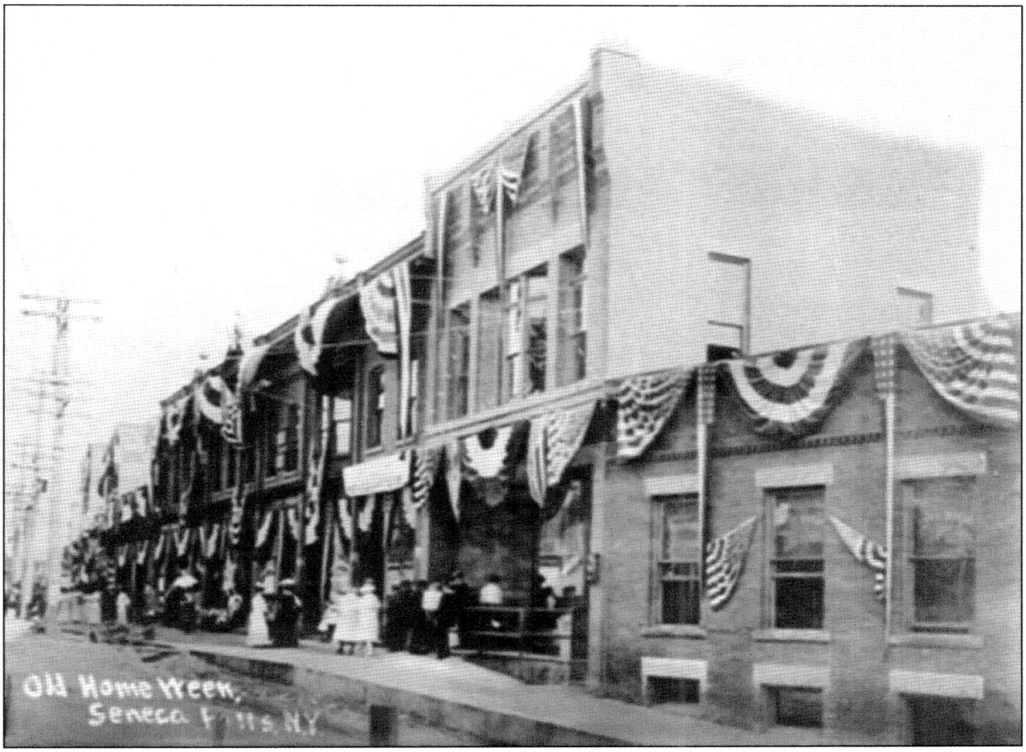

Fall Street is seen here in 1906 decorated with bunting on both sides from one end to the other to welcome back former residents. There were fireworks and parades all week long in the various towns. The event was very successful because of the cooperation of all of the towns.

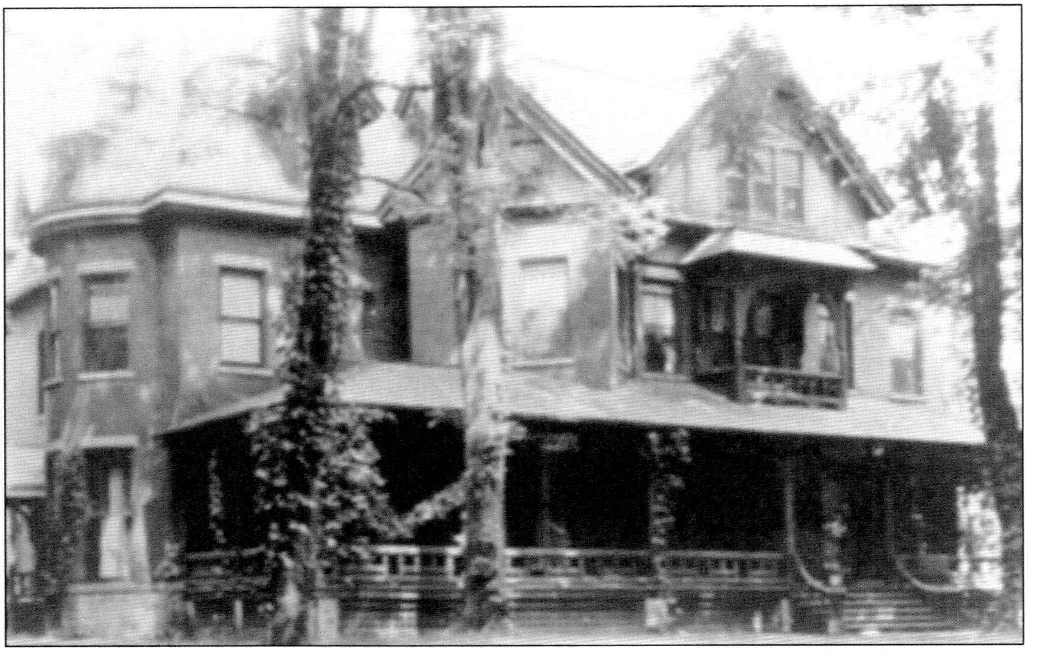

Cayuga Street was once known as millionaires row, as the wealthiest families lived in large stately houses on this tree-lined street. The Becker house was one of these, once owned by Edward Mynderse and then extensively remodeled in the 1880s by Ellen Partridge. For 70 years, the Beckers enjoyed the house, and now it is enjoyed by all who visit the Seneca Falls Historical Society.

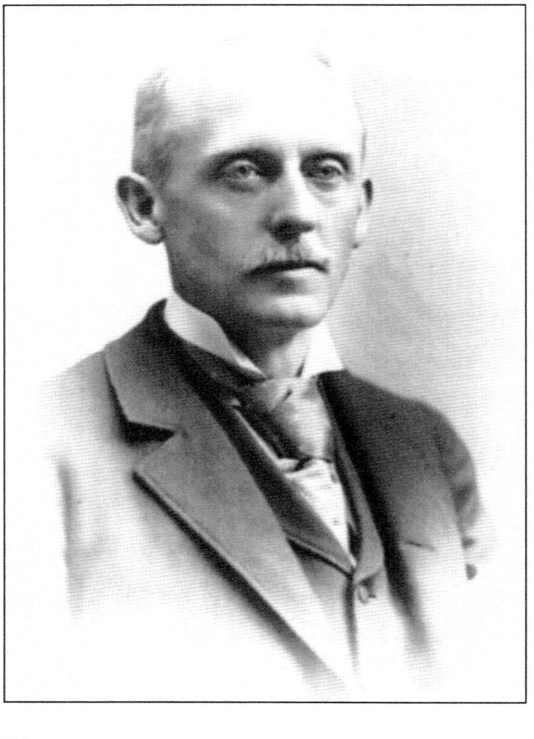

Norman Haines Becker was born in Fayette, New York, in 1842. The family then moved to Waterloo. After graduating from Hamilton College, he taught for a short time at Whitestown Seminary. On his return to Seneca County, he was appointed the teller of the National Exchange Bank in Seneca Falls. He was known as being frank and assured in all business dealings. He died while abroad in Turkey in 1900.

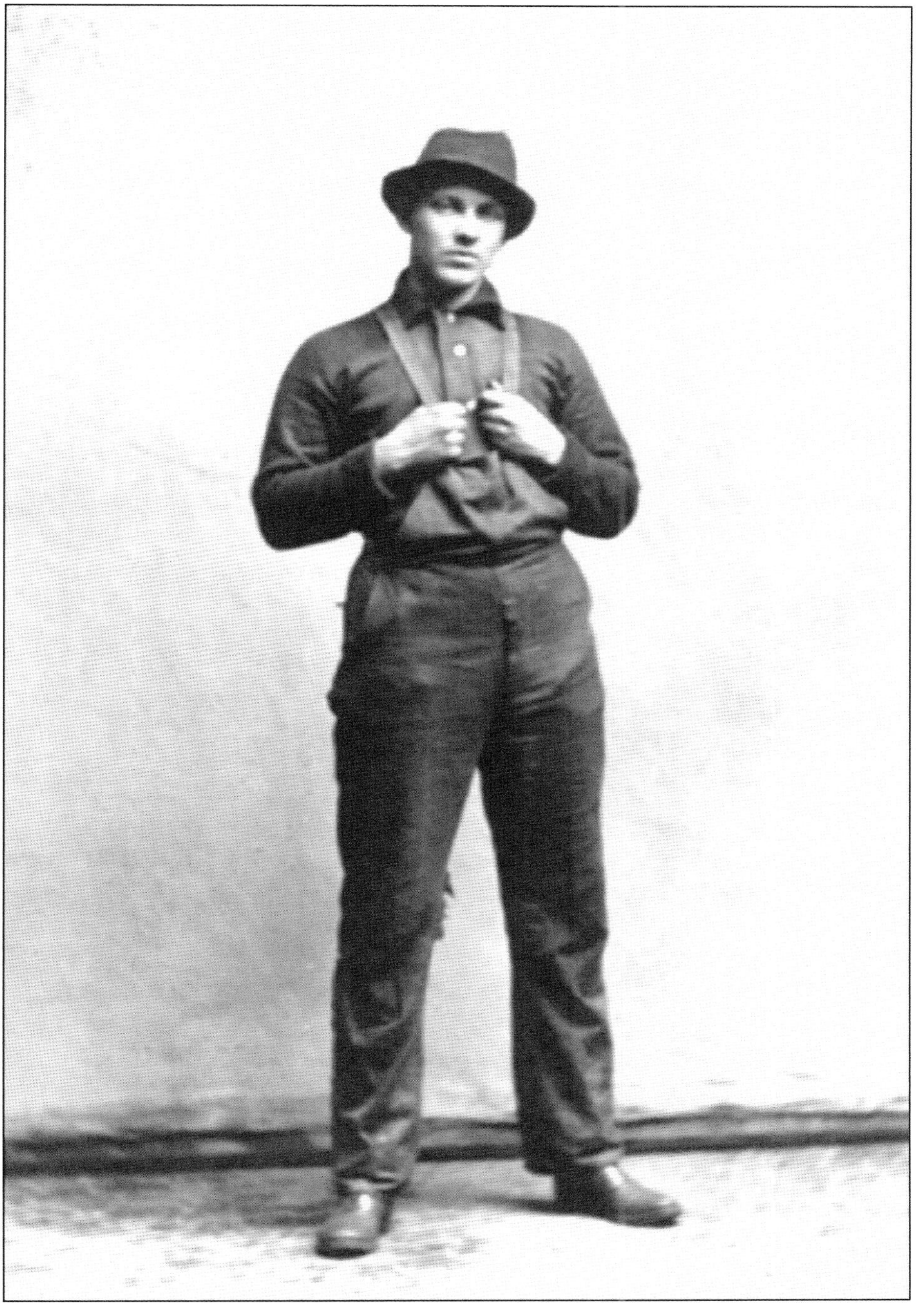

Norman Judd Gould, grandson of Seabury Smith Gould of Goulds Pumps, was the last of the Gould family to run the company. His maternal grandfather, Judge Norman Buel Judd, placed Abraham Lincoln's name into nomination in Chicago in 1860. During his youth, Norman worked in every department at Goulds, even the foundry. He graduated from Cornell University, became the president of Goulds, was a congressman, and could say hello to all of the Goulds employees as he met them on the street.

GOULDS SPANISH-AMERICAN STEEL AMALGAM BELLS.

These Bells are made so as to be fastened from the top and to remain stationary. They are to be rung by a cord fastened in the eye at the end of the clapper, after the manner of chime bells, and they are *Real, Ringing Merry Bells.*

No farm, plantation or factory should be without one.

FIG. 354.

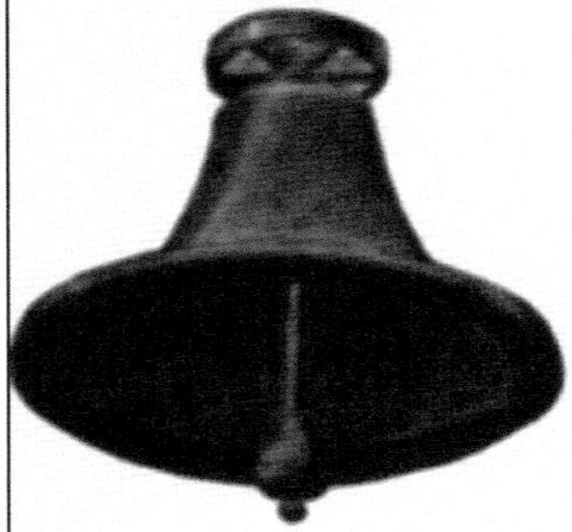

FIG. 354. Sizes, Prices, Etc.

No.	Dia.	Weight Bell only.	Cipher.	Price.
1	15½ in.	38 lbs.	Fagot	$ 4.80
2	16½ "	51 "	Fall	6.00
2½	17½ "	57 "	Fain	7.00
3	18½ "	65 "	Faint	7.75
4	21 "	80 "	Fell	10.00
5	24 "	134 "	Felt	14.00
6	28 "	247 "	Fen	30.00
7	30 "	325 "	Fence	36.00
8	33 "	414 "	Fern	55.00

GOULDS LARGE STEEL AMALGAM BELLS.

WITH HANGINGS AND FRAME.

FIG. 353.

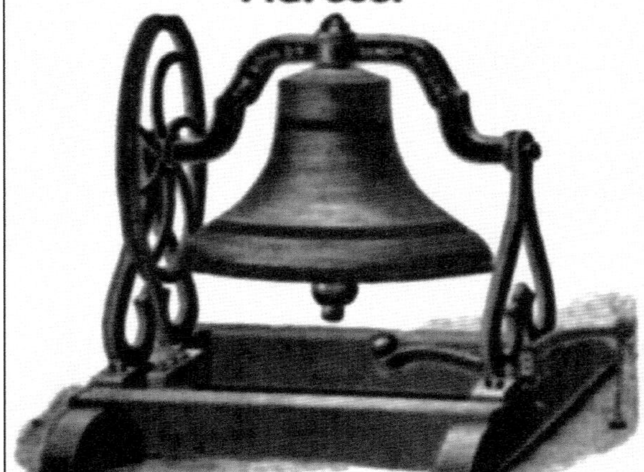

Fig. 353 represents our Steel Amalgam Bells as we mount them in the larger sizes for churches, schoolhouses, factories, engine houses, etc. We have sent thousands of these Bells to various portions of the United States, as their cheapness places them in the reach of any church, and they have always given splendid satisfaction.

We send all our Bells to market richly gilded.

We put tolling attachment as shown in cut, on Nos. 6 and 7 at $4.00 extra, and on No. 8 at $5.00 extra list.

FIG. 353. Sizes, Prices, Etc.

No.	Dia.	Weight of Bell only.	Weight Complete.	Size of Frame.	Cipher.	Price.
3	18½ in.	65 lbs.	172 lbs.	27 x 41½ in.	Fabric	$16.00
4	21 "	80 "	186 "	30 x 41½ "	Fabrile	20.00
5	24 "	134 "	240 "	32½ x 41½ "	Fable	25.00
6	28 "	247 "	306½ "	36 x 48 "	Face	40.00
7	30 "	325 "	487 "	36 x 48 "	Fact	50.00
8	33 "	414 "	689½ "	38 x 48 "	Fade	75.00

Bells from the Goulds foundries are found in every state of the union and in many countries around the world. The other pump producers in Seneca Falls also made bells, and in their catalogs they extolled the virtues of their steel amalgams. This is a page from the 1885 Goulds catalog, but it could be from any catalog because the bells and their prices changed very little over the years.

Jeptha Wade was born in Romulus, New York, in 1811 and was a portrait painter and made daguerreotypes for a short time in Seneca Falls. In 1840, he moved his family first to Michigan and then settled in Cleveland. His interest in telegraphy was the start of Western Union. Over the years, Wade's generosity helped to create Cleveland's educational and cultural foundations.

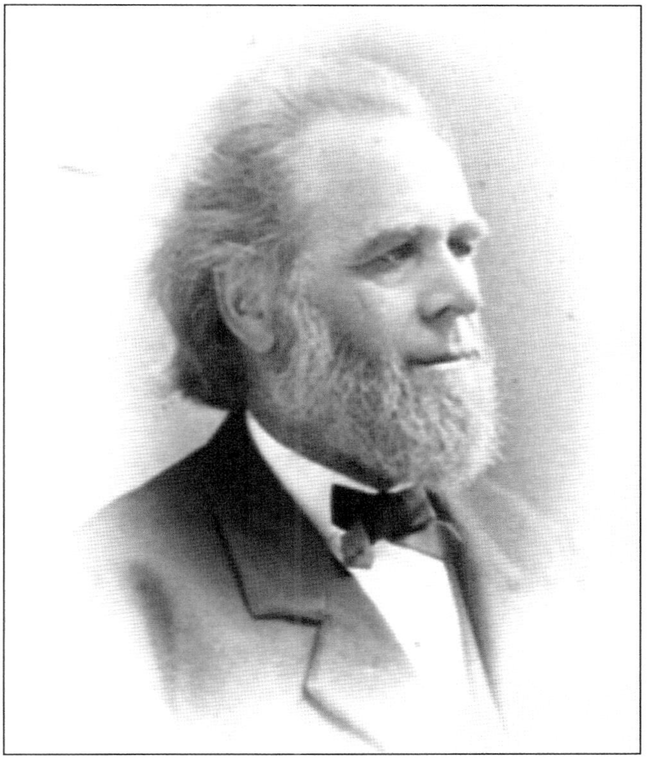

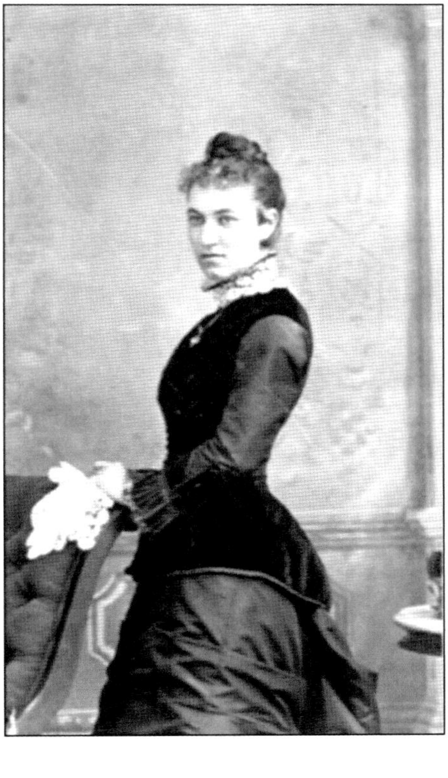

Janet McKay Cowing, the daughter John P. Cowing, was one of the founders of the Sa-Go-Ye-Wat-Ha chapter of the Daughters of the American Revolution and the Seneca Falls Historical Society. She was born in 1852 in Seneca Falls. She researched and wrote several articles about early families, business, and events of Seneca Falls that have been published.

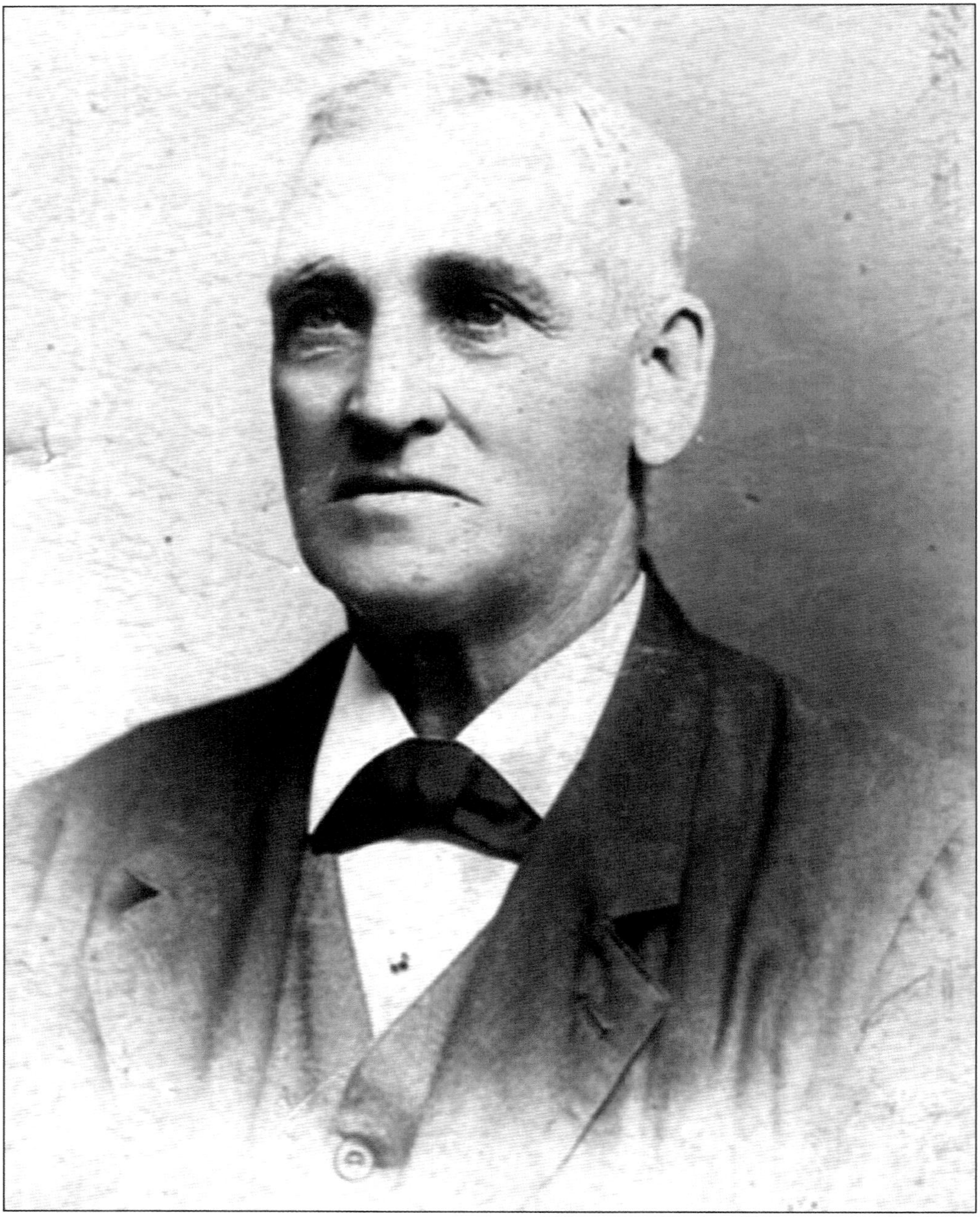

Milton Hoag, at one time the president of the Exchange National Bank and also the owner of a great deal of real estate in Seneca Falls, was very instrumental in building up the village. Trained as a butcher, he later worked in the grocery business. Upon his arrival in Seneca Falls in 1851, he was in the whiskey business with his brother. In 1866, he sold out of the whiskey business and bought Carr's Hotel and renovated the building. After the fire of 1890, the Hoag House, his real estate holdings, and business were wiped out. This effectively caused him to retire.

Five

Newcomers Help to Build and Rebuild Seneca Falls

As Seneca Falls rebuilt, it relied on the newest wave of immigrants to help. These new arrivals were the Italians, and they contributed to the community just as the first wave of immigrants, the Irish, had done.

The Irish had arrived just as Seneca Falls began to grow. They worked on the canal, railroads, and in the young factories. The young women who came to America often alone took jobs as domestics or shop girls. Soon the Irish were store owners, businessmen, policemen and firemen, and community leaders.

After the fire of 1890, the factories still needed hands, but many of the men were busy rebuilding Seneca Falls. A young Italian came to Seneca Falls by mistake and found that it provided plenty of opportunity, so he stayed. Charles Fornesi became an established businessman, and he then encouraged family and friends to leave Italy and come to Seneca Falls.

The Italian immigrants arrived ready to work and build a new life. Many found jobs in the factories and mills; some grew vegetables, and some opened grocery stores selling familiar foods to their friends. Today the Italians are a strong and vital part of Seneca Falls.

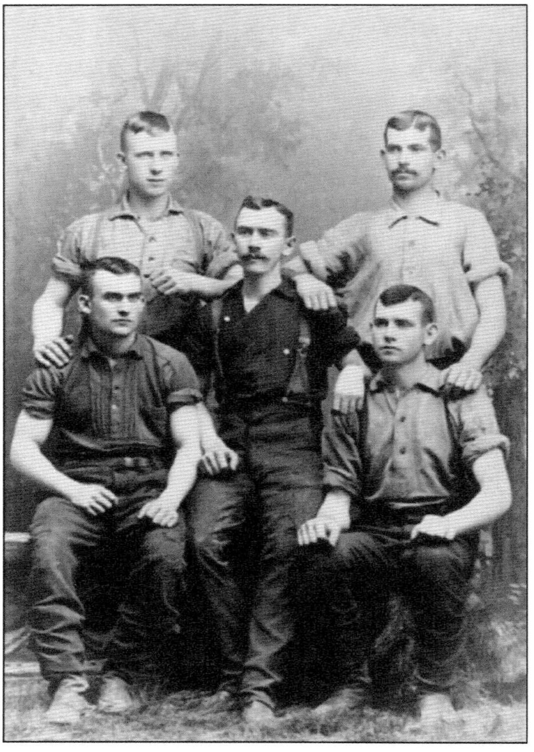

The McKeon men are seen in a studio portrait taken at the J. E. Hale Studio in Seneca Falls. Seen here are iron molder James McKeon (center) with his sons Frederick, Joseph (born 1866), James Jr. (born 1871), and Patrick (born 1864). All but James Jr. were iron molders; he was a barber.

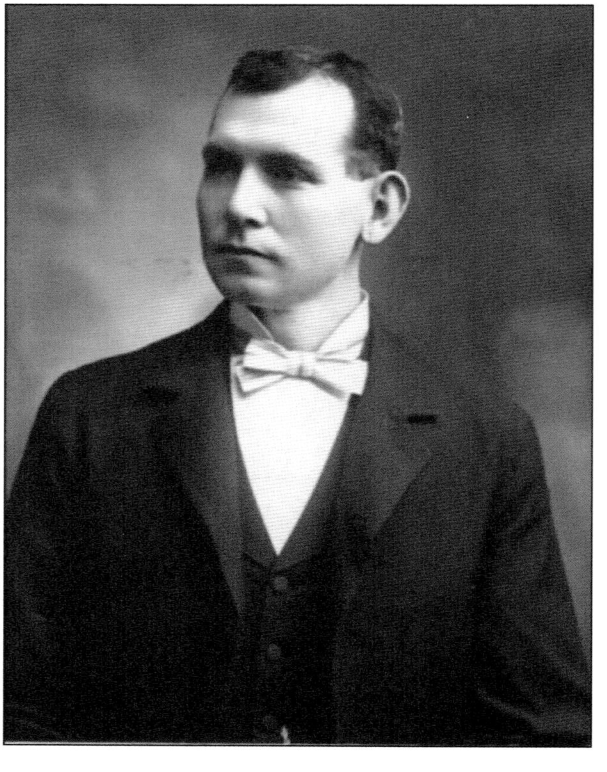

Patrick became a policeman on the Seneca Falls Police force. He had the misfortune of being the first officer killed in the line of duty in 1902.

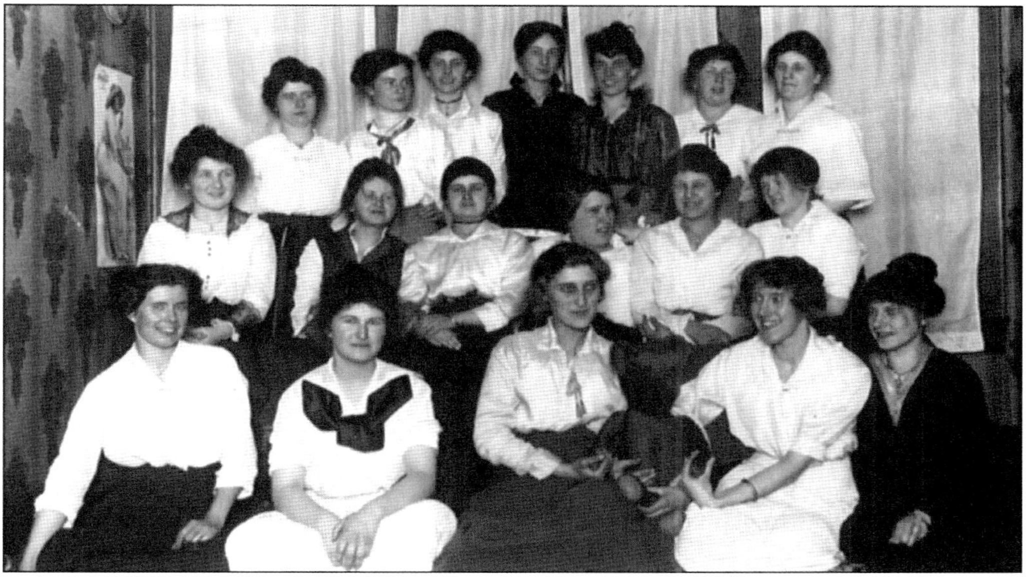

Many of the Irish girls worked outside the home in offices or shops. Here is a group of young women who worked in an office. Seen here are, from left to right, Ellen Galvin Covert, Isabelle Freer, Katherine McDonald, Florence Galvin Pow, and unidentified; (second row) Eve Campbell, Francis Greer, Anna Young Brady, unidentified, Mildred Perkins, and Marie Campbell; (third row) Mary Rice Trowbridge, Mary Ryan, two unidentified, Gerladine Ryan Oaks, Catherine Lyman, and unidentified.

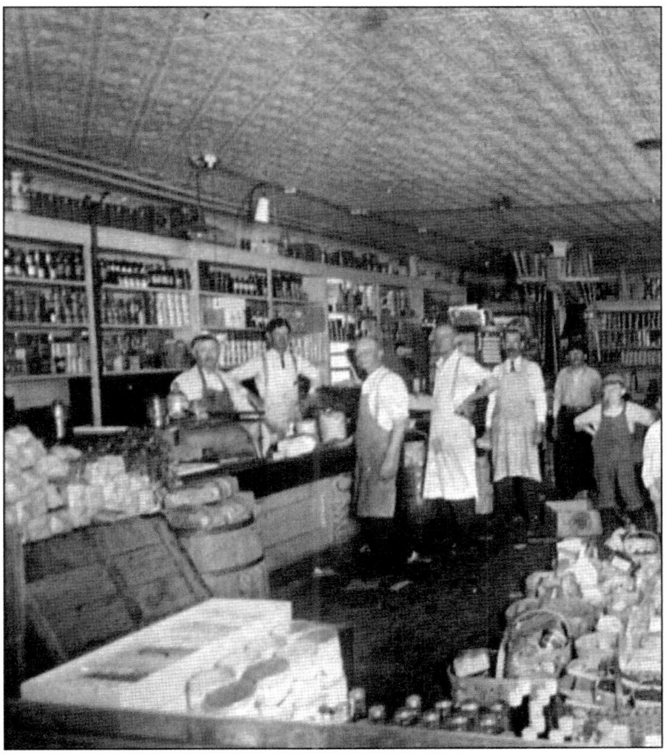

John McGraw is the tall clerk behind the counter. He managed to increase his trade in the store by personally walking to all of his customers' homes to take their orders.

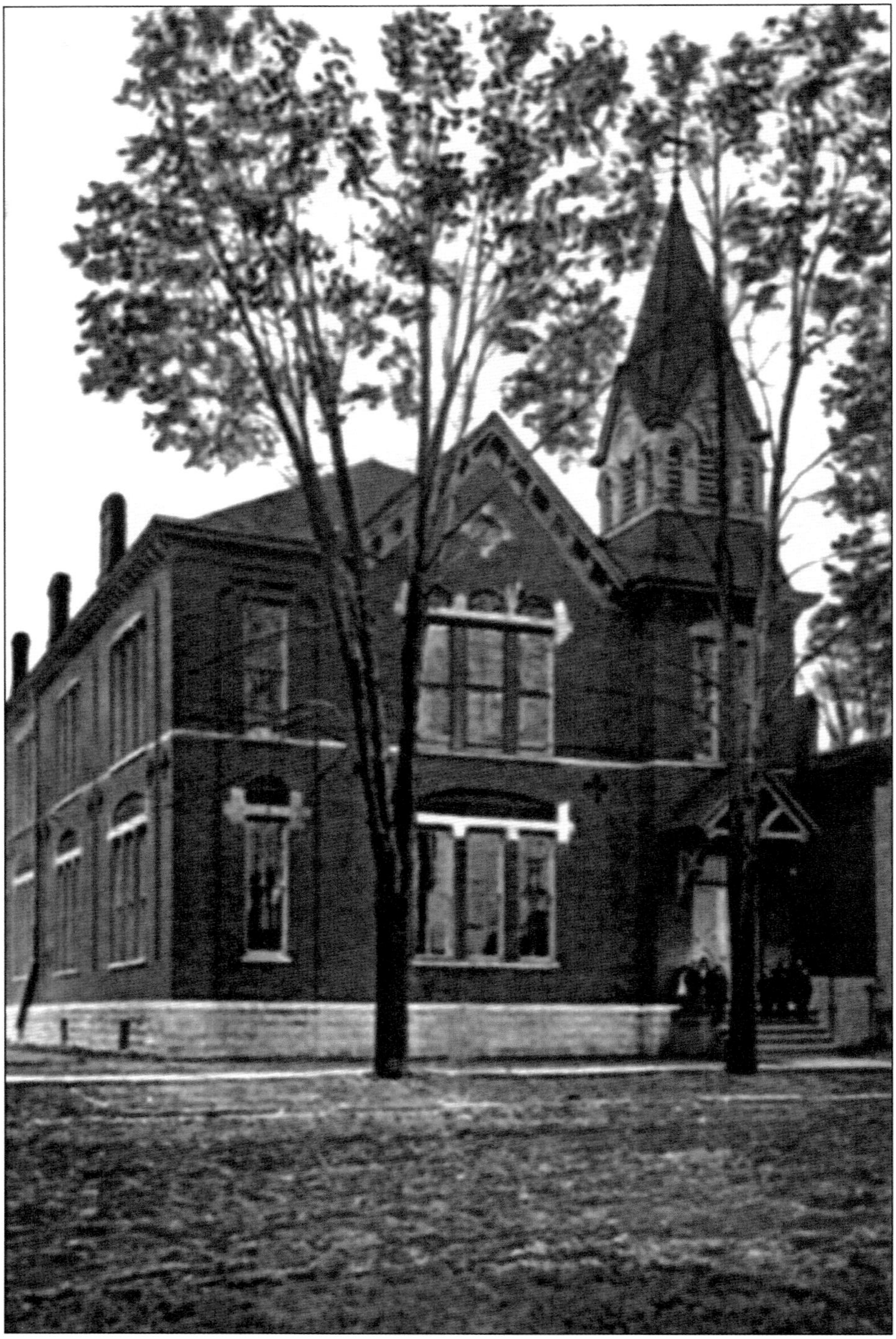

St. Patrick's School was first built in the late 1880s, as there were more Irish students that wanted a Catholic education. As the years went by, the school grew larger, and soon the parish needed a convent for the nuns. At one time, there was talk of moving St. Patrick's School to the north side of the canal, but nothing ever came of it.

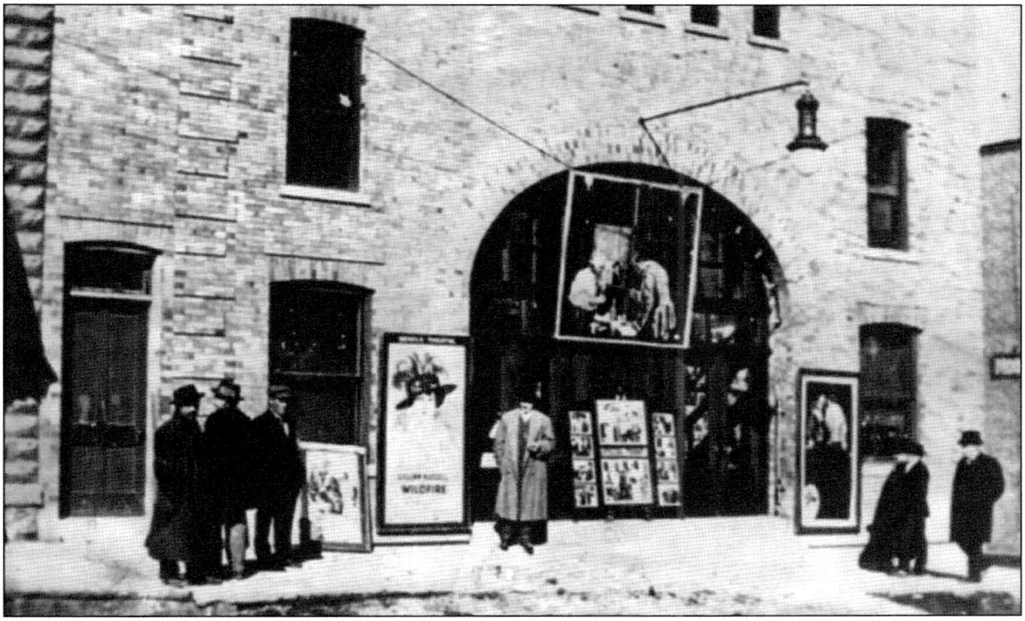

The first movie theater was located on lower Fall Street and was owned by Charles Fornesi. The building has a nice arched entryway that was good for showing the broadsides and posters for the coming features.

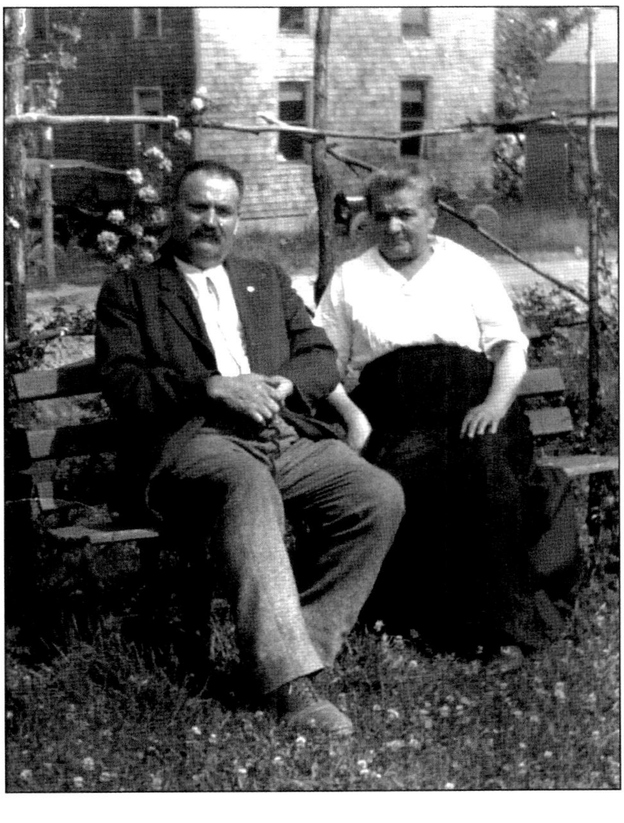

Fornesi and his wife, Erena, are enjoying their garden. After settling in Seneca Falls their family grew to 10 children: David, Julia, Charles, Rose, Erena, Catherine, Frank, Fred, Paul, and Louis. Fred would serve in the U.S. Army during World War I.

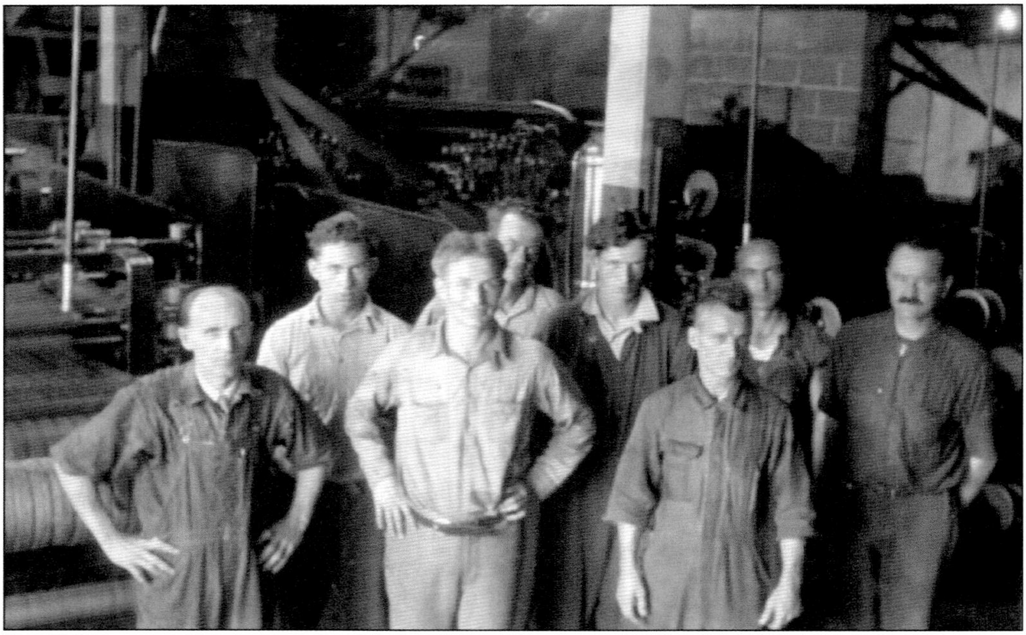

Many of the new arrivals took jobs in the knitting mill, where they learned new skills and English. The drive belts can be seen in the upper part of the photograph. All of the machines were run by these belts that were connected to the main power source. In the early days, that would have been the mill wheel.

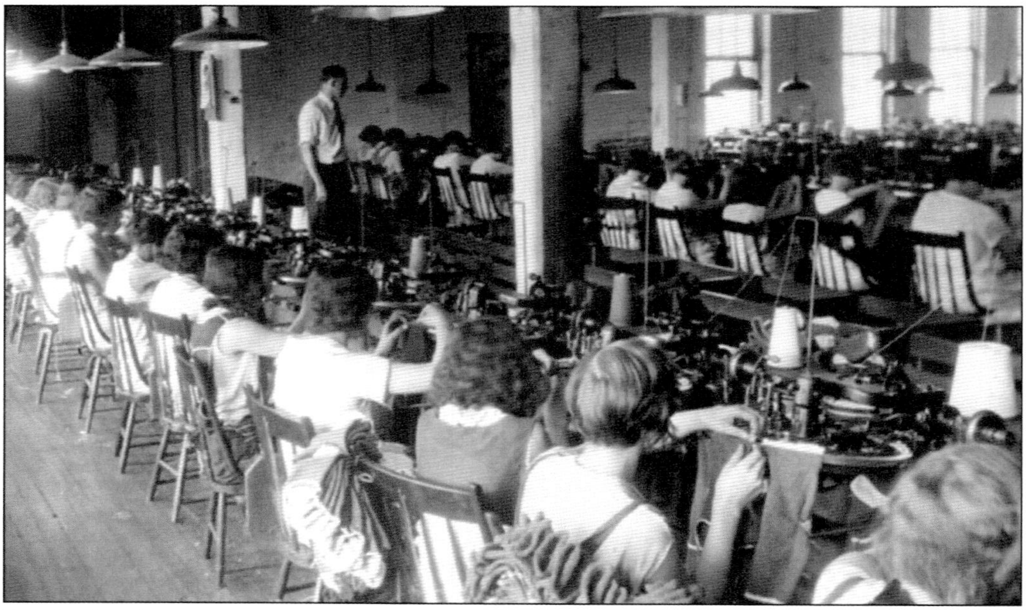

For the first few years, the Italian women were reluctant to work outside the home. There were plenty of jobs available in the knitting mill. All of the women were paid by the piece; the faster one worked, the more one made. They are working knitting machines that make socks. The finished socks can be seen on the backs of their chairs; someone will come and take the socks to the washing room next.

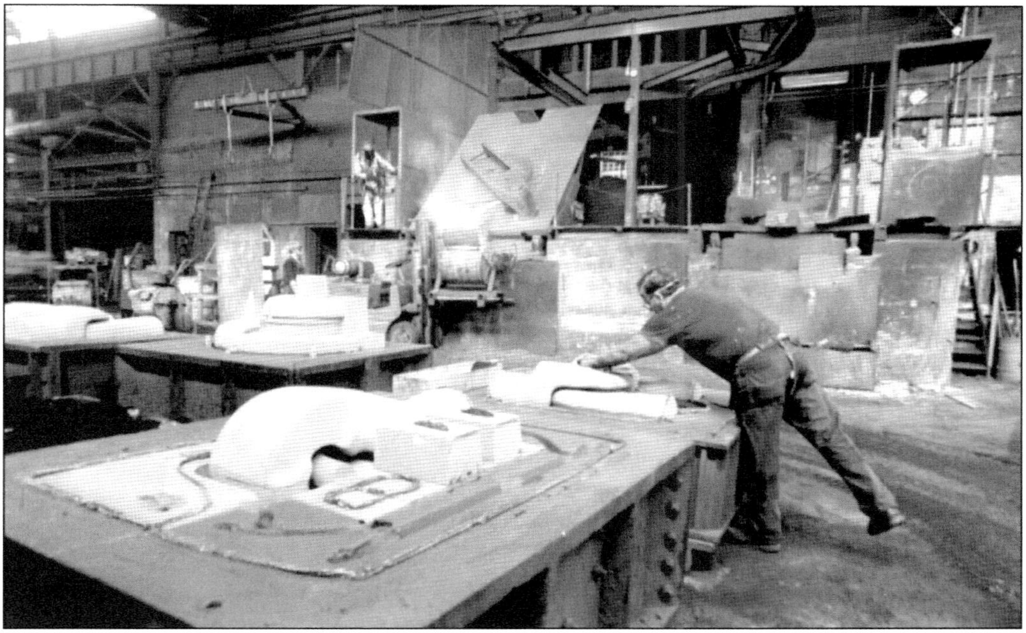

Anthony Barbieri, a core setter at Goulds, makes last-minute adjustments to a mold before a pour. Working temperatures that can be well over 100 degrees and having tons of molten metal all around can be a very difficult work situation. These highly-skilled core setters were considered vital to the war effort in the 1940s.

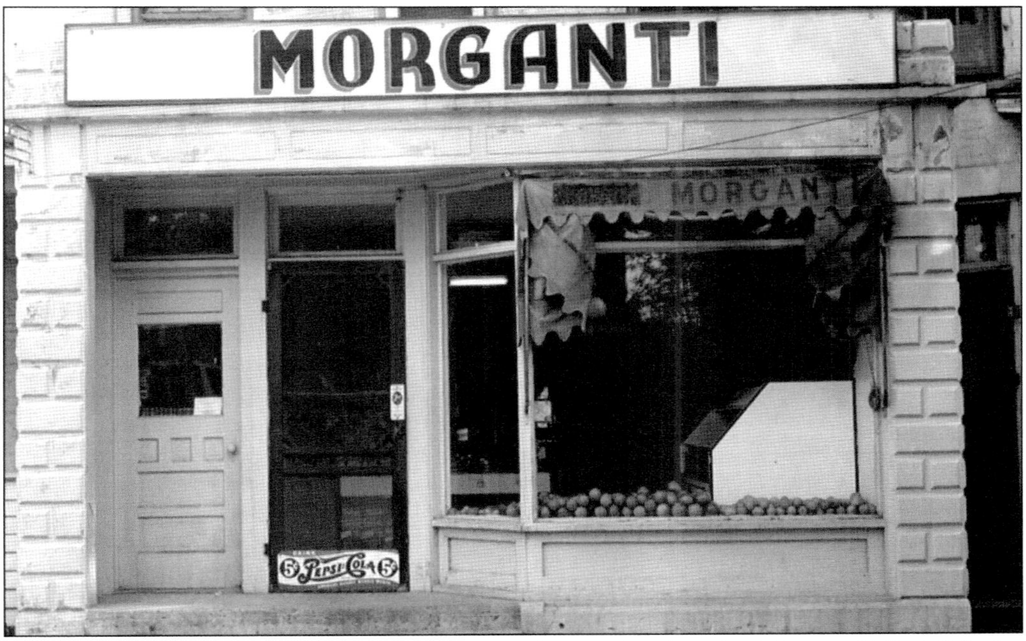

There have always been small grocery stores in the neighborhoods of Seneca Falls. With the increase of Italians moving in, many of the stores were owned by Italian families, and they carried foods that were familiar to the recent immigrants and also broadened the tastes of their American neighbors.

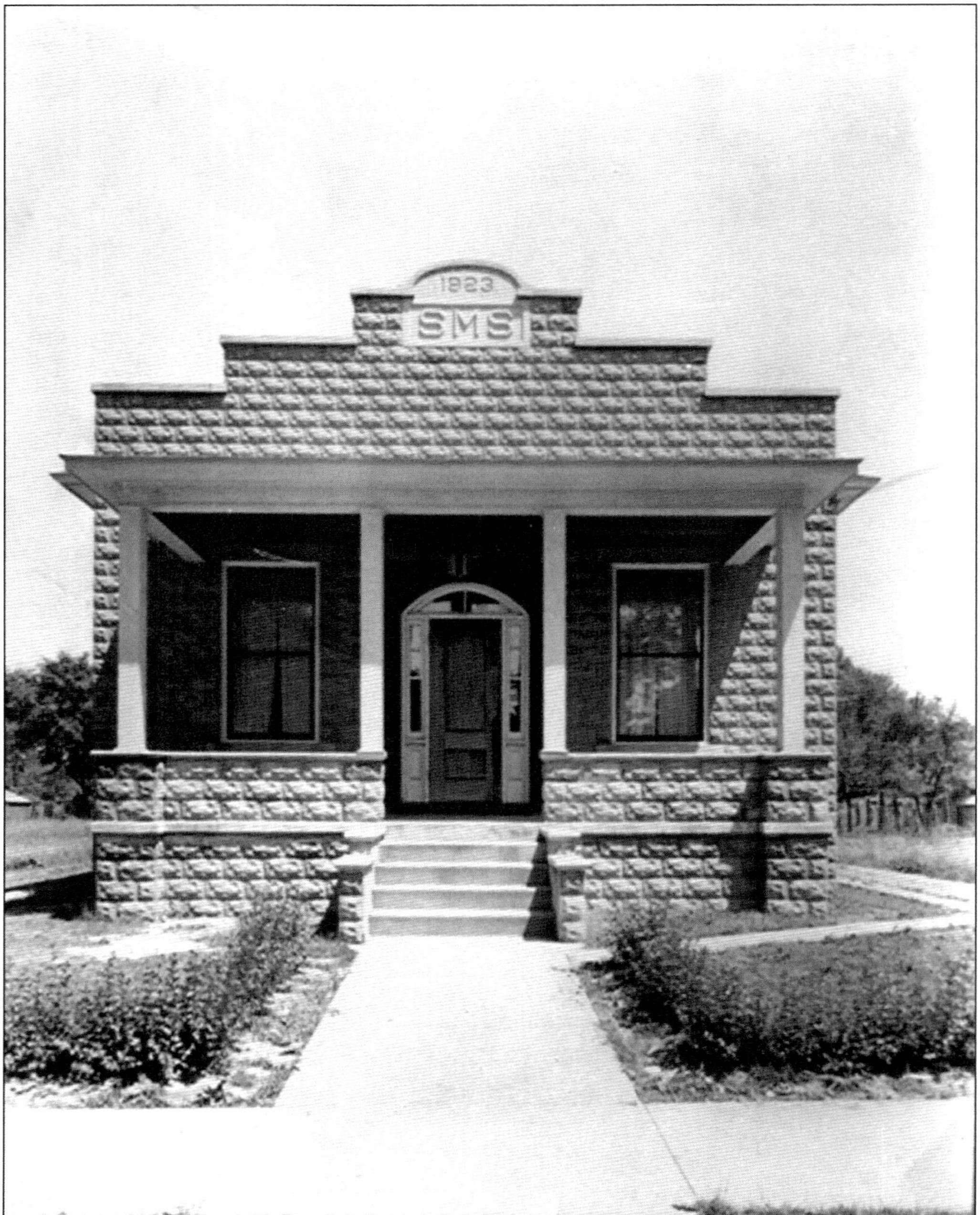

The Societa di Mutuo Soccorso (SMS) was a group formed by the first immigrants to assist each other, as well as being a social club. This building was their first meeting place and was built in the 1920s. This was a gathering place for families; there were picnics and bocce tournaments. Today the SMS is a charitable organization as well.

Six

THE 20TH CENTURY BRINGS MORE CHANGE TO SENECA FALLS

Even as Seneca Falls was rebuilding and moving into the new century, there were still changes to come.

As the Erie Canal had been enlarged so larger barges and tugs could carry more goods, the Cayuga-Seneca Canal had stayed about the same size that it had always been. The state engineers felt that it was necessary to make this canal larger. In 1910, a meeting was held in Seneca Falls to discuss the changes. A notice that went out to "The citizens and business men of Seneca Falls" to meet at the Johnson Opera House Friday evening, May 6, to give expression upon the subject of the location of the proposed Cayuga and Seneca Barge Canal. All in favor of the canal passing through the village of Seneca Falls were urged to attend this meeting as it was desirable that the state canal board at Albany should understand the sentiment of the people as a guide for its action in locating the canal.

With this meeting would come many changes to Seneca Falls: the flats would disappear, some businesses would leave Seneca Falls, some would relocate with in the village, and several would loose their homes.

There were other changes that did not come with the canal, and on the whole, Seneca Falls has survived in good shape.

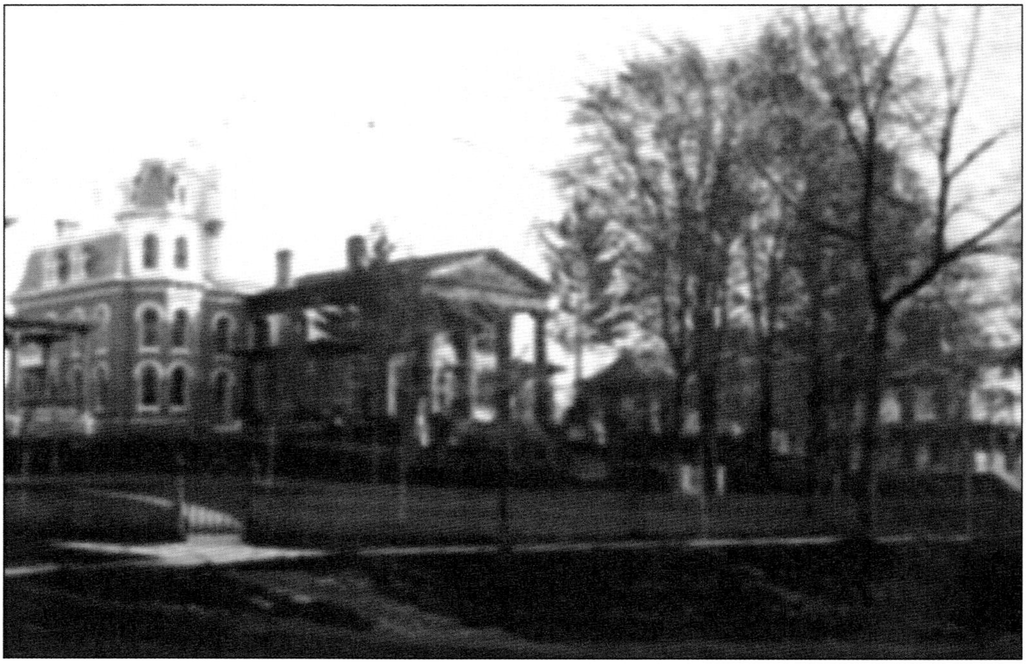

Terrace Row, overlooking the flats, contained the homes of the Goulds, Rumseys, and Silsbys. They were grand houses that had been built during the heyday of industry in Seneca Falls. Rumsey Hall is to the left, and it later became a private school before it was demolished. The Silsby home was the Seneca Falls Hospital for 50 years before it was demolished to make room for a new hospital.

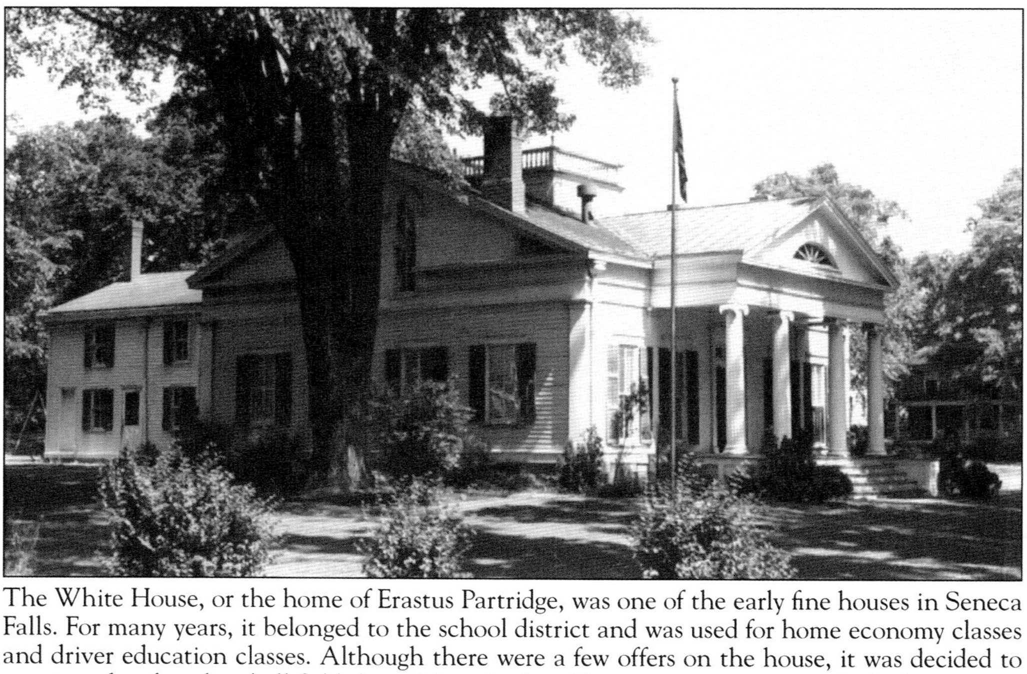

The White House, or the home of Erastus Partridge, was one of the early fine houses in Seneca Falls. For many years, it belonged to the school district and was used for home economy classes and driver education classes. Although there were a few offers on the house, it was decided to raze it and make a baseball field there. Many in the village were very upset with the loss.

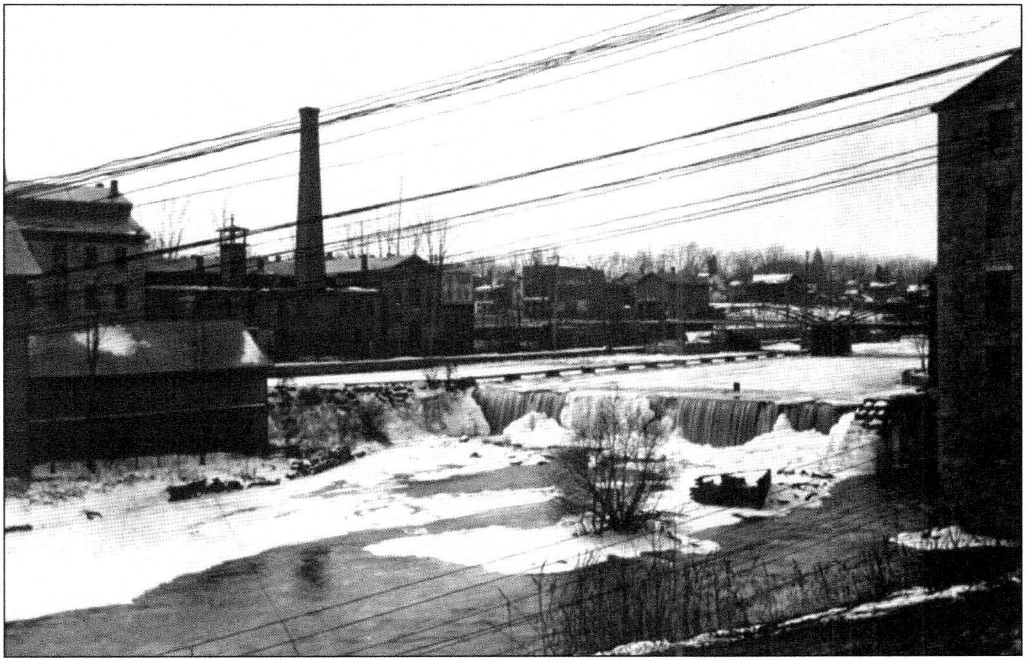

The upper falls of the Seneca River were created by placing dams to create provide power for the mills. All of the waterpower generated was very carefully measured and accounted for. No one was to take more water for their millruns than they were allotted.

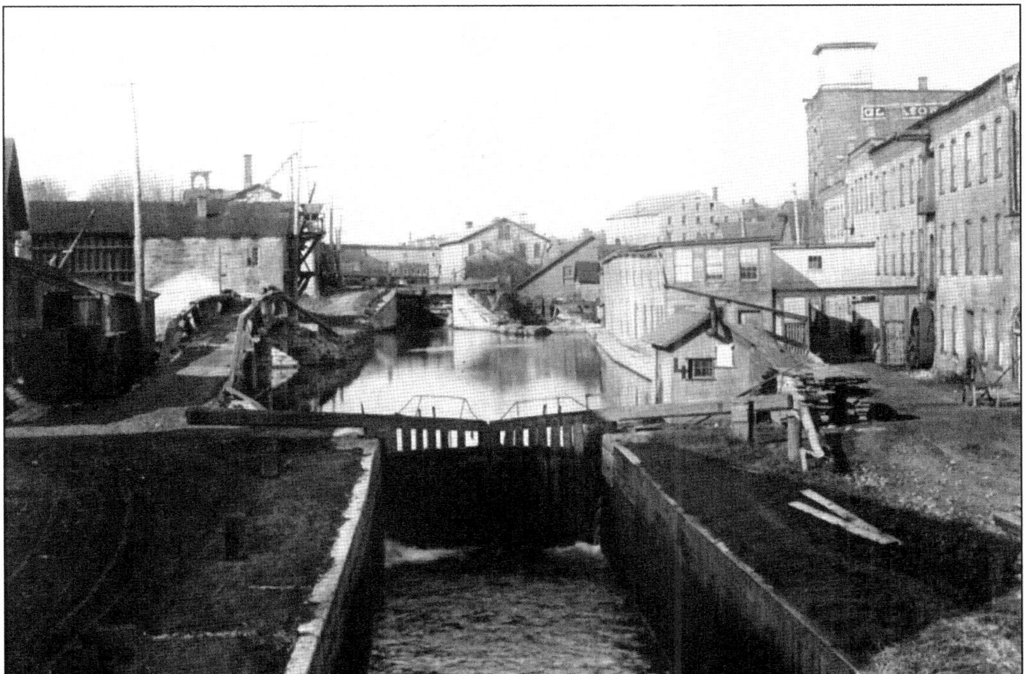

This is the lock on the Cayuga-Seneca Canal looking west. The towpath bridge crosses over an outlet, and the Phoenix Mill bell tower can be seen in the background.

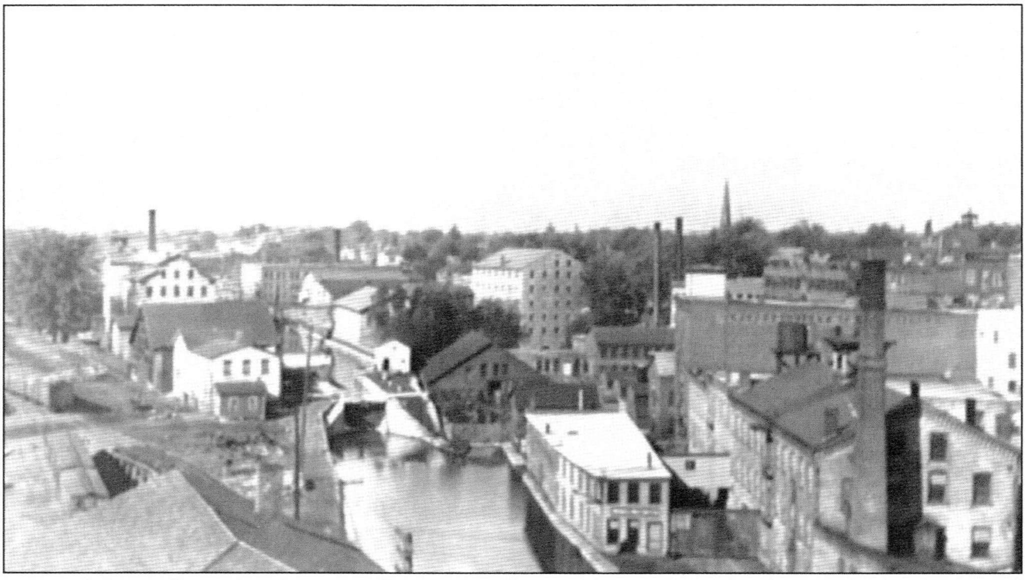

Most of the mills and industries of Seneca Falls were located on the flats and islands created by the dams on the river and the canal. Phoenix Mill is on the left, a lock and the City Mill building are in the center, and the steeple seen is part of the Wesleyan Methodist Church.

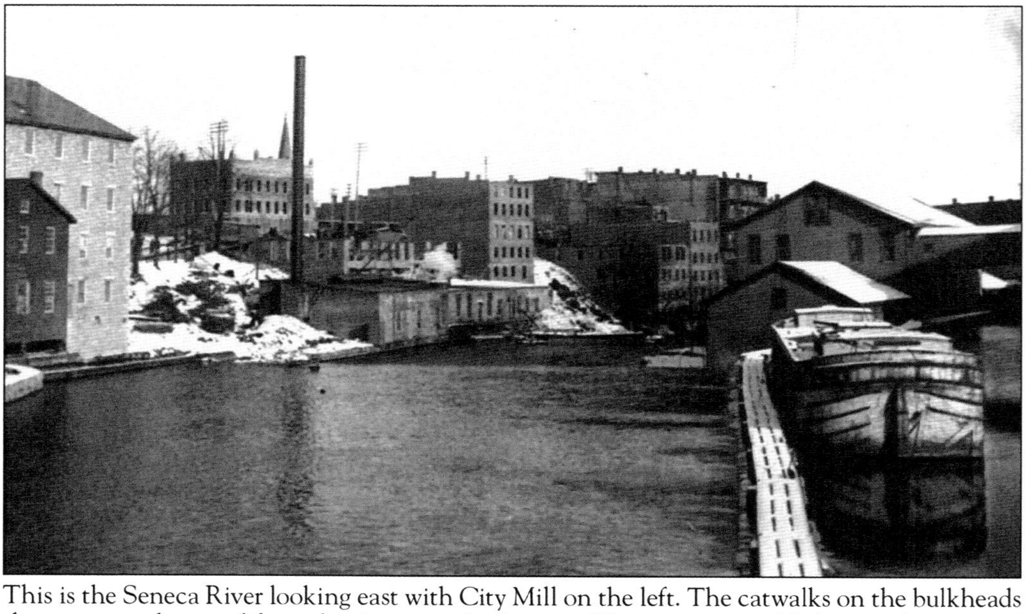

This is the Seneca River looking east with City Mill on the left. The catwalks on the bulkheads that separate the canal from the river can also be seen. These were most likely very slippery and very tricky to walk on.

The Seneca River is seen here as it passes between the buildings on the mainland and the islands. Openings for millraces can be seen at the foot of the building in the center. Wooden walkways were built to make it easy to get from one building to the next.

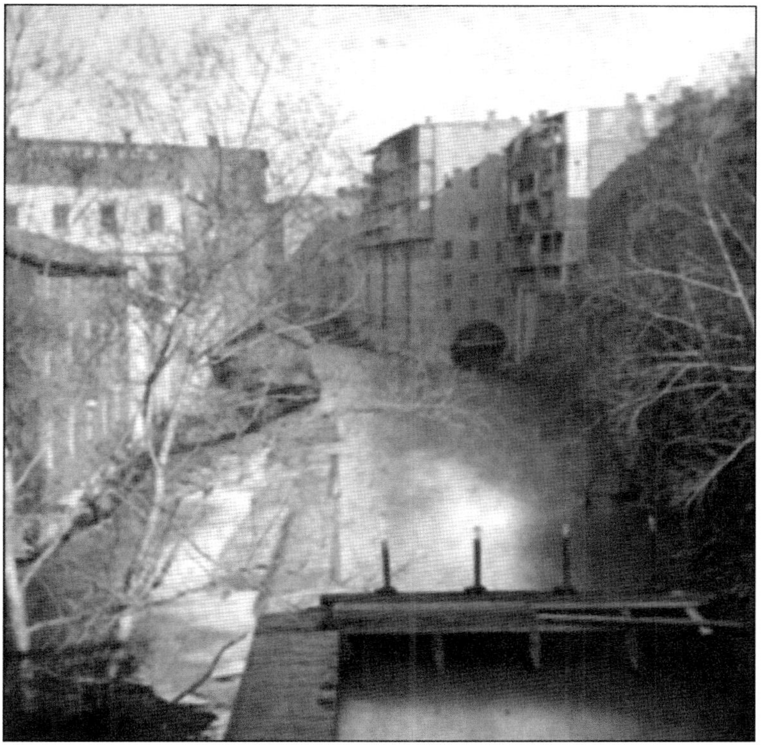

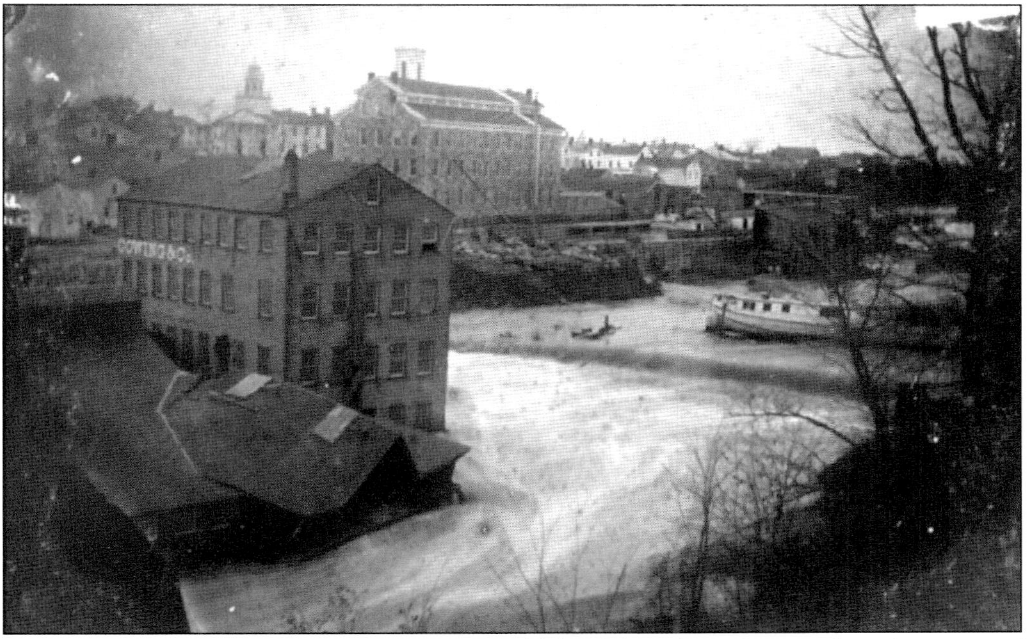

Very often, in the spring, the Seneca River would flood, breaching dams and sending some of the buildings down river. This view shows part of the Cowing and Company building collapsed, and a canal boat is adrift in the river. The bell tower of the Baptist church can be seen in the upper right.

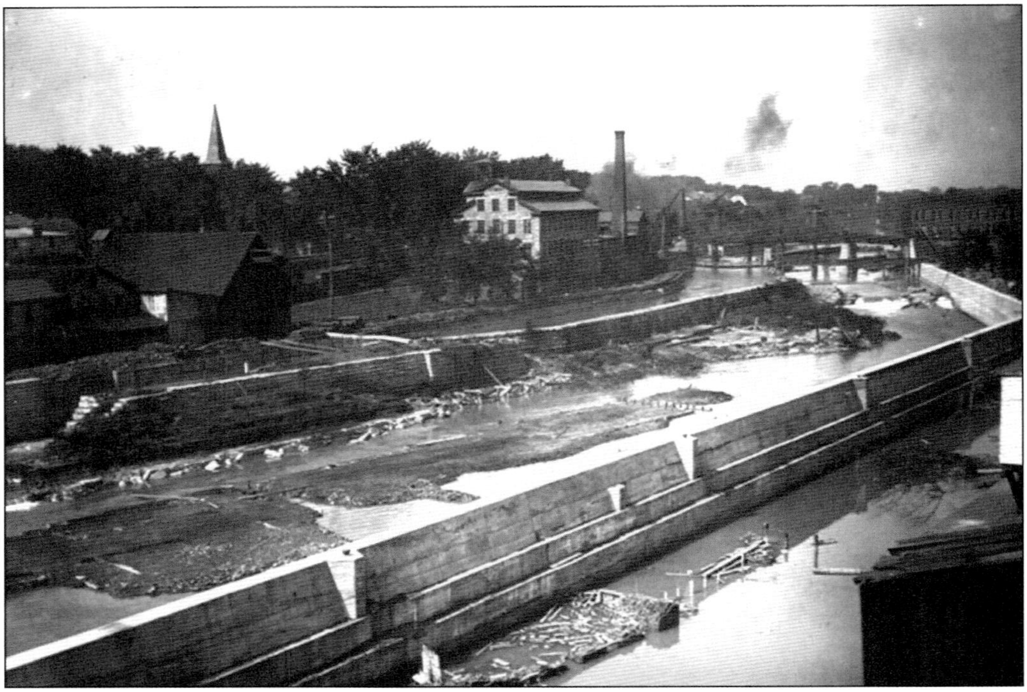

As construction begins on the canal enlargement in 1912, the old canal, raceways, and foundations are exposed. The steeple above the trees is part of the new Baptist church, and the original Bridge Street bridge is seen in the background.

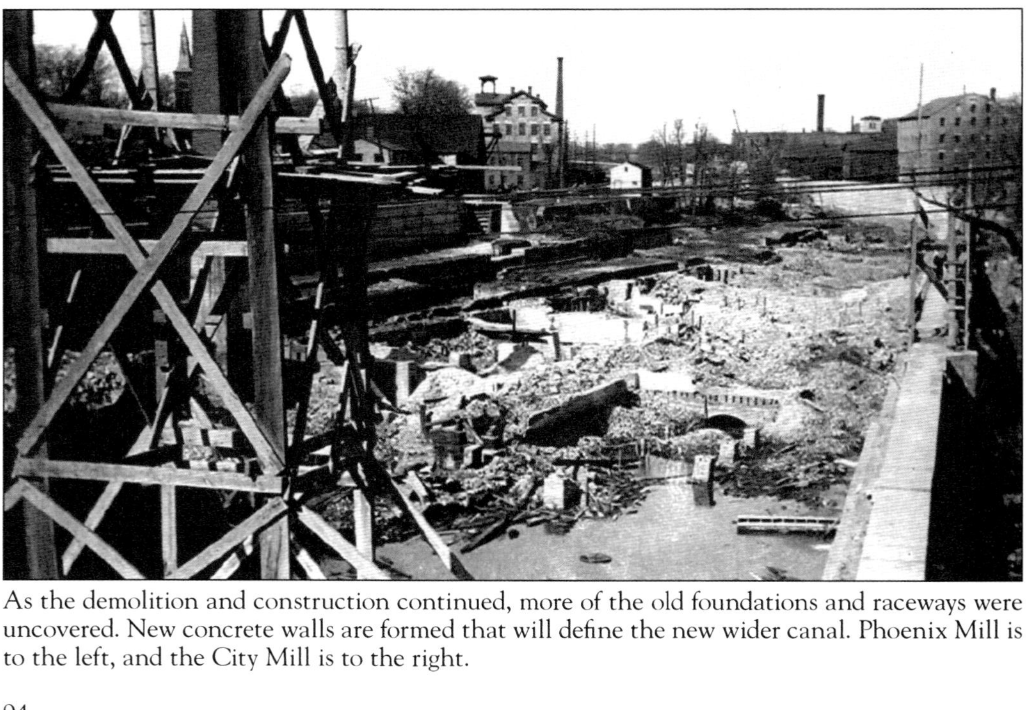

As the demolition and construction continued, more of the old foundations and raceways were uncovered. New concrete walls are formed that will define the new wider canal. Phoenix Mill is to the left, and the City Mill is to the right.

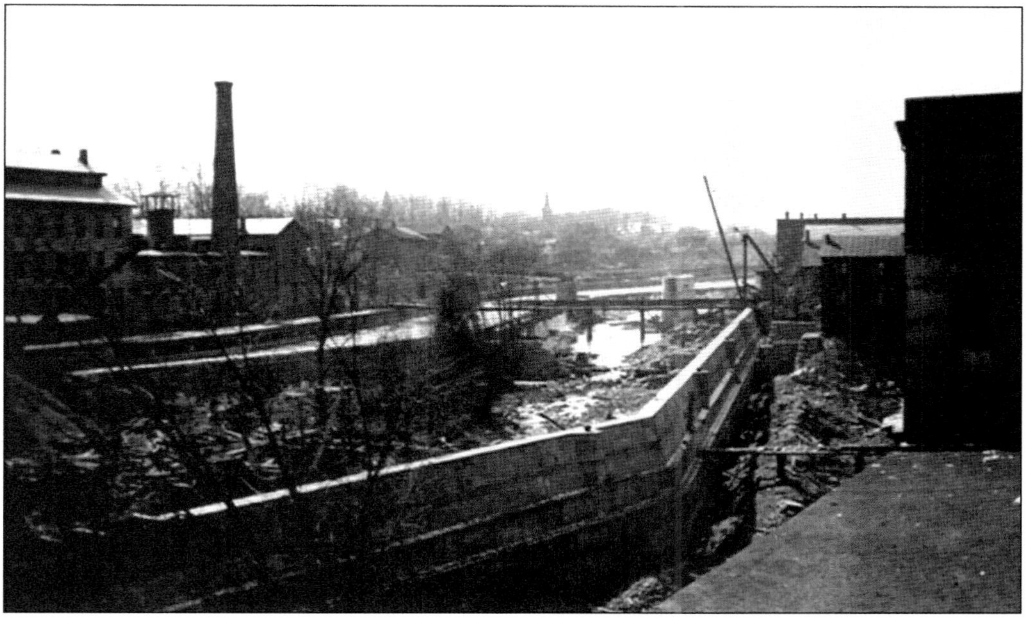

New concrete walls were built, and the space between the wall and the buildings filled in to create Cowing Street. Phoenix Mill is on the left and the steeple to St. Patrick's is in the background.

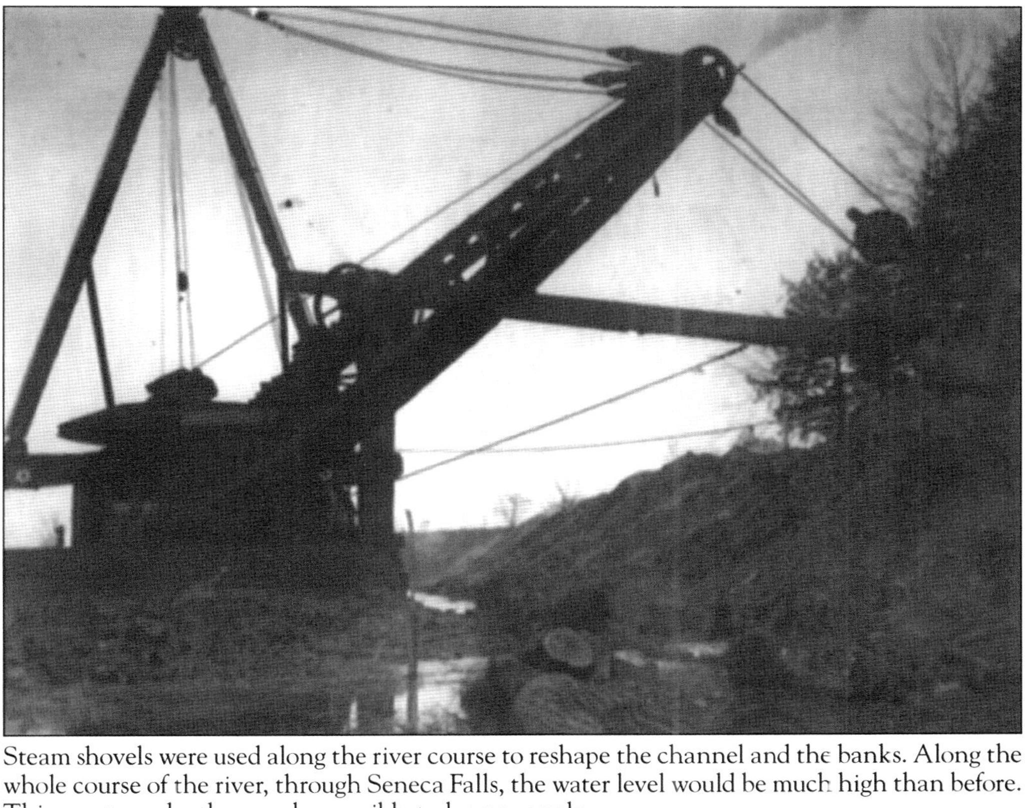

Steam shovels were used along the river course to reshape the channel and the banks. Along the whole course of the river, through Seneca Falls, the water level would be much high than before. This was to make the canal accessible to larger vessels.

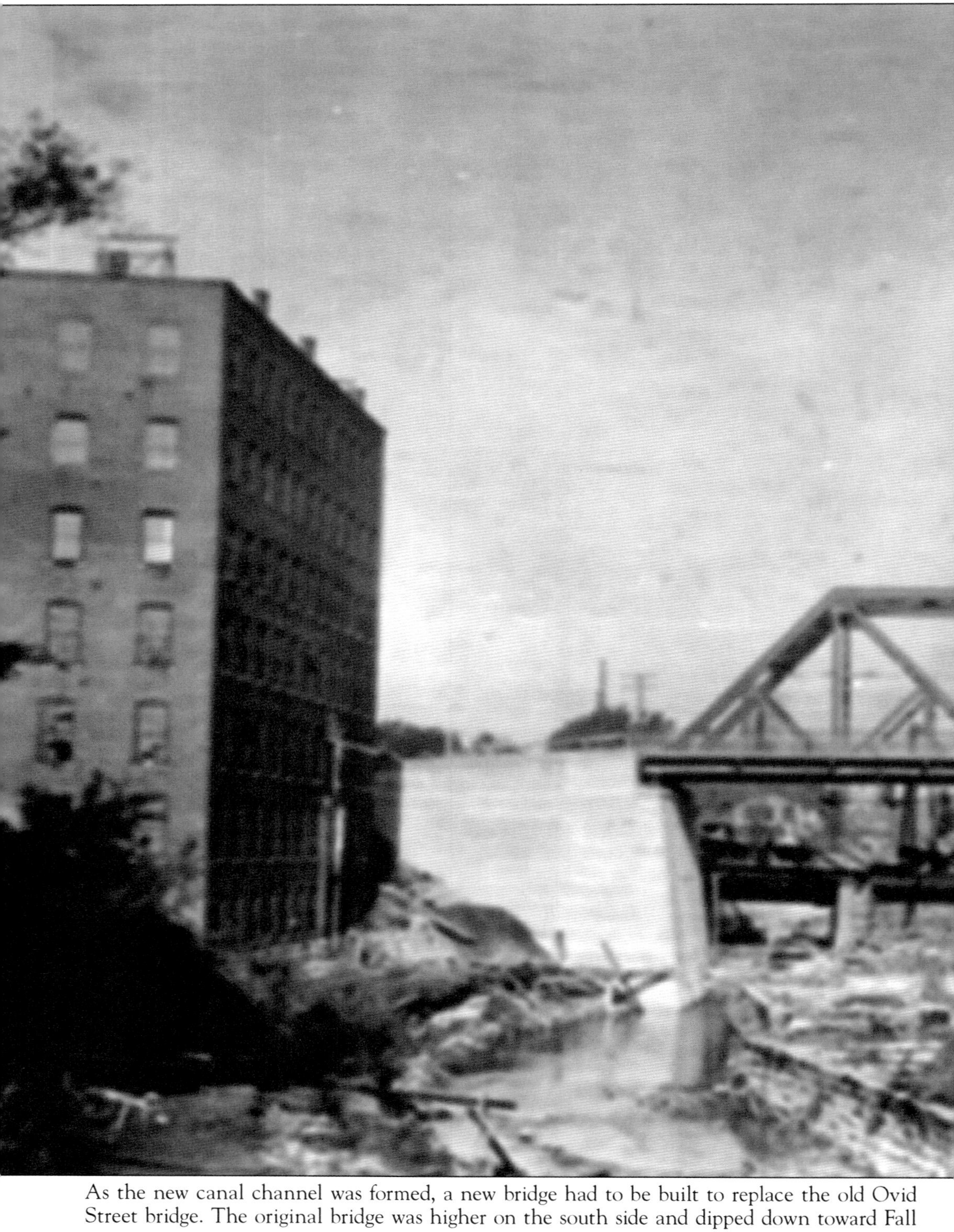

As the new canal channel was formed, a new bridge had to be built to replace the old Ovid Street bridge. The original bridge was higher on the south side and dipped down toward Fall

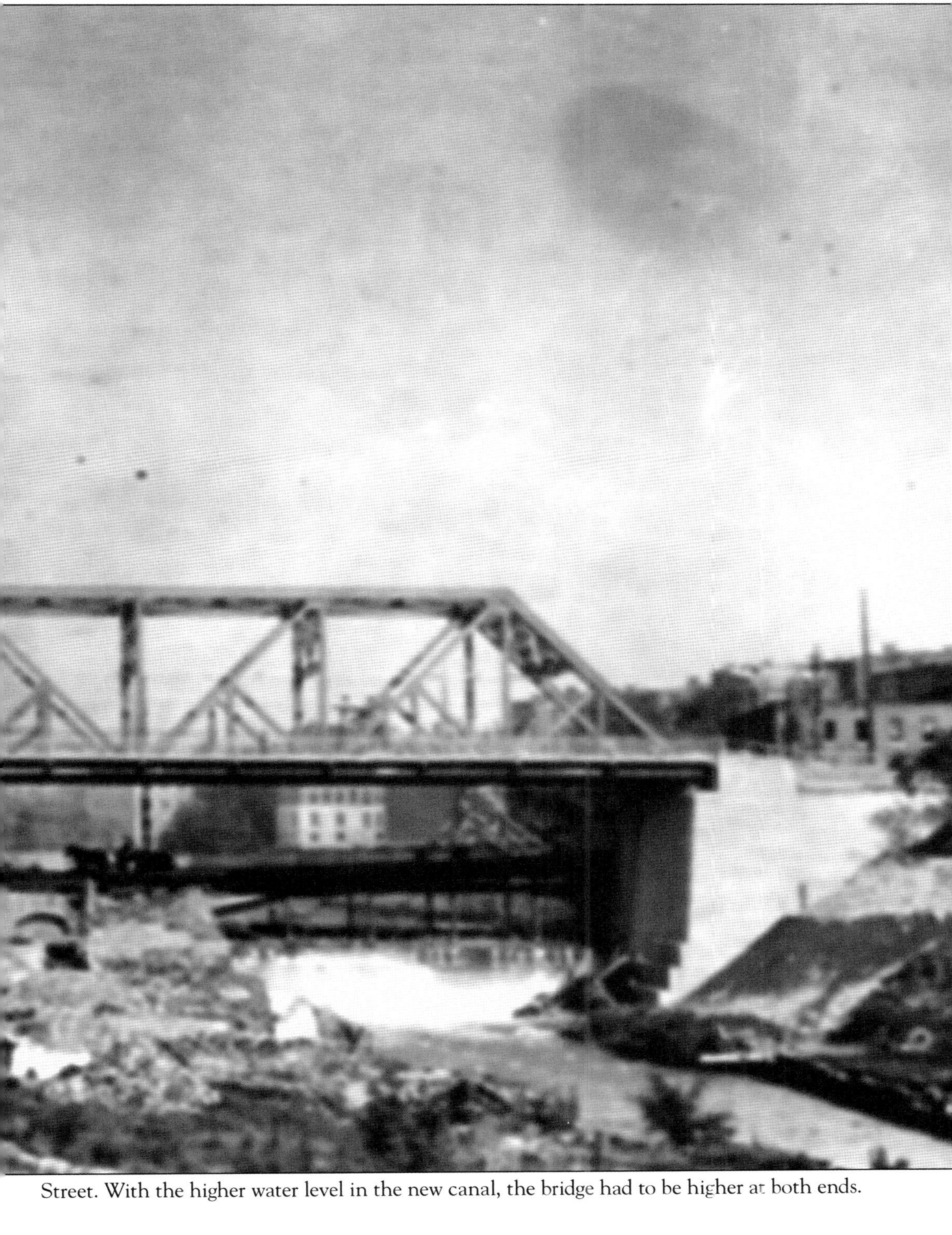

Street. With the higher water level in the new canal, the bridge had to be higher at both ends.

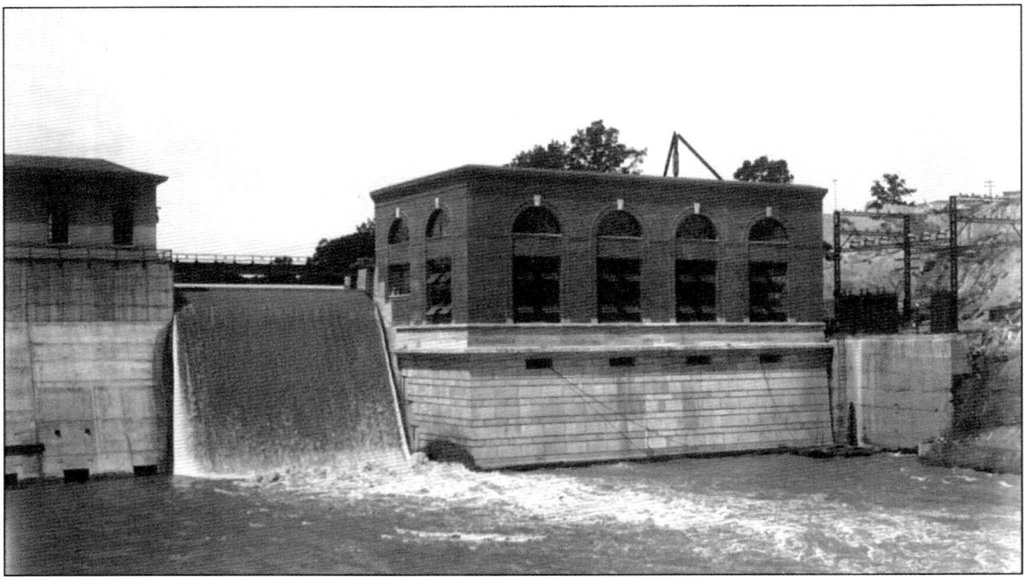

With the new canal, the double lock at the east end of the village created a waterfall to generate sufficient electricity for the whole town. A power plant was built, and the electricity was used by everyone. The plant is still generating power, but with today's demand there is only enough for about 20 households.

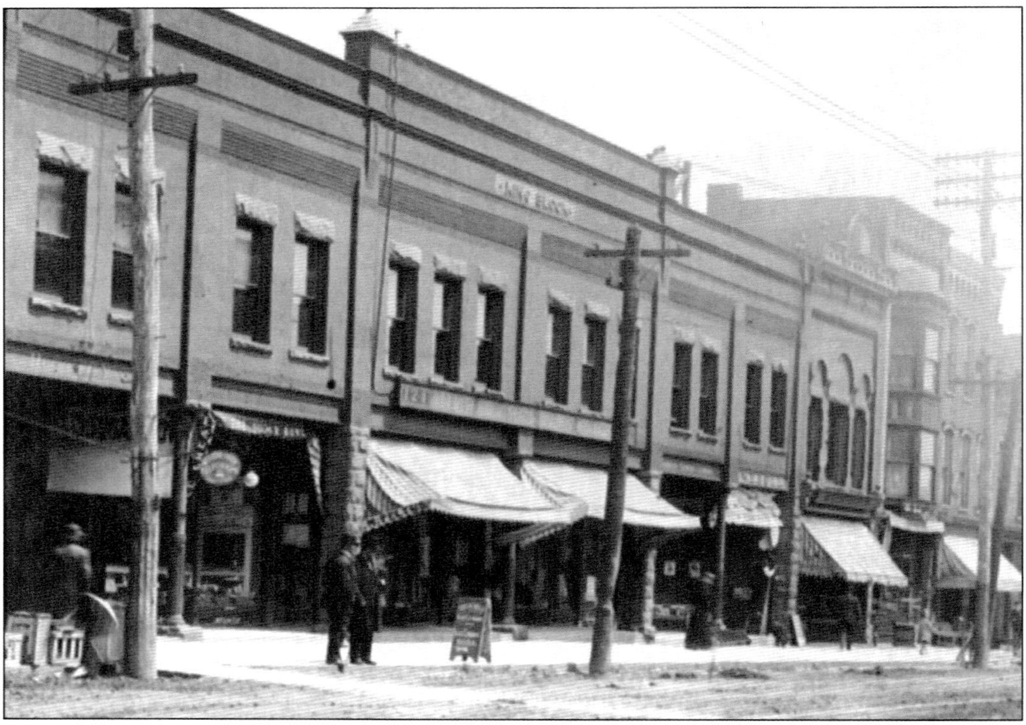

Fall Street was still being rebuilt several years after the fire, but the need for the new buildings did not slow down. Even as Seneca Falls progressed, there were still a few things that needed to be improved, such as paving the streets.

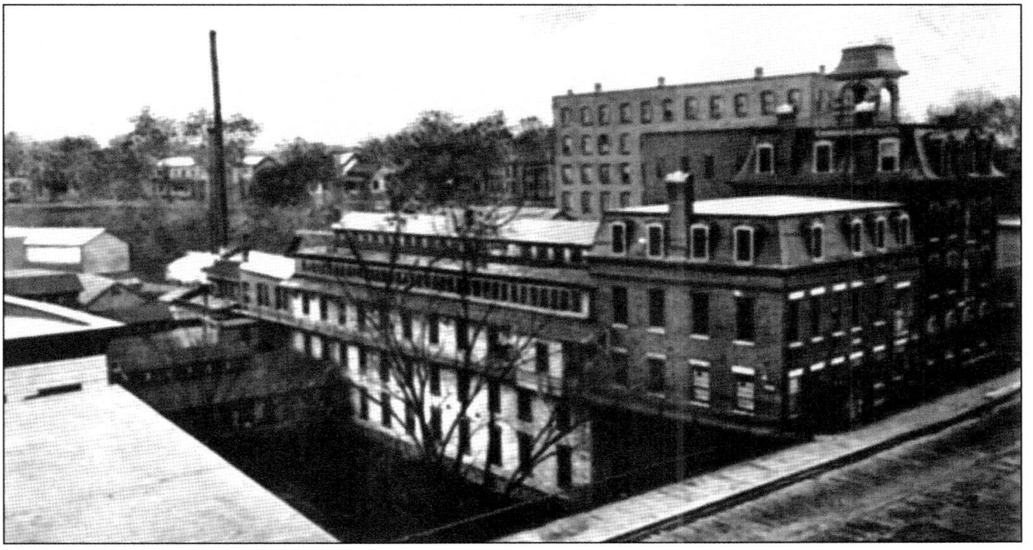

The Goulds warehouse along the Ovid Street bridge is seen here before the warehouses and foundries were moved to the west side of the village. Notice the various levels above and below street level. All of these buildings were lost when the canal was finally completed.

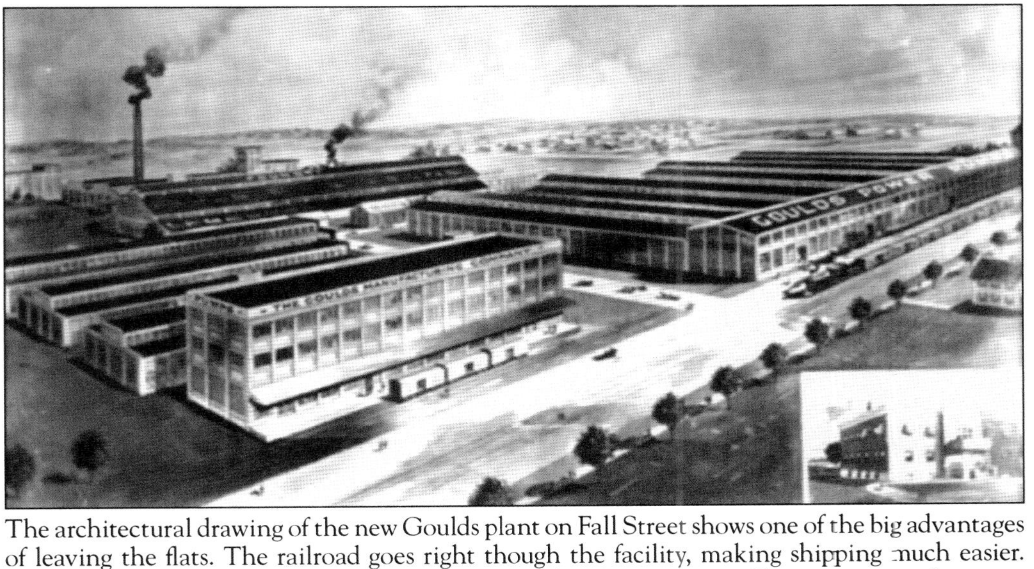

The architectural drawing of the new Goulds plant on Fall Street shows one of the big advantages of leaving the flats. The railroad goes right though the facility, making shipping much easier. Also all of the buildings would be on the same level and not separated by river or canal.

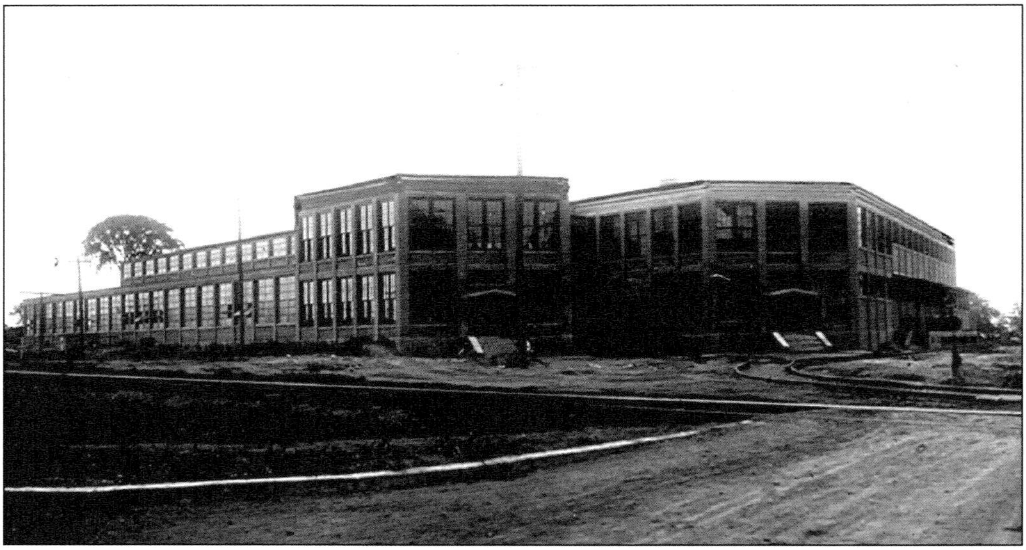

Rumsey Pump Company moved their plant to Prospect Hill, which overlooked the flats (now Cleef Lake). Again the railroad goes right by the warehouse making receiving and shipping very easy. The move was very hard on the bottom line for Rumsey, and they sold the buildings to Sylvania in 1947. Picture tubes for televisions were manufactured there for 39 years.

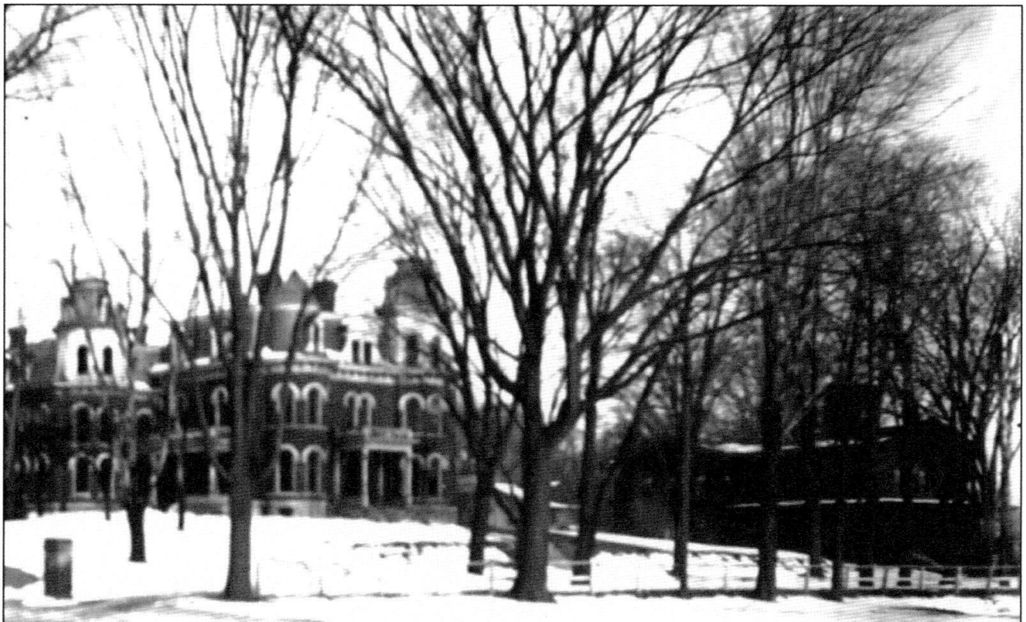

Rumsey Hall on Terrace Row (the house on the left) was the home of John Rumsey. It was not until the canal was enlarged that the view from his front porch became beautiful; originally it looked out over the factories on the flats. Maybe he was just keeping an eye on his business.

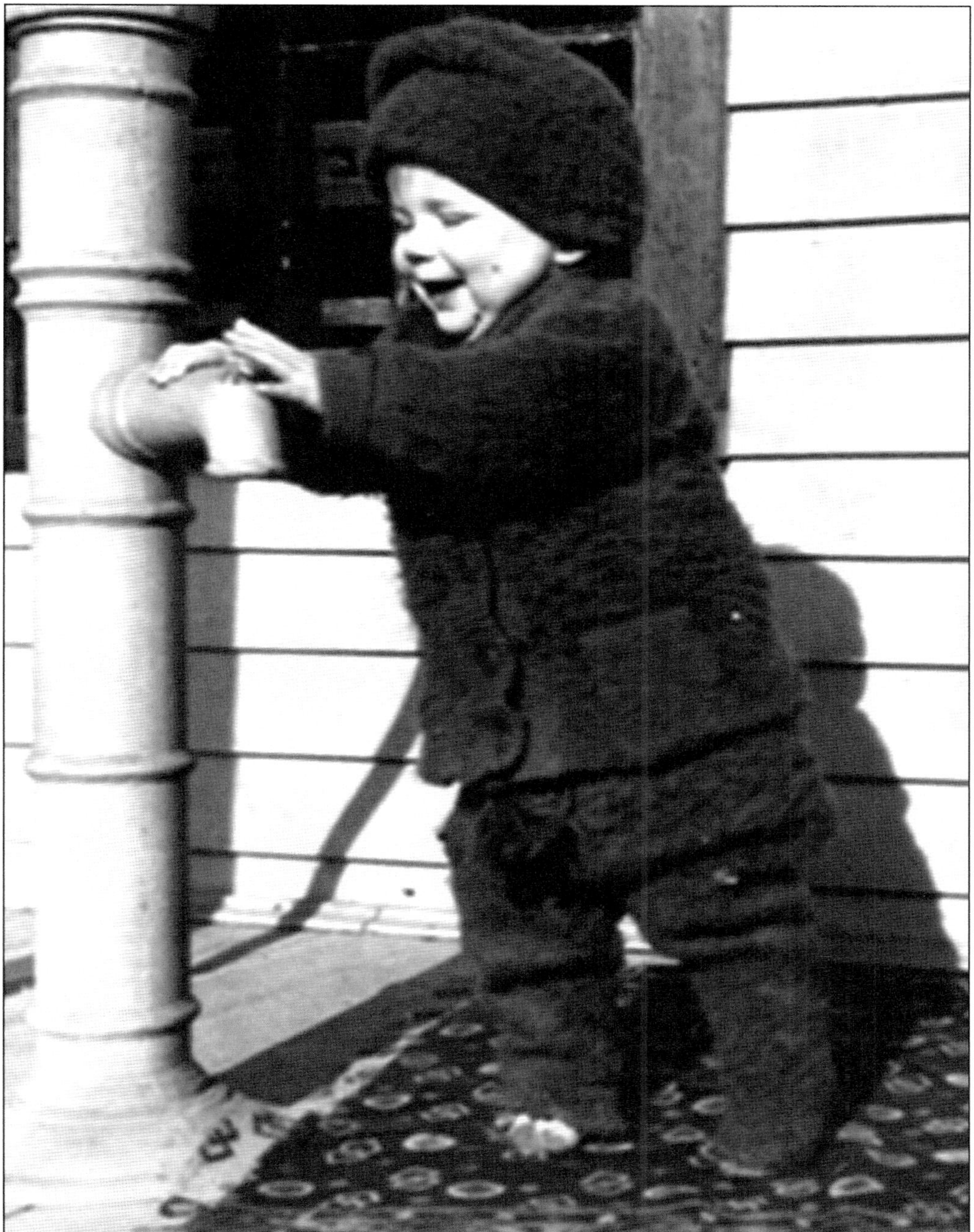

A very young Seabury S. Gould IV is learning all about pumps on his porch. This snapshot was published in the local newspaper as well as in Goulds' publications. Seabury did go on to work at Goulds for a short time.

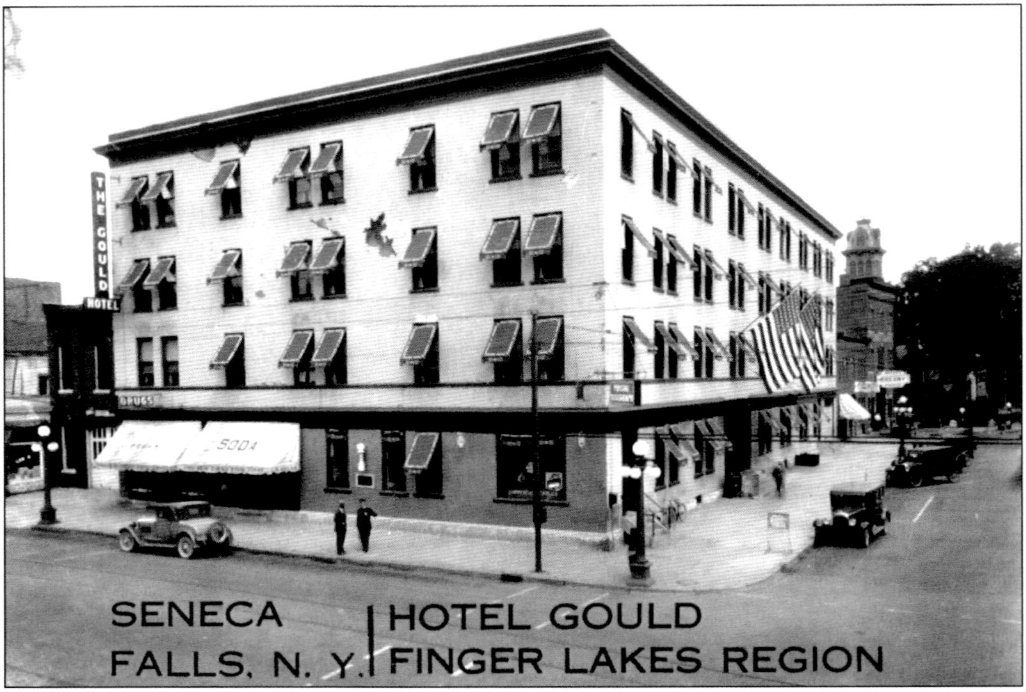

The Gould Hotel was built on the site of the Hoag Hotel after it burned in 1919. The building was touted as fireproof in all of the advertisements. The hotel was to have the very best in appointments, with a bar, restaurant, candy shop, and a reading room.

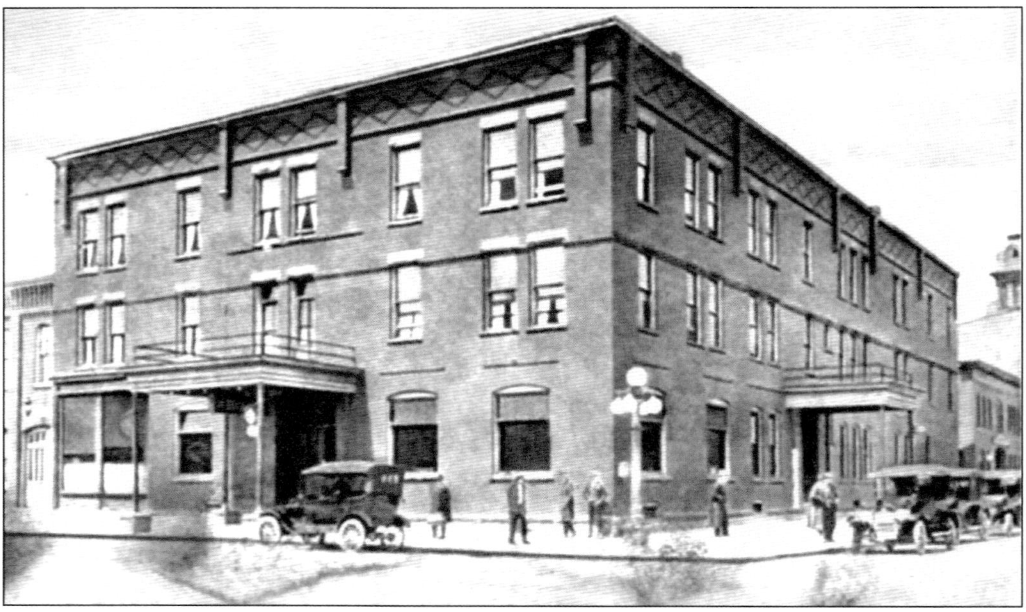
The second Hoag Hotel was not destined to last very long. After being rebuilt in the 1890s, the hotel was again struck by fire in 1919. The Hoag Hotel and the new Gould Hotel look very similar, and the only way to tell the difference is to count the floors. The Hoag Hotel was three stories, and the Gould Hotel was four.

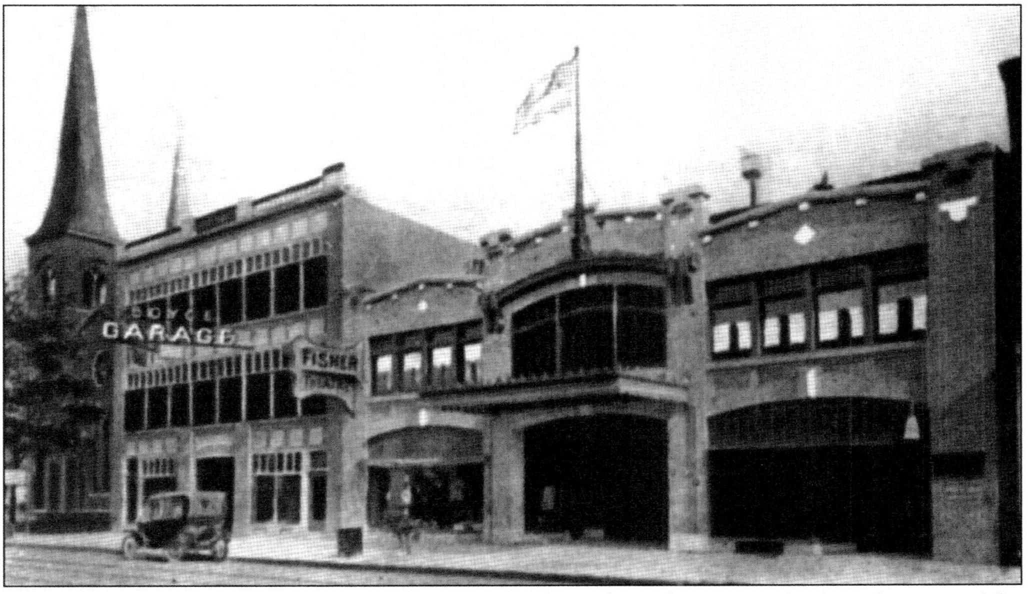

After the Fornesi Theater proved to be a success, the Fisher Theater was built and equipped for sound; it proved to be very popular. The three-story building on the right was Boyce's garage. Today it is the visitor center for the Women's Rights National Historic Park.

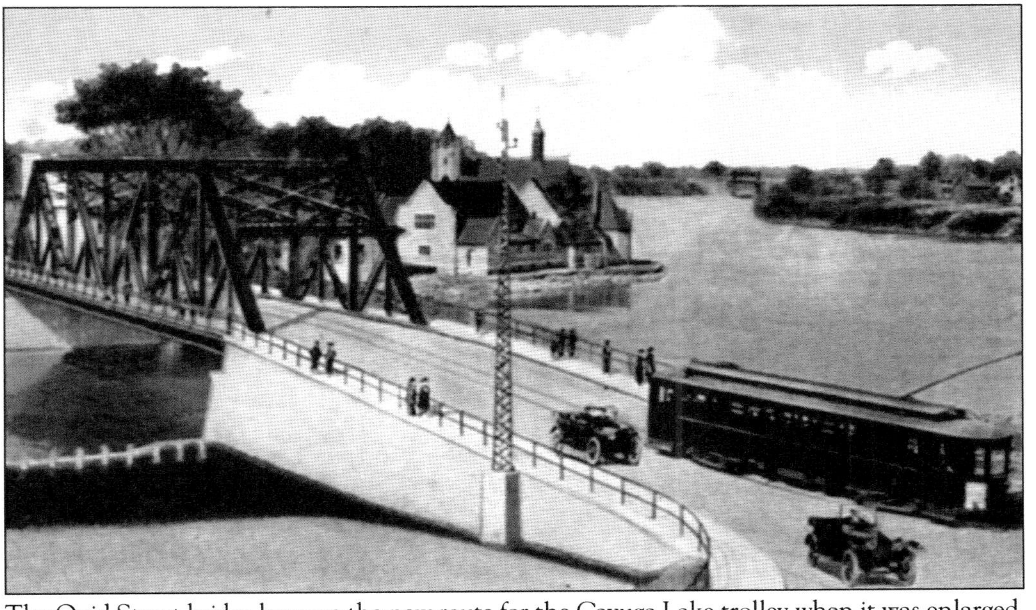

The Ovid Street bridge became the new route for the Cayuga Lake trolley when it was enlarged. Previously the trolley stopped at the Hoag Hotel, and the passengers had to walk across and board a new trolley at the Franklin House.

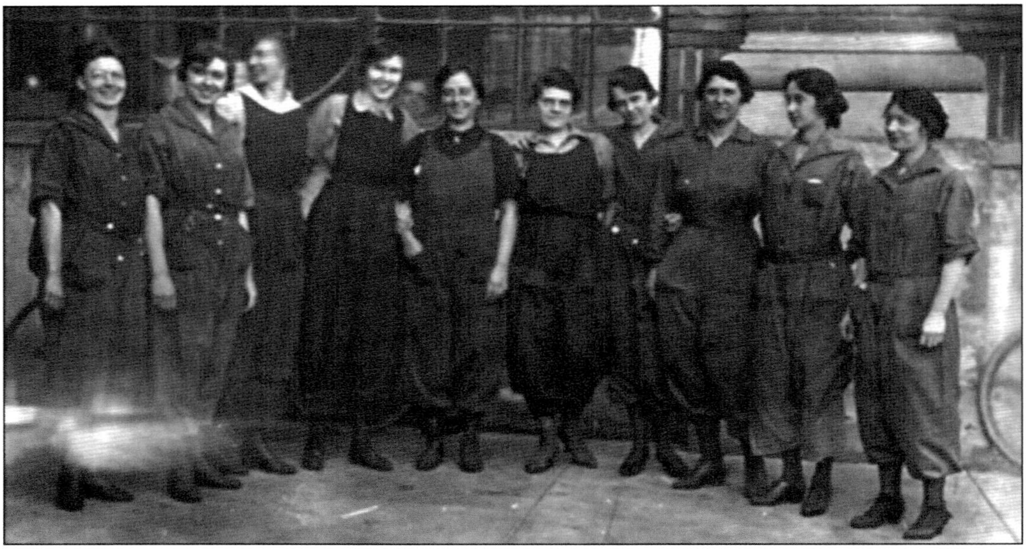

During World War I, the women of Seneca Falls did their part by working in the factories. These ladies worked at Seneca Falls Machine, making machine tools and equipment. The U.S. Navy thought very highly of the lathes that were produced here. The bloomer outfits were the forerunner of the coveralls that Rosie the Riveter wore during World War II.

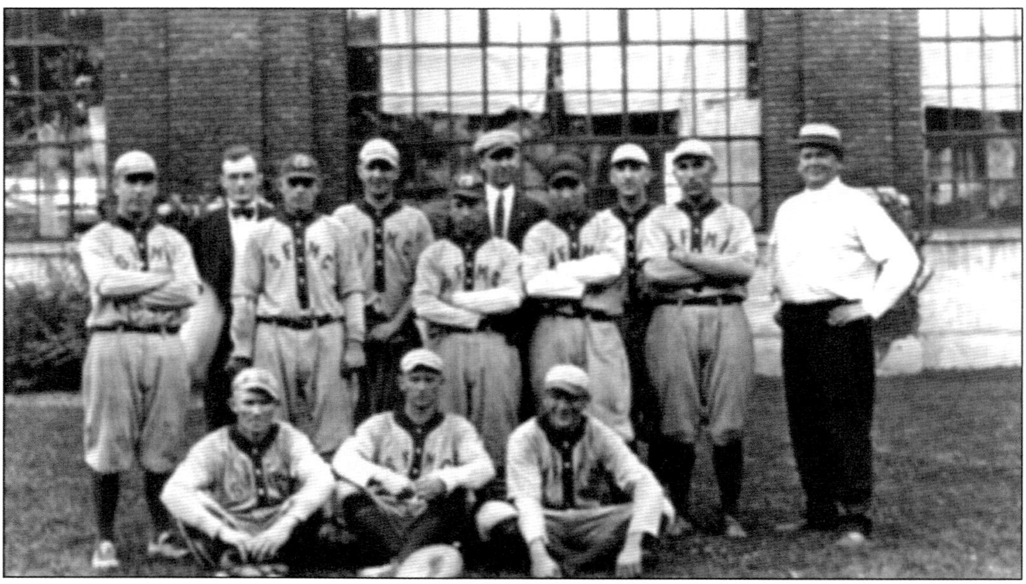

The Seneca Falls Machine men were not playing baseball while the women worked, but they did have very good team. There were lots of company teams in the area as well as semiprofessional teams. The House of David team even came to the area to play a few games. The local papers were good about reporting the results of the games.

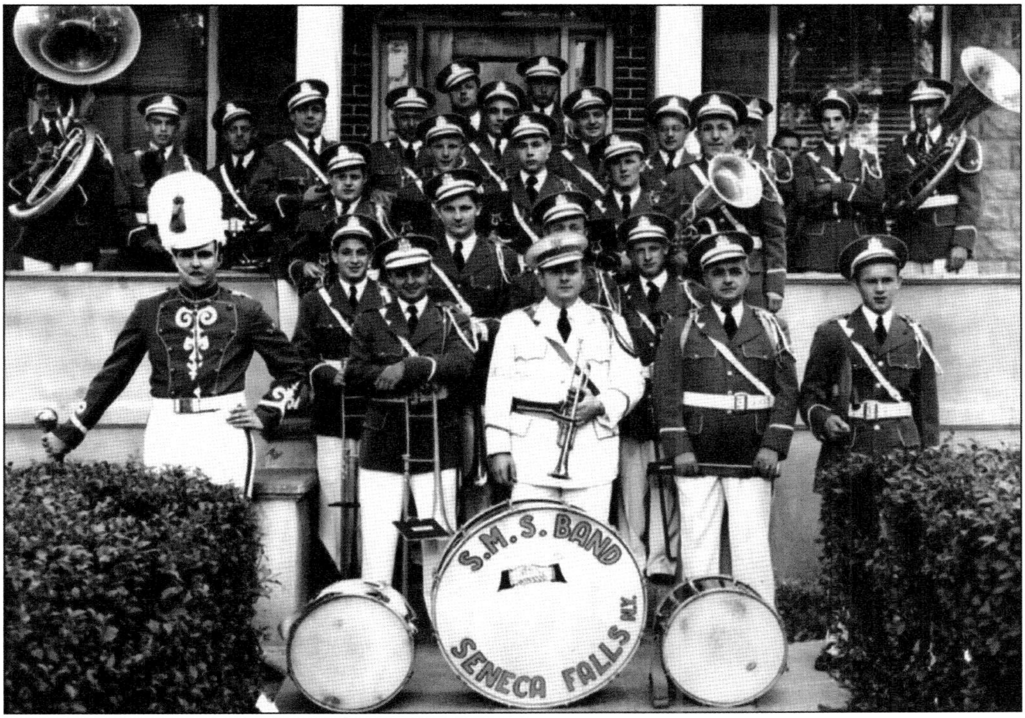

The SMS band was formed to perform at parades and compete with the other local bands. Many a hopeful musician tried out for the band, whose standards were high. The band was very successful and won several trophies.

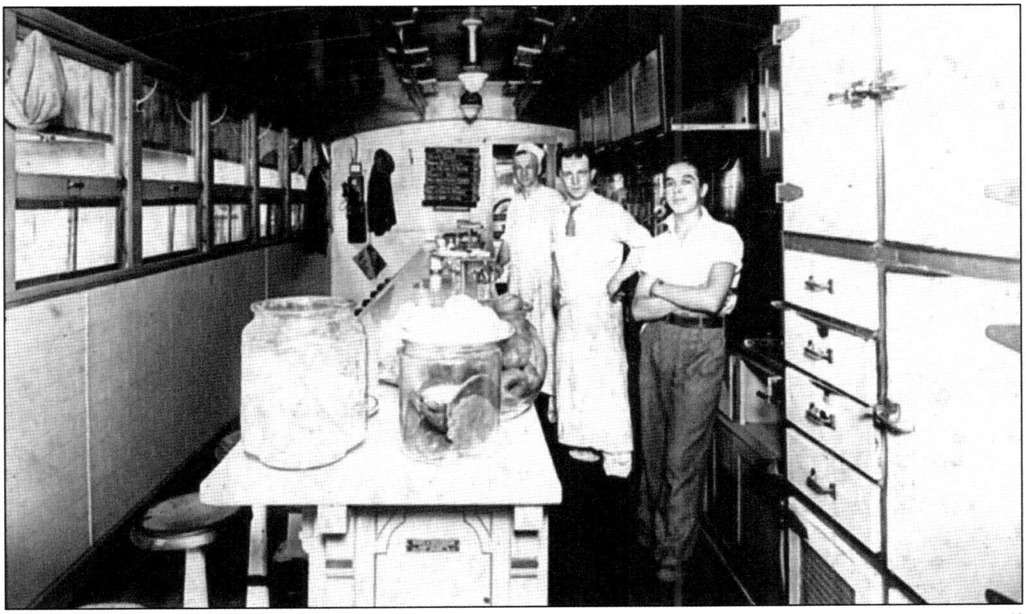

The Homestead Diner was located on a small triangle of land where Water Street intersects Fall Street. Seen here are, from left to right, Harvey Amidon, Bill Seward, and unidentified. This diner was moved to Canoga where it was very popular. It was then moved to Buffalo a few years later.

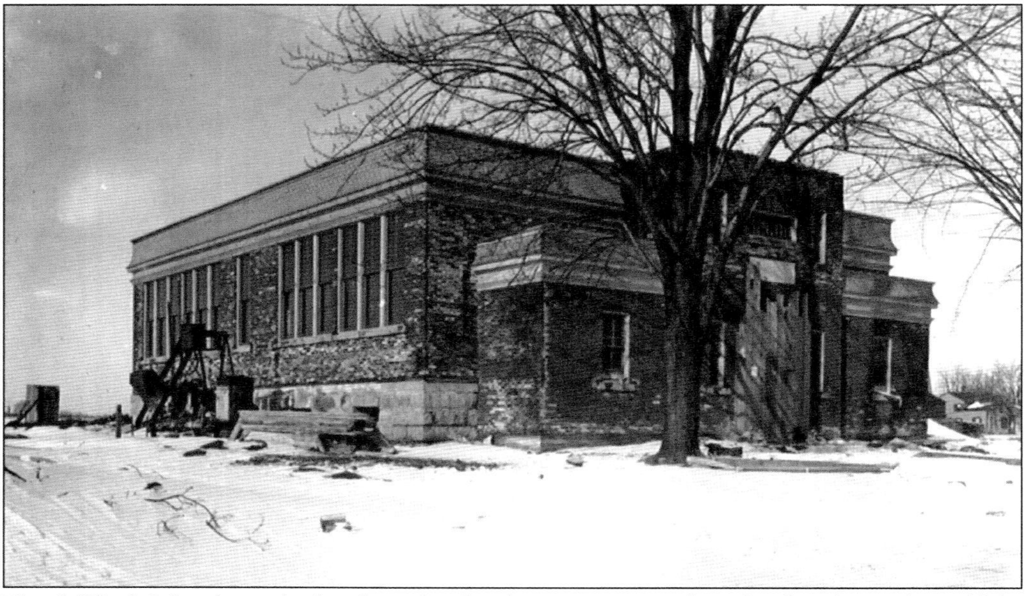

Third Ward School was built when the families were upset that the fourth ward would be getting a new school. The original school had been located on Bayard Street, but the new school was placed further south in the third ward. The building has been a factory and an apartment building.

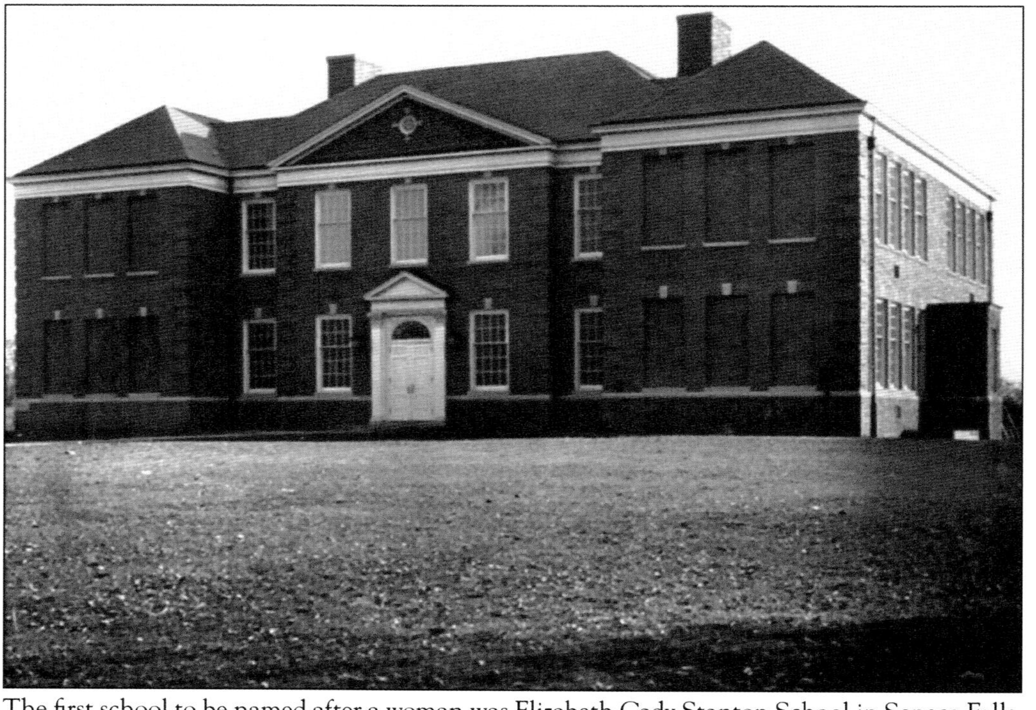

The first school to be named after a woman was Elizabeth Cady Stanton School in Seneca Falls. Built as a WPA project during the 1930s, it replaced the original Fourth Ward School.

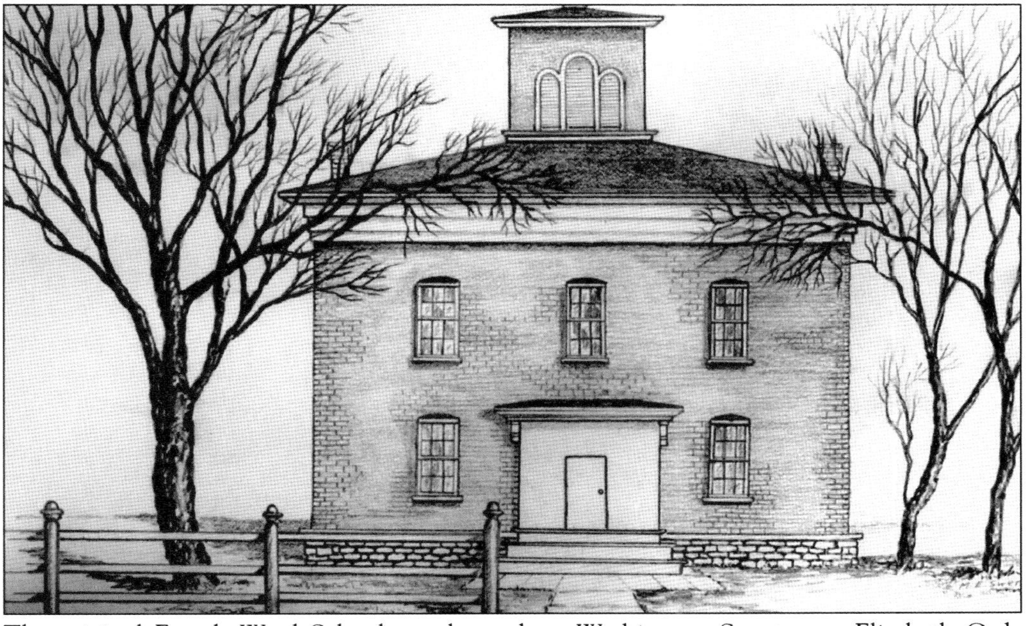

The original Fourth Ward School was located on Washington Street near Elizabeth Cady Stanton's farm. The village was divided into four wards; the first and second wards were on the north side of the canal, and the third and fourth were on the south side. Today the school is an apartment building.

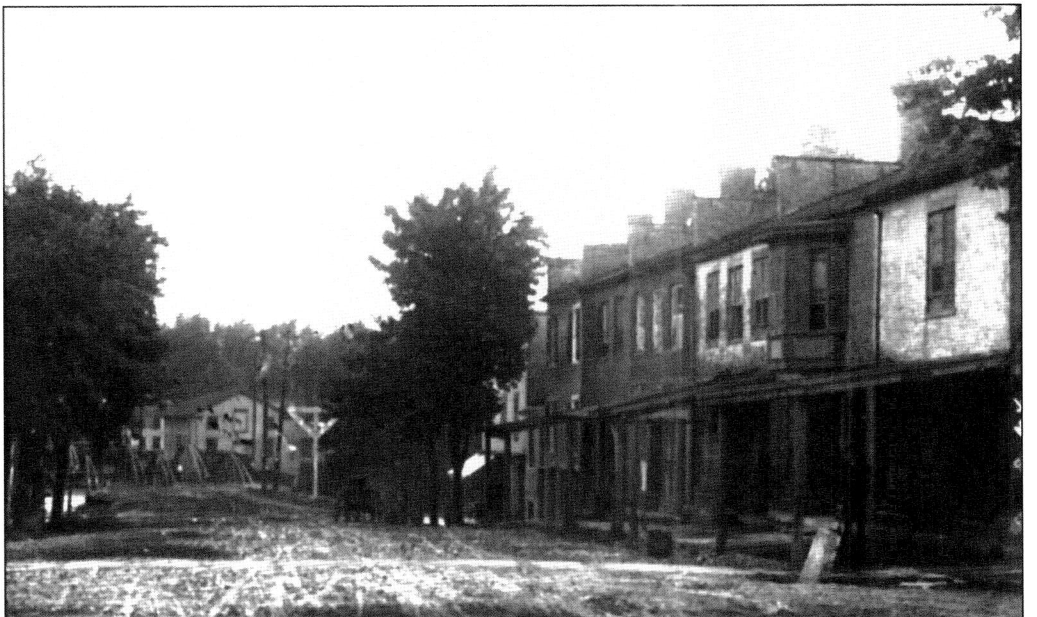

The Sackett district is one of the oldest areas of the village, located on the south side of the canal near the Seneca Woolen Mill. Judge Gary V. Sackett owned several lots in the area. The buildings that are left were originally his, built in the 1830s. The judge kept very good records about his properties, noting things such as who rented them and for how much.

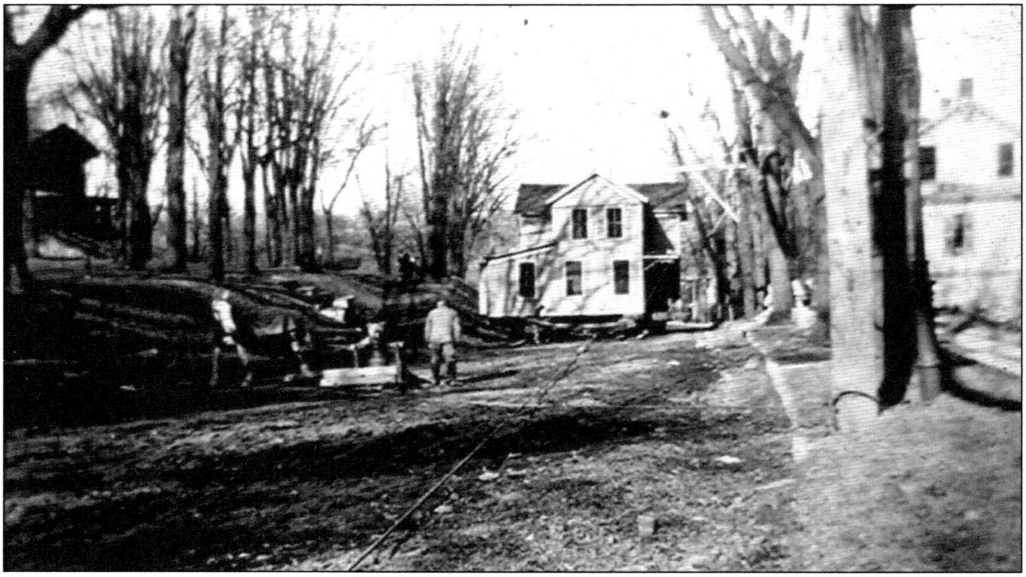

As work progressed on the canal, families needed to move out and find a new house or move the house. Horses or mule teams were used to pull the houses up Fall Street to their new locations. Dey Street would have been too steep for the teams.

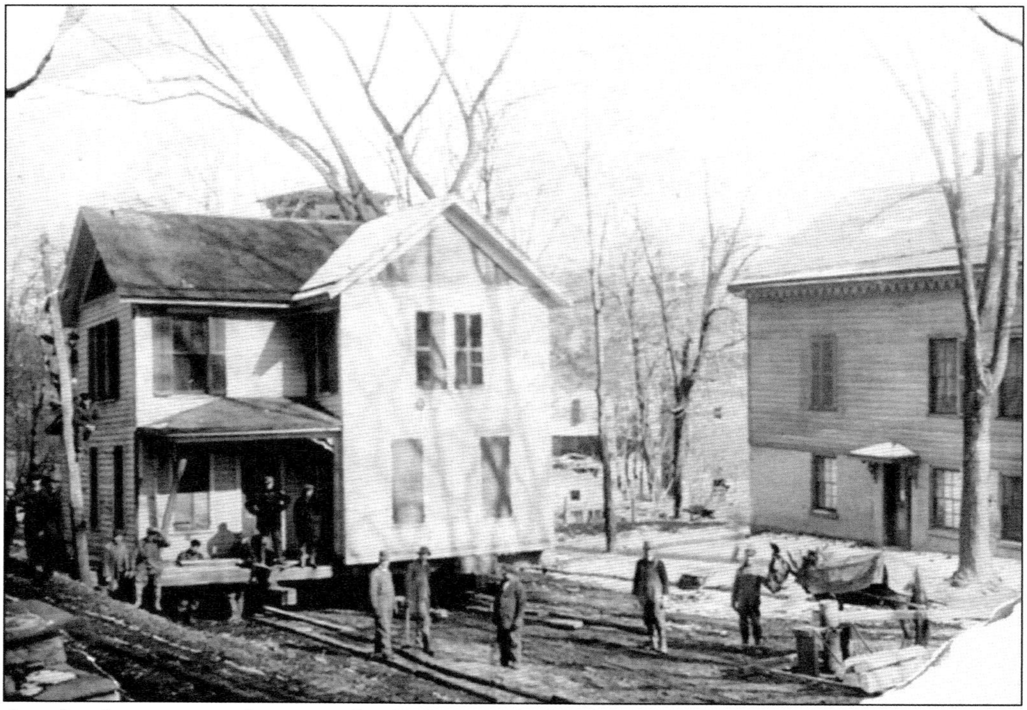

Another house is on the move. In 1915, a total of 76 houses were moved to new locations in the village and 100 houses and industries were destroyed to accommodate improvements to the Cayuga-Seneca Canal.

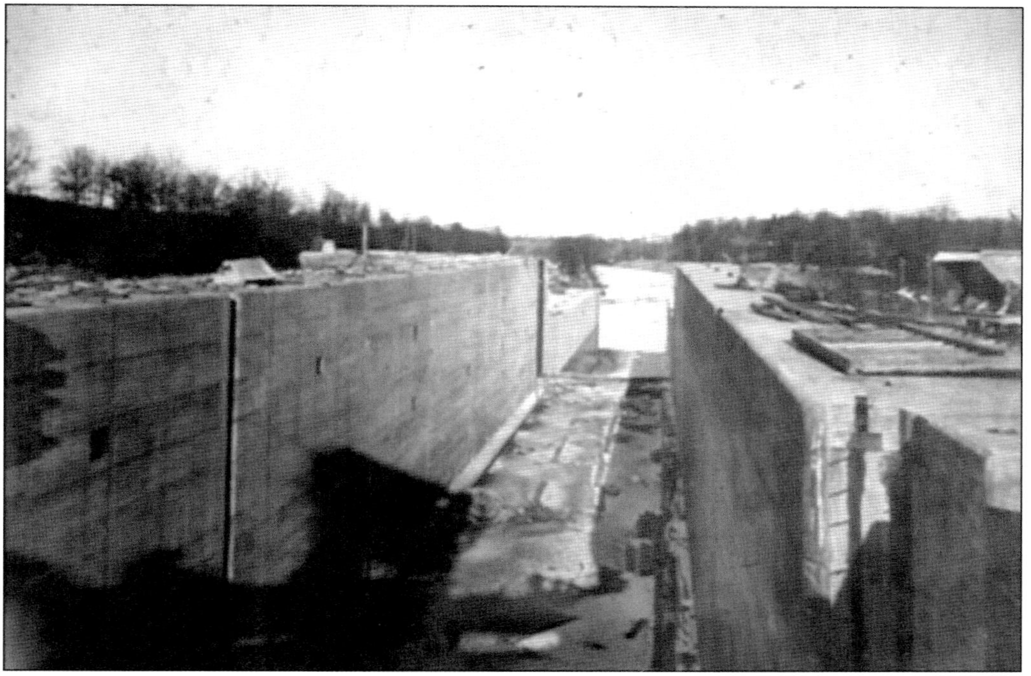

The plan for the new Cayuga-Seneca Canal called for 2 large locks instead of 11 small ones. These would be placed at the east end of Van Cleef Lake. To create the new locks, Nos. 2 and 3 of the Cayuga-Seneca Canal, concrete walls had to be built. This took thousands of barrels of cement and hundreds of thousands of dollars to complete.

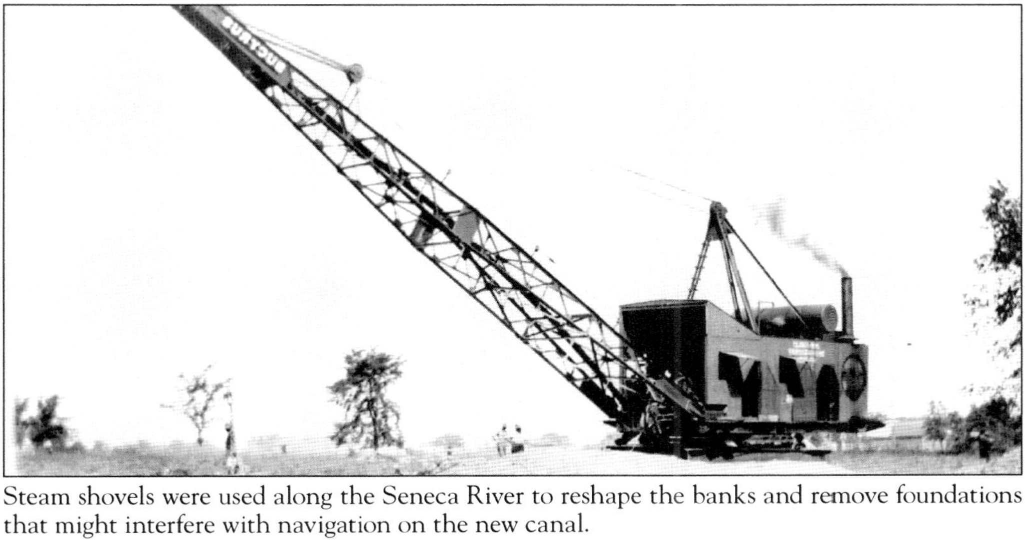

Steam shovels were used along the Seneca River to reshape the banks and remove foundations that might interfere with navigation on the new canal.

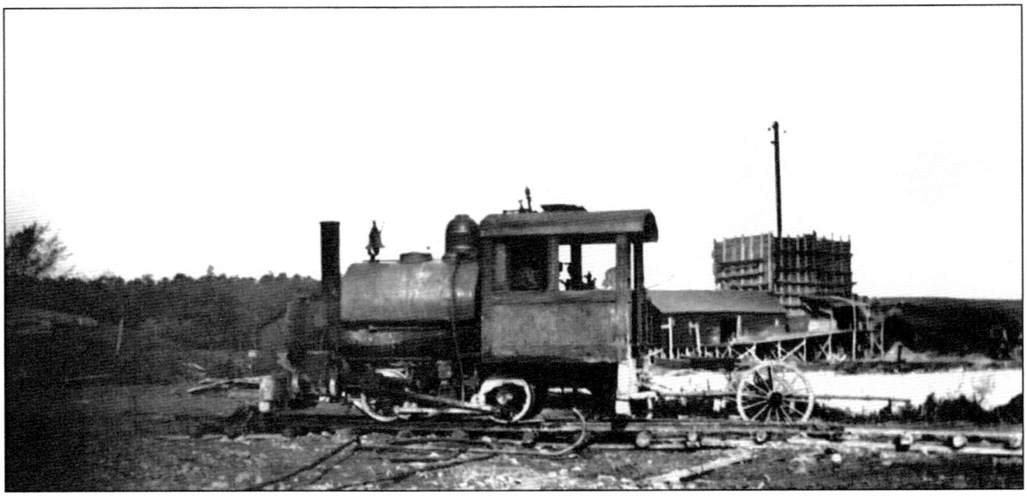

Small steam engines were used to help move rubble and equipment as the construction in the old riverbed progressed. When the old mills and factories were removed from the islands and the flats, there were huge amounts of material to be moved, and there was no canal or river to move it.

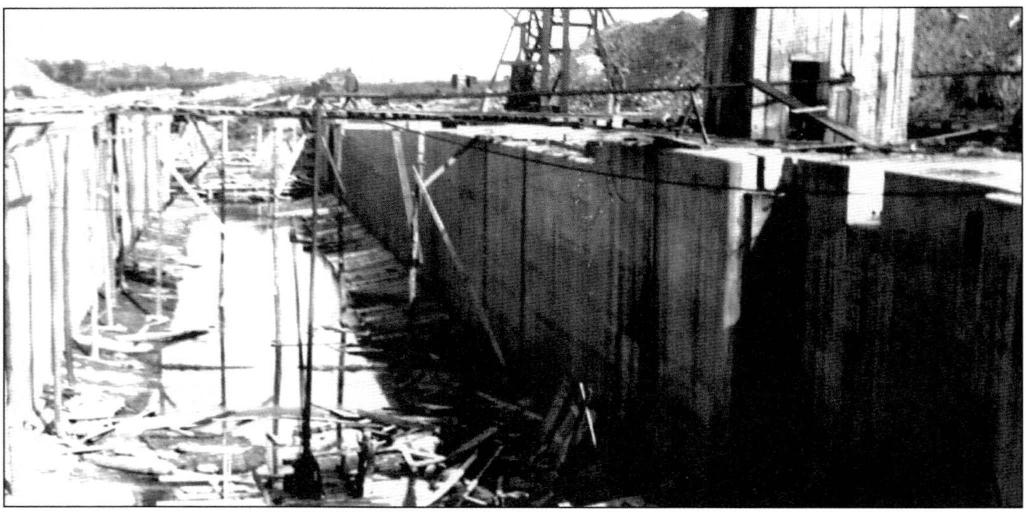

Lock Nos. 2 and 3, with a 40-foot drop, meant that each lock had to lift 20 feet. The construction progress was reported weekly in the *Seneca Falls Reveille*, including things like the amount of dirt moved, the number of barrels of concrete used, and of course the amount of money spent. In the meantime, work kept on, and by 1916, the job was completed.

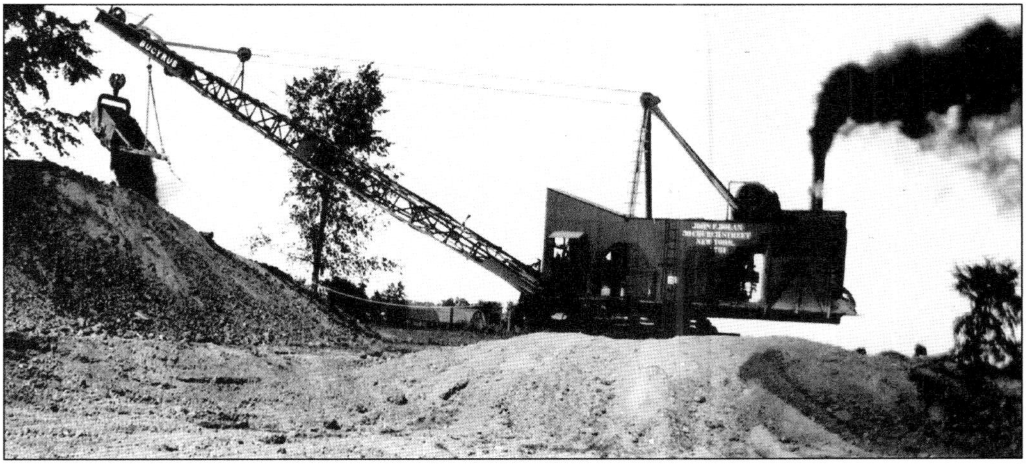

A steam shovel was able to move tons of dirt much faster and place it right where it needed to be.

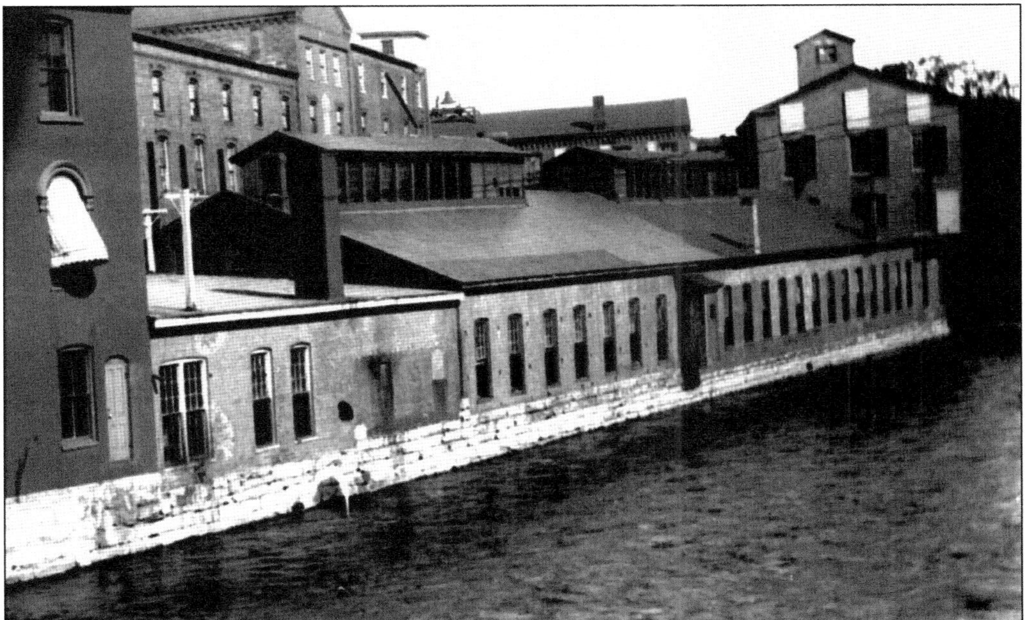

Factories and businesses built right on the sides of the canal and the river. This made it easy to bring in raw materials and ship the finished product. It made it easy to dump the waste, but efforts were made to clean up the canal. One can see the bell on the rooftop, which let the workers know when it was time to go to work and time to go home.

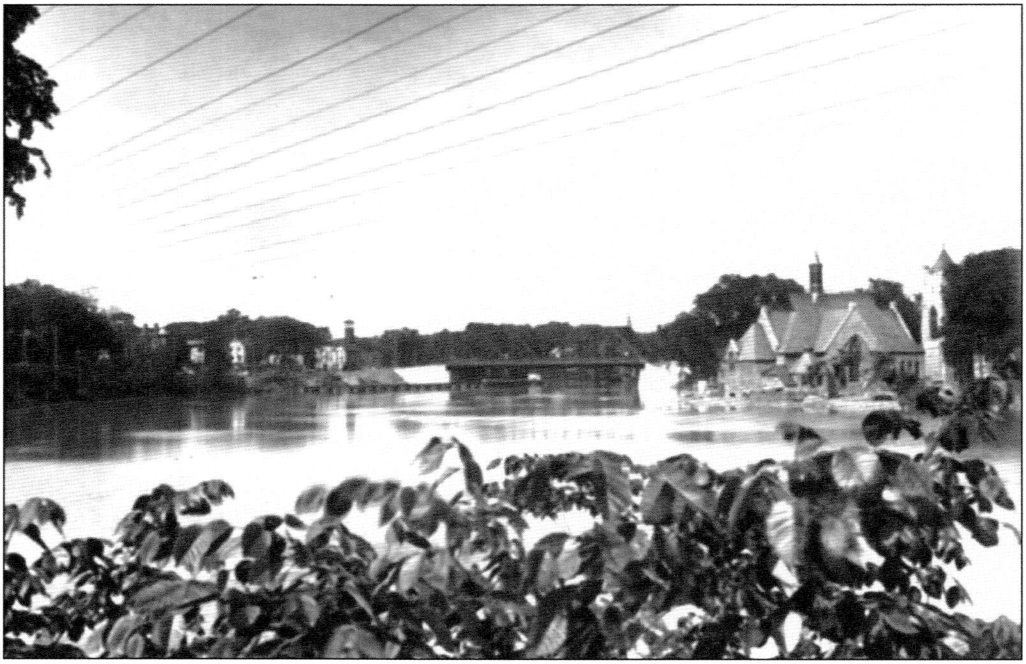

The resulting lake from the dam caused a bit of a stir; because it was a main reservoir, the state did not want to call it a lake. But while the state deliberated on a name, the citizens of Seneca Falls had ideas of their own. They thought it should be named after George VanCleef, the first European child born here.

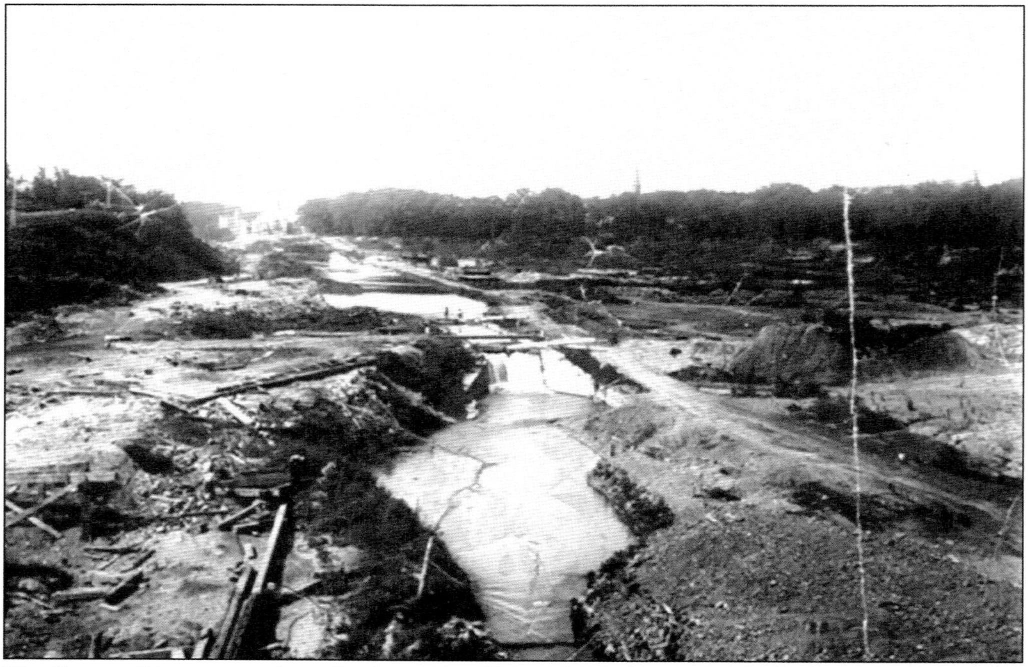

The Seneca River is seen here, looking west during the construction of the new Cayuga-Seneca Canal between 1912 and 1916. This is now Van Cleef Lake.

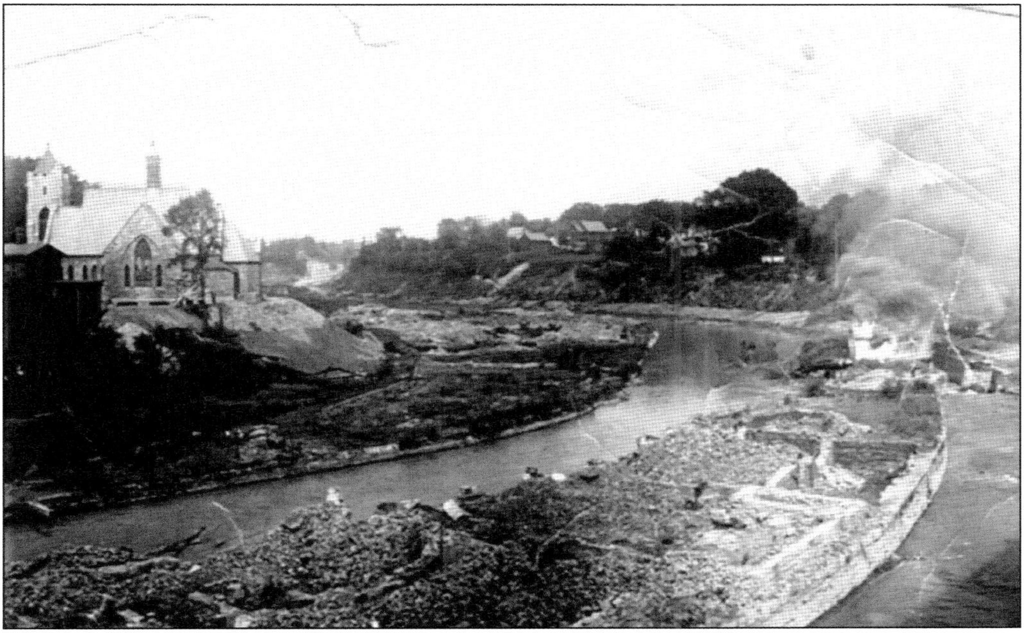

As work continued on the canal project, the original channel and the canal can be seen among what is left of the foundations.

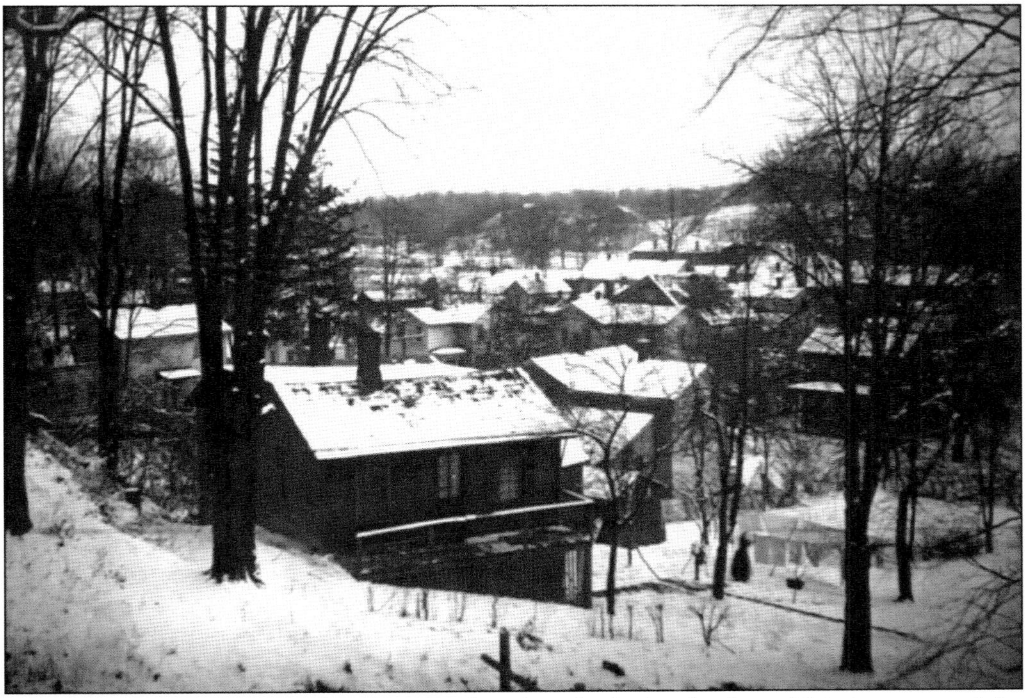

Even during the winter months, chores such as laundry had to be done. This is a scene of the neighborhood in the flats, now under Van Cleef Lake.

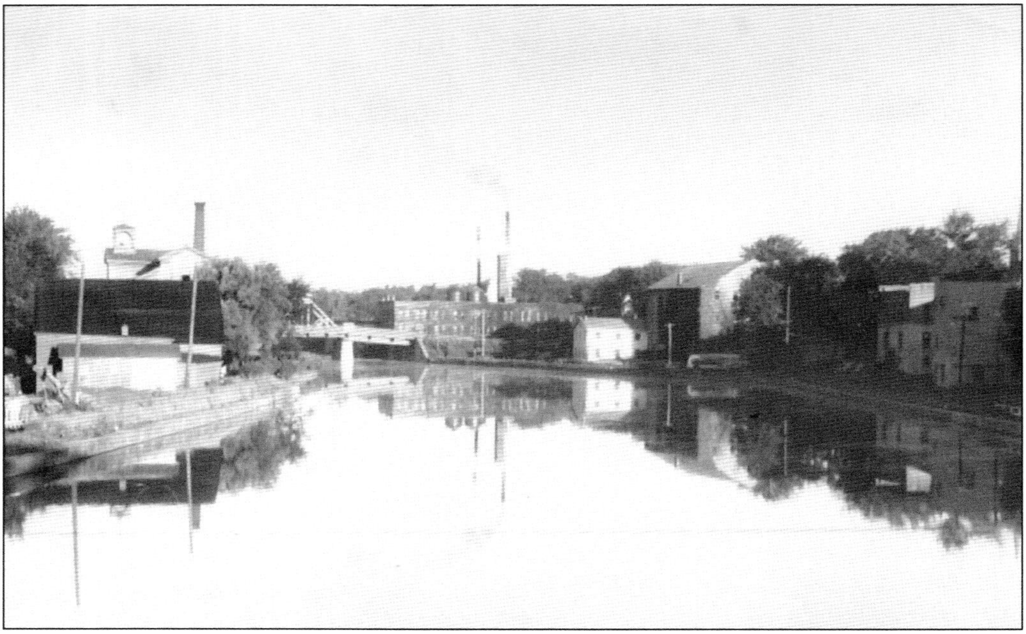

Looking to the west along the new canal, the Bridge Street bridge can be seen, and the Methodist church steeple can be seen in the distance.

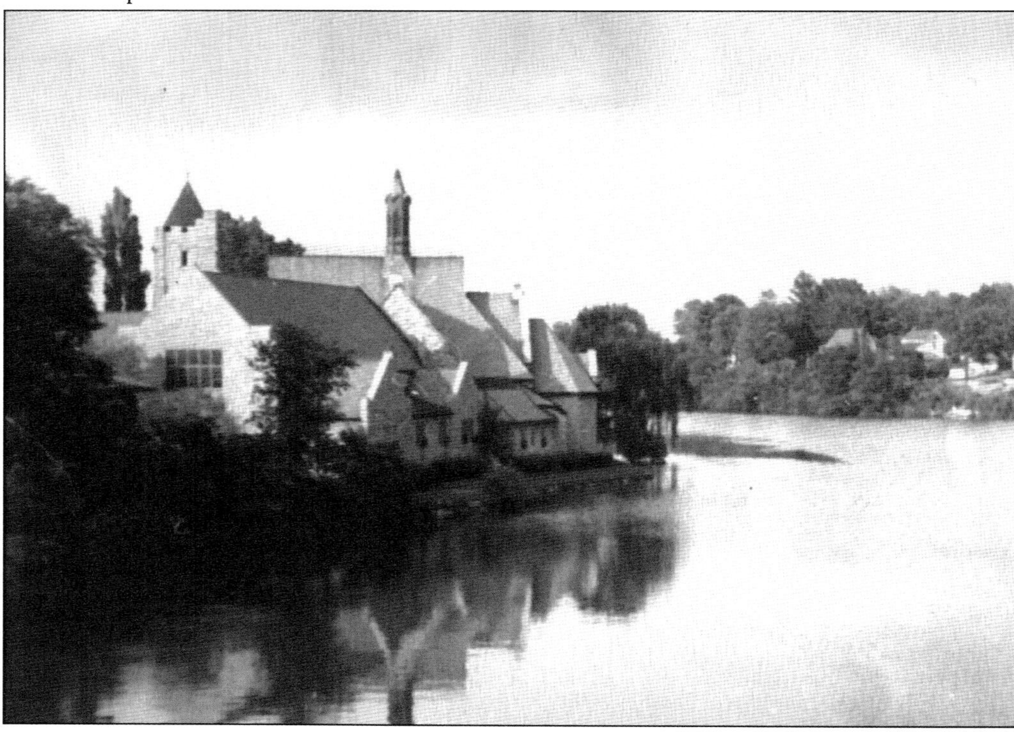

The new Trinity Episcopal Church on Van Cleef Lake is one of the most photographed places in New York. This beautiful building was almost sold to the state and demolished to make way for the canal. At the last minute, it was decided that the church would stay.

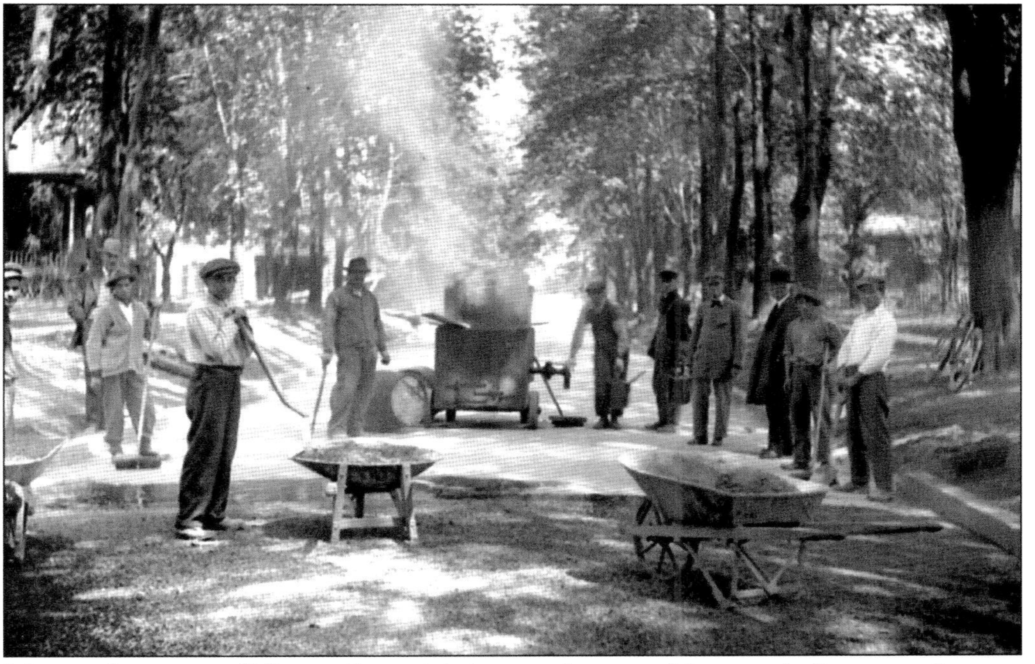

Johnston Street, just off Cayuga Street, is being paved as part of the move by Rumsey to Prospect Hill. Paving the streets made shipping a bit easier.

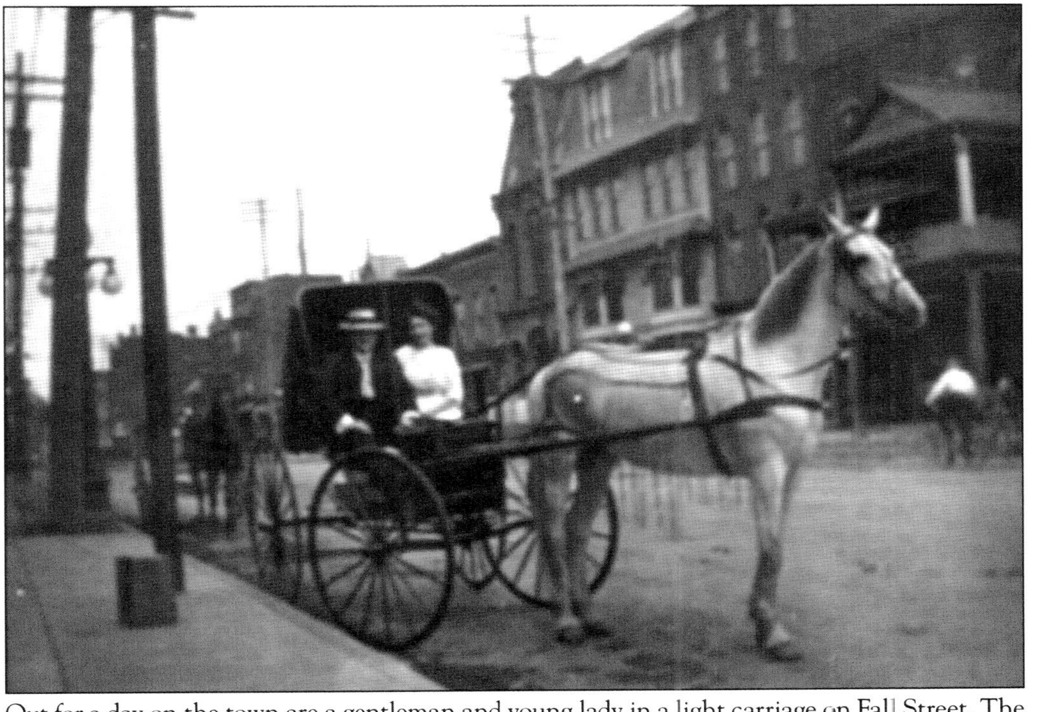

Out for a day on the town are a gentleman and young lady in a light carriage on Fall Street. The Stanton House's covered entry is seen across the street. The horse is kept comfortable with fly netting, thin strips of leather that move easily to keep the flies off.

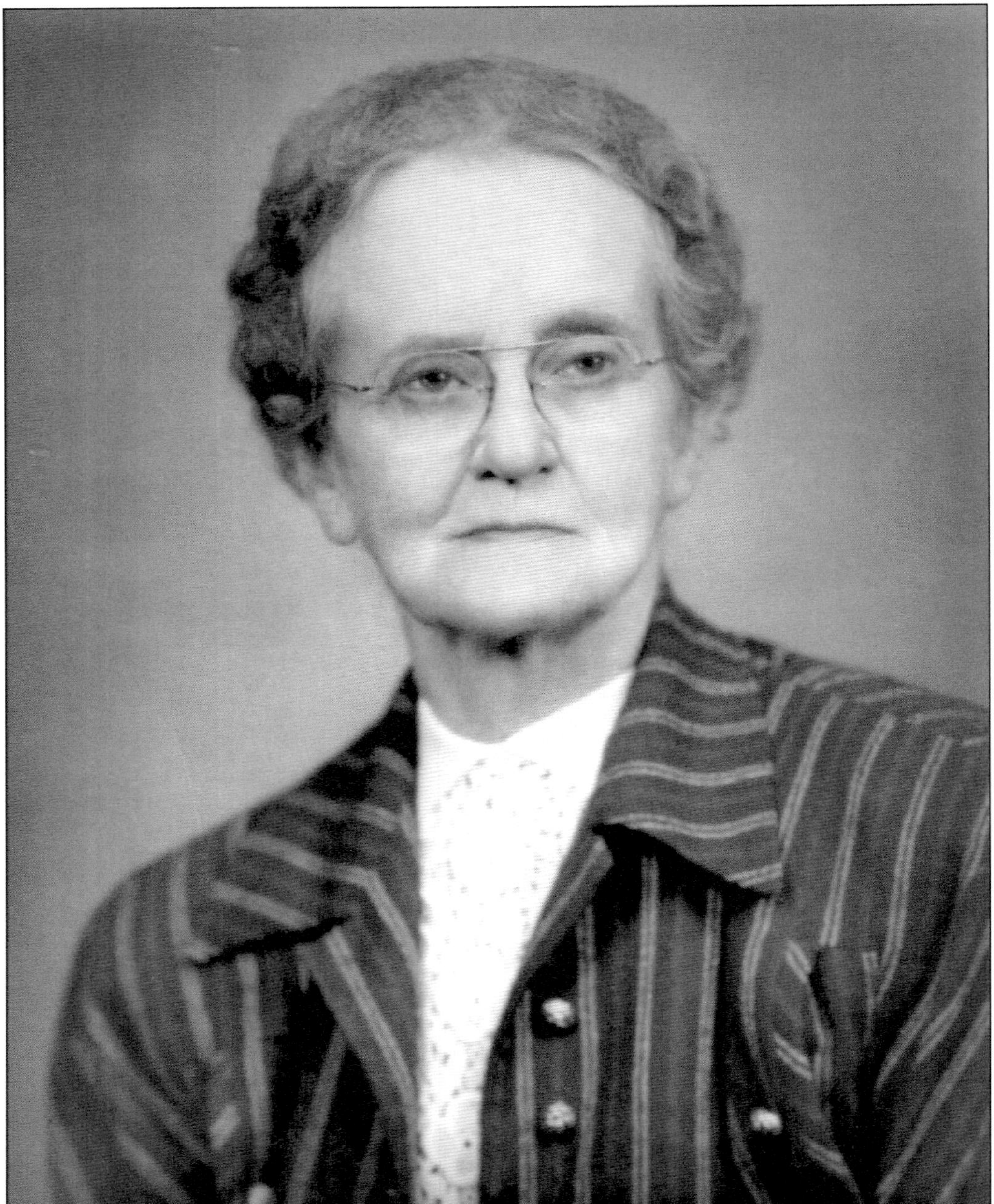

Dr. C. Anna Brown, a doctor with a busy practice in Seneca Falls, realized that there was no hospital locally. Feeling that it was important that a village the size of Seneca Falls have a hospital, Dr. Brown purchased the Silsby house on Terrace Row and remodeled so it was suitable as a hospital. Opened in 1910, it would be used for the next 50 years.

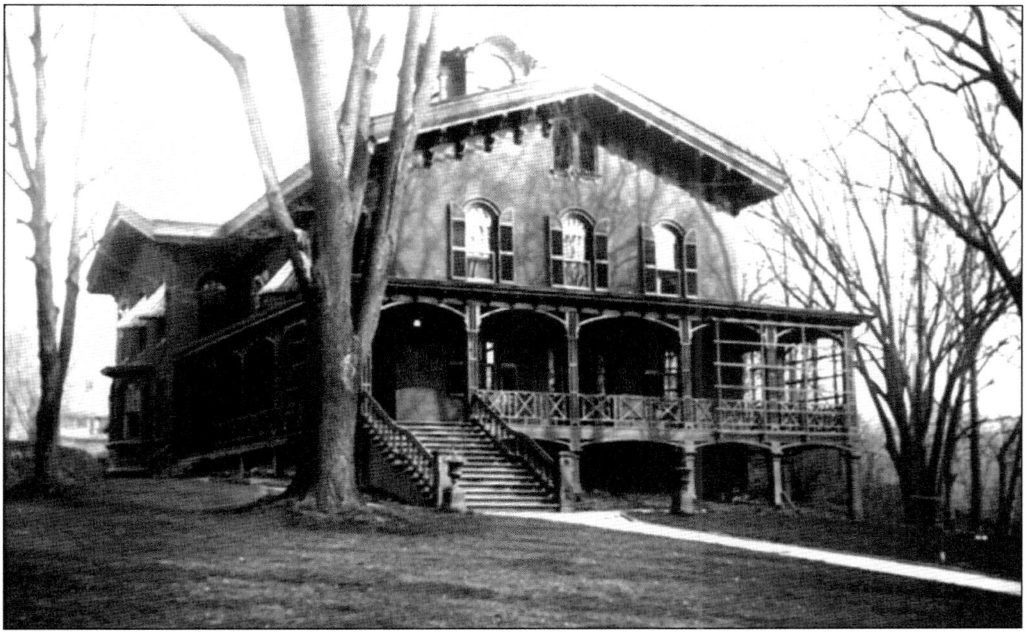

This is the Silsby house before it became the Seneca Falls Hospital. Dr. Brown would use her own money to keep the hospital going until she was too busy trying to practice medicine and run the hospital. The Town of Seneca Falls stepped in and the hospital became the Seneca Falls Hospital.

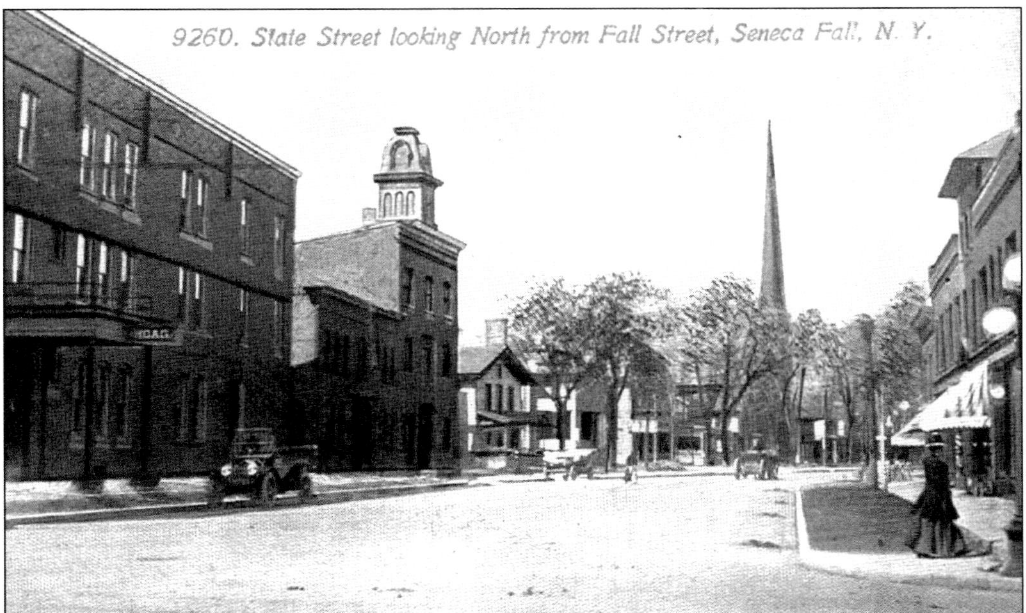

This is a postcard view of Fall Street and State Street after the Hoag Hotel has been rebuilt. The building to the right is a livery stable that will become a garage as automobiles become more popular.

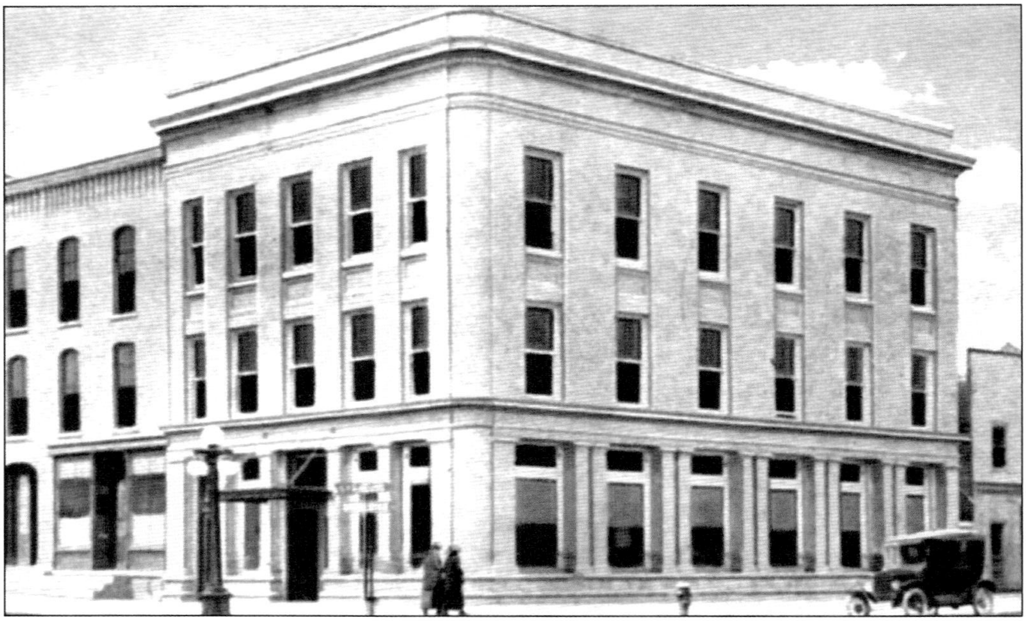

This building was built by Thomas James in the 1860s for his barbershop on the corner of Fall and Cayuga Streets. In the 1920s, the state bank purchased the building and did an extensive face lift. The brick was covered with a material called litholite, which looks like granite, and the interior floors and walls were reinforced. The building is still being used as a bank today.

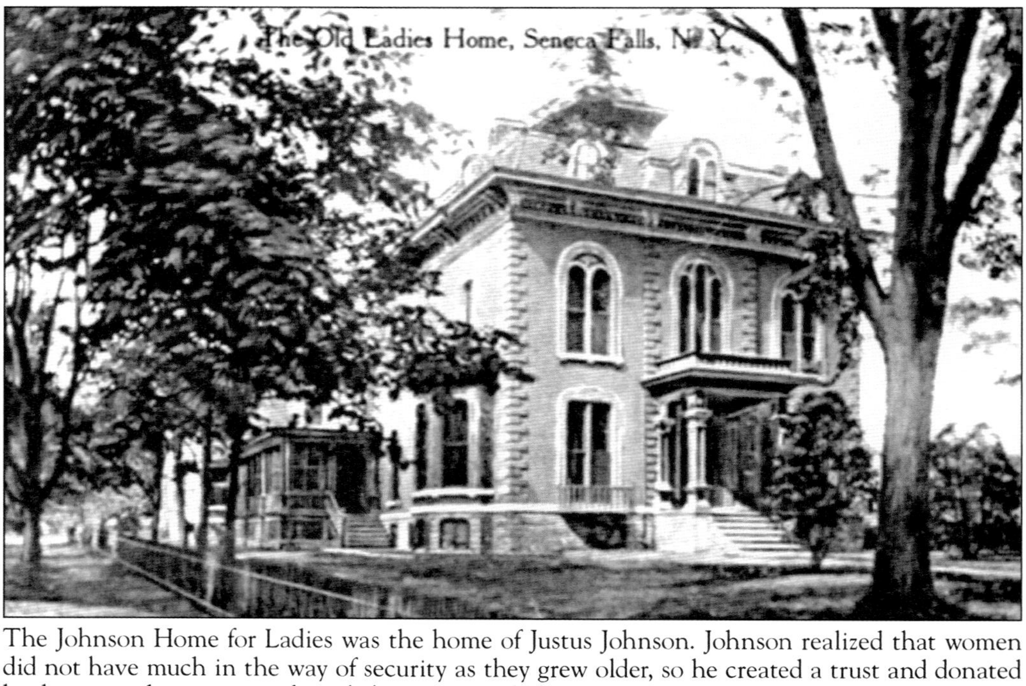

The Johnson Home for Ladies was the home of Justus Johnson. Johnson realized that women did not have much in the way of security as they grew older, so he created a trust and donated his home so that women of good character would have a place to live. Opened in 1898, women could live in comfort for the rest of their lives.

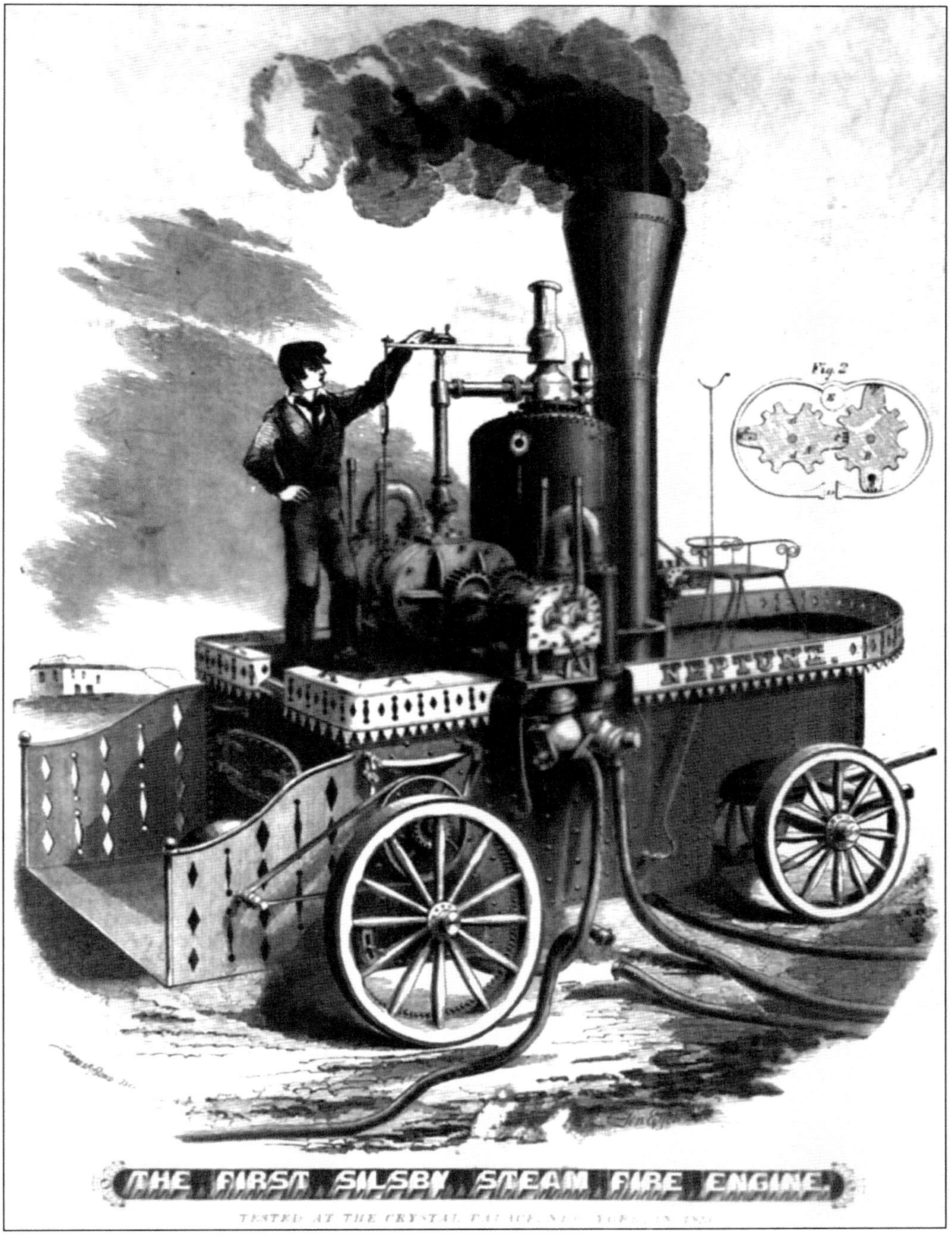

This is a page from one of the early Silsby catalogs showing one of the first steam fire engines. The boiler need a sturdy support platform, and no one was very sure about the safety of the boilers. The early machines were noisy, dirty, and dangerous, but a good idea did win out, and the rotary steam fire engine became a common tool for fighting fires.

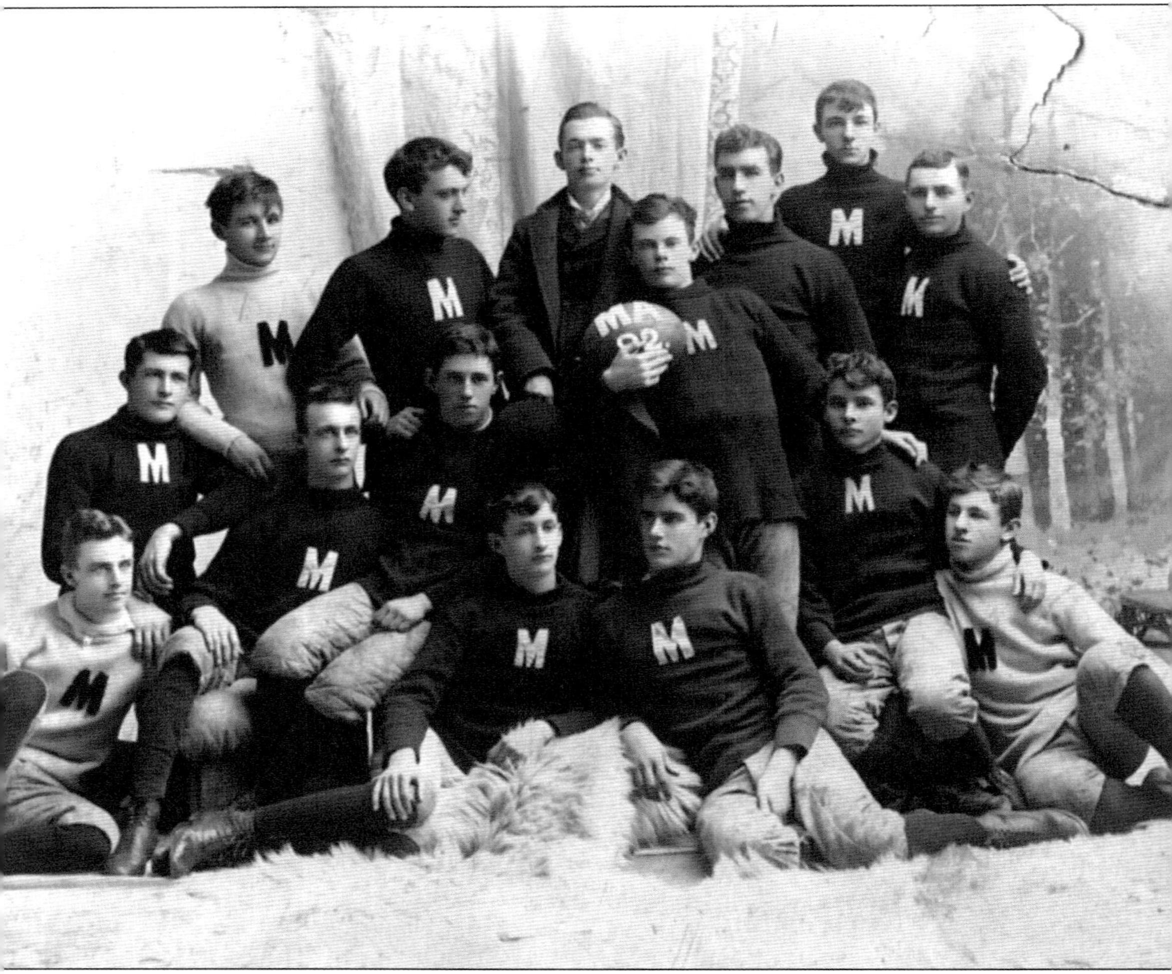

The first Mynderse Academy football team in 1898 is pictured here, though none of the players are identified. Notice how fat the ball is; the forward pass was not used, and the helmets and pads were almost non-existent. Over the years, Mynderse Academy would have many good teams.

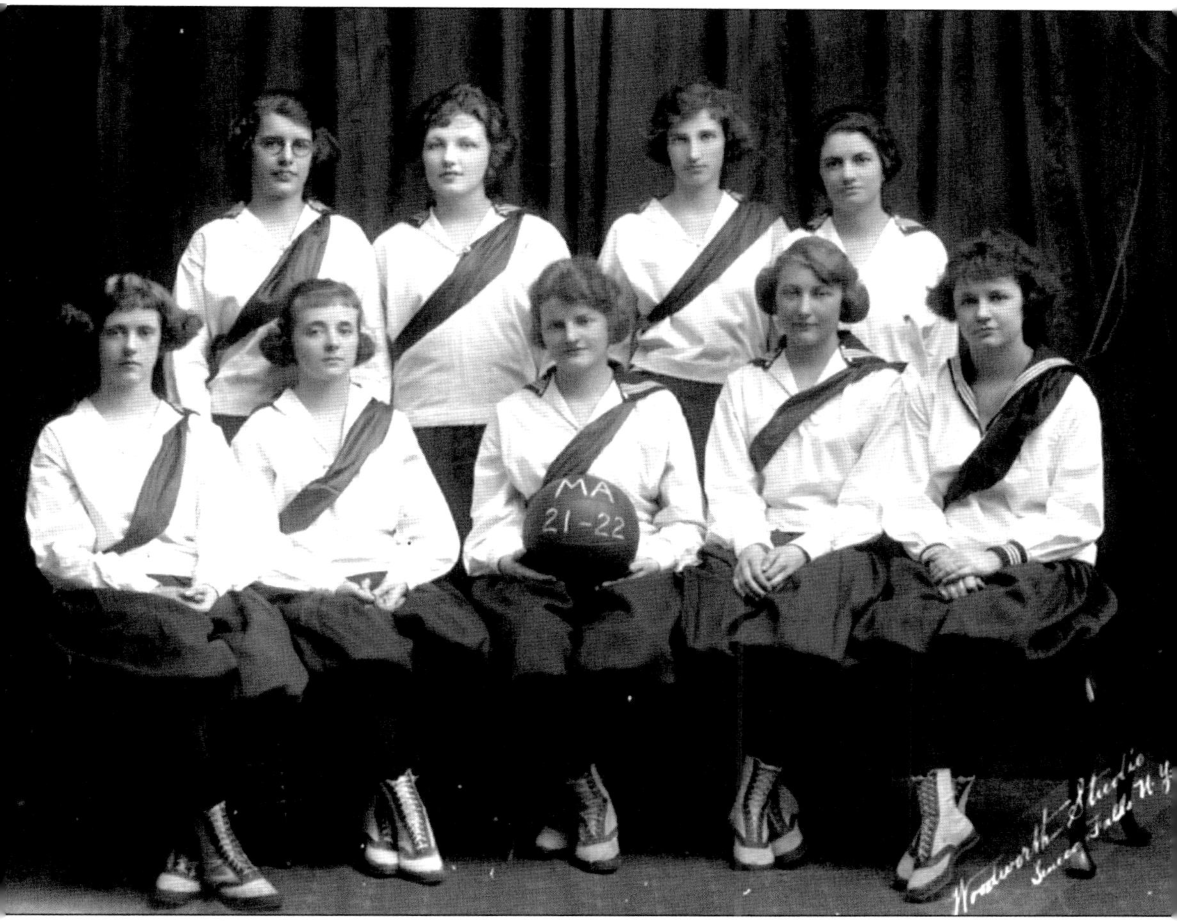

In 1921–1922, the Mynderse Academy girl's basketball team was coached by young teacher Lillian "Billie" Battenfield Oliver. Over several generations, she became a much-loved teacher and friend. Seen here are, from left to right, (first row) Gladys Maxon, Florence Fegley, Dorothy King, Elizabeth Van Seckle, and Alice Fegley; (second row) Gertrude Garnsey, Beryle Tenant, Marjorie Price, and coach Oliver.

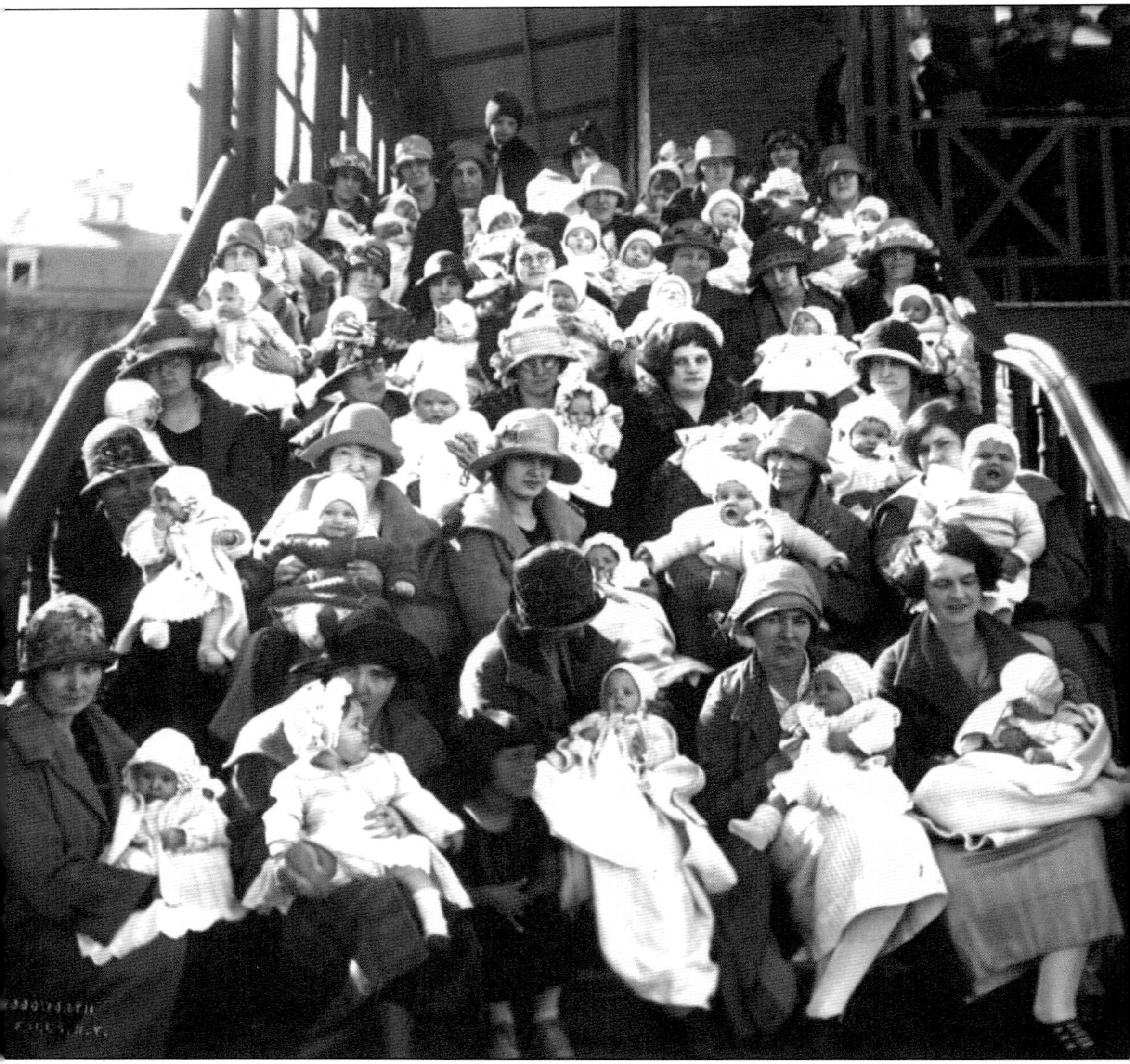

Seen here are mothers and babies born in Seneca Falls in 1928 on National Hospital Day 1929. Grace Woodworth would take a photograph each year of the babies born the year before. They are sitting on the front steps of the Seneca Falls Hospital.

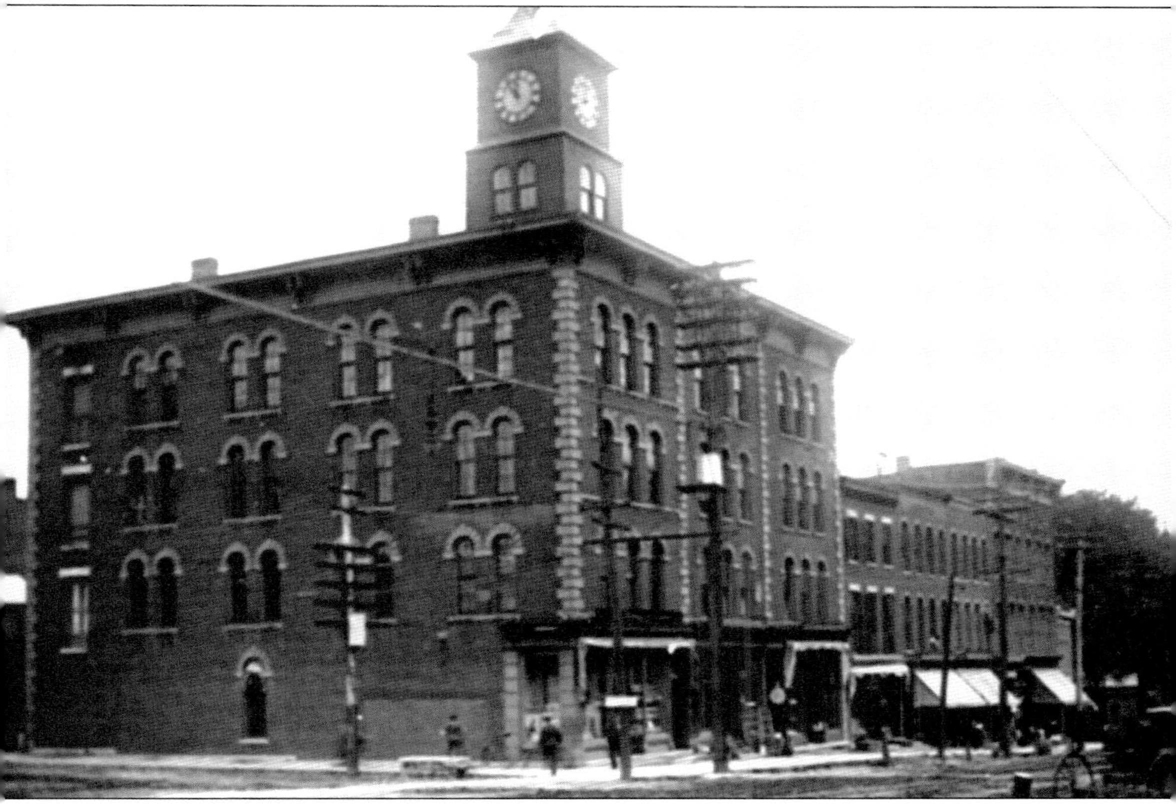

The Hoskins building at the corner of Fall and Cayuga Streets was owned by one of the earliest merchants in town. The clock in the tower was placed after the clock in the Partridge building was destroyed by fire. A Seth Thomas clock that was weight driven kept very accurate time. It also provided a challenge to local boys, who climbed the tower and signed the face of the clock. When the building was demolished, the clock was given to the Seneca Falls Historical Society.

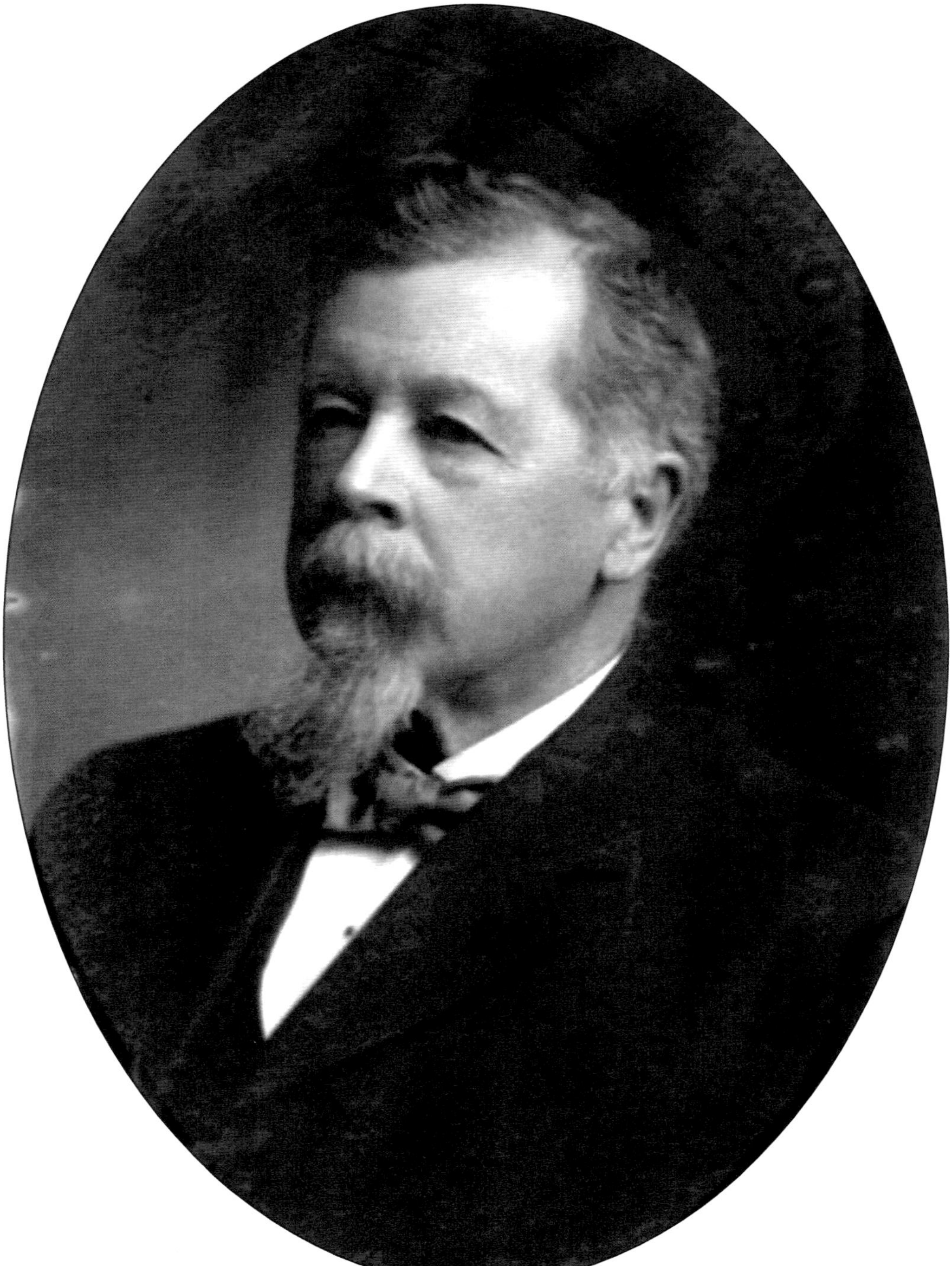

Henry Stowell had been the editor and proprietor of the *Seneca Falls Reveille* since the paper was four years old and made it a spirited, influential family journal. Stowell began to contribute articles to the local papers when he as only 17. He was also interested in the preservation of local history and served as the Seneca Falls historian during the centennial celebration.

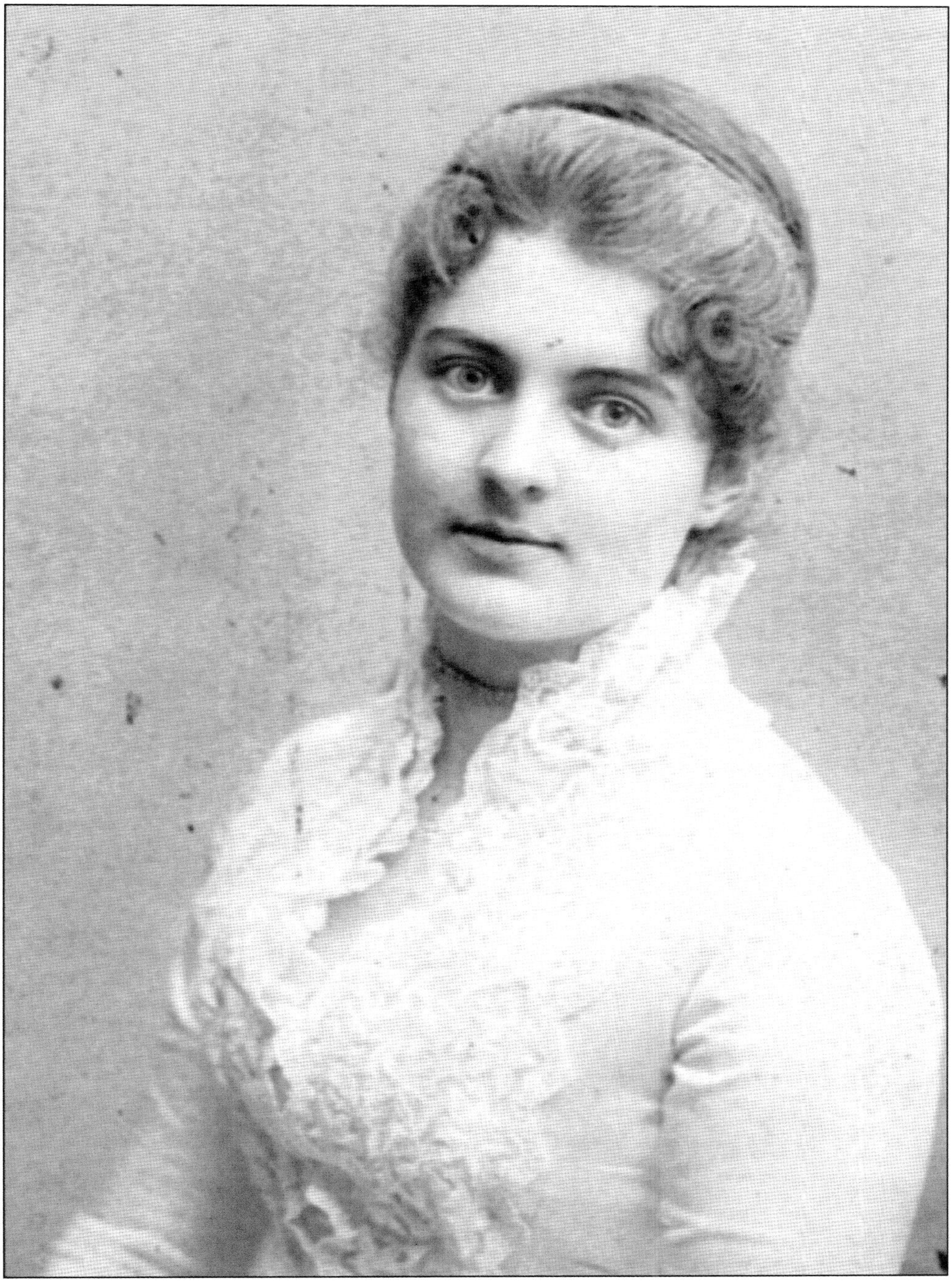

This lovely photograph of Frances Folsom Cleveland was taken by J. E. Hale of Seneca Falls one summer when Cleveland was visiting cousins. This was such a nice likeness of Cleveland that Hale won a prize at the National Photographers Convention. Hale then would not release the photograph to the *New York World* for publication without first the lady's permission. She very graciously gave permission to Hale to use the photographs as he saw fit, as his were by far the best she had ever had taken.

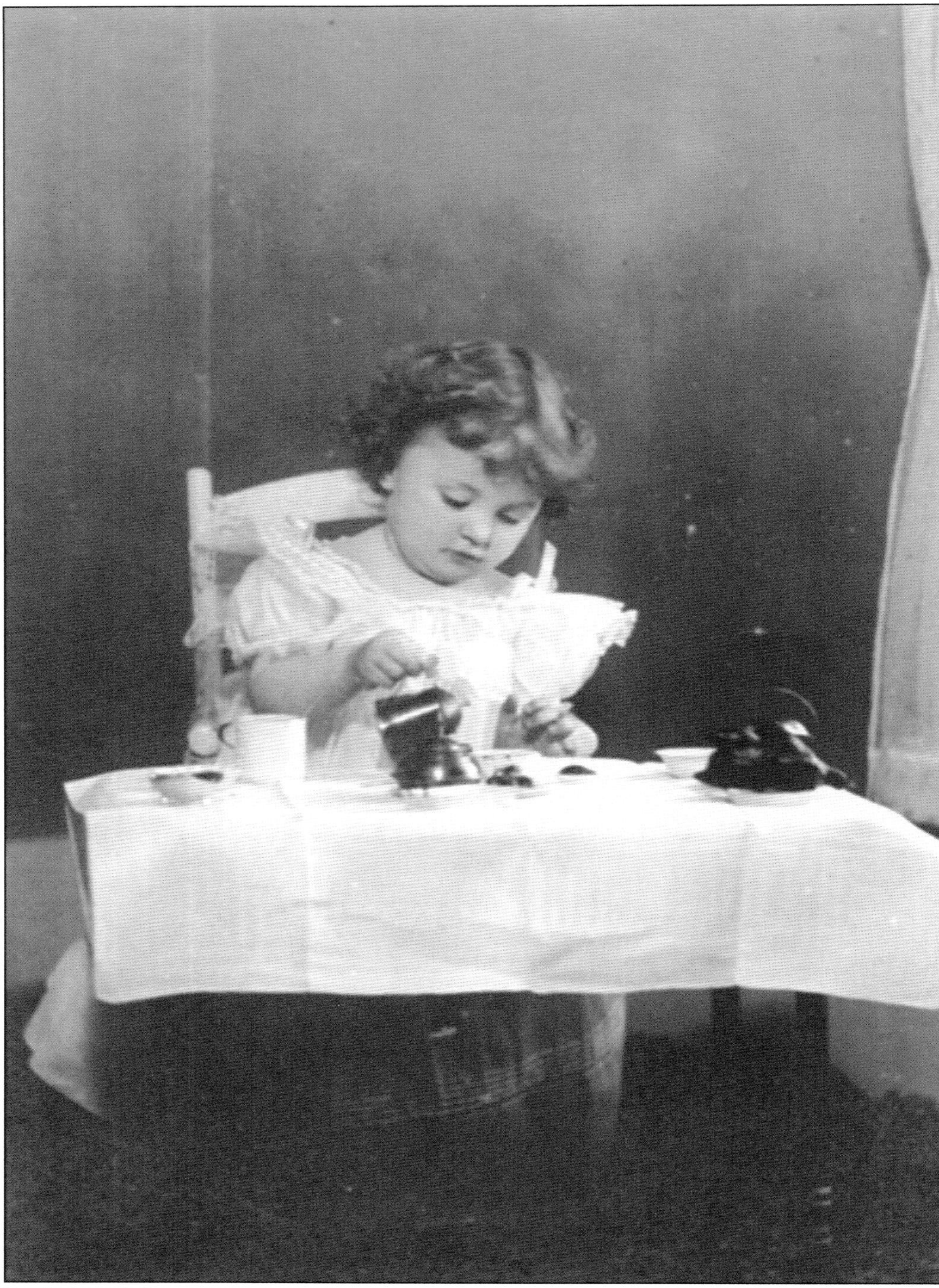

Emily (Knight) Huntington grew up on Cayuga Street, a delightful place to spend a trouble-free childhood. She is about to have tea, a charming custom that was practiced in most of the homes on Cayuga Street in the early 20th century.

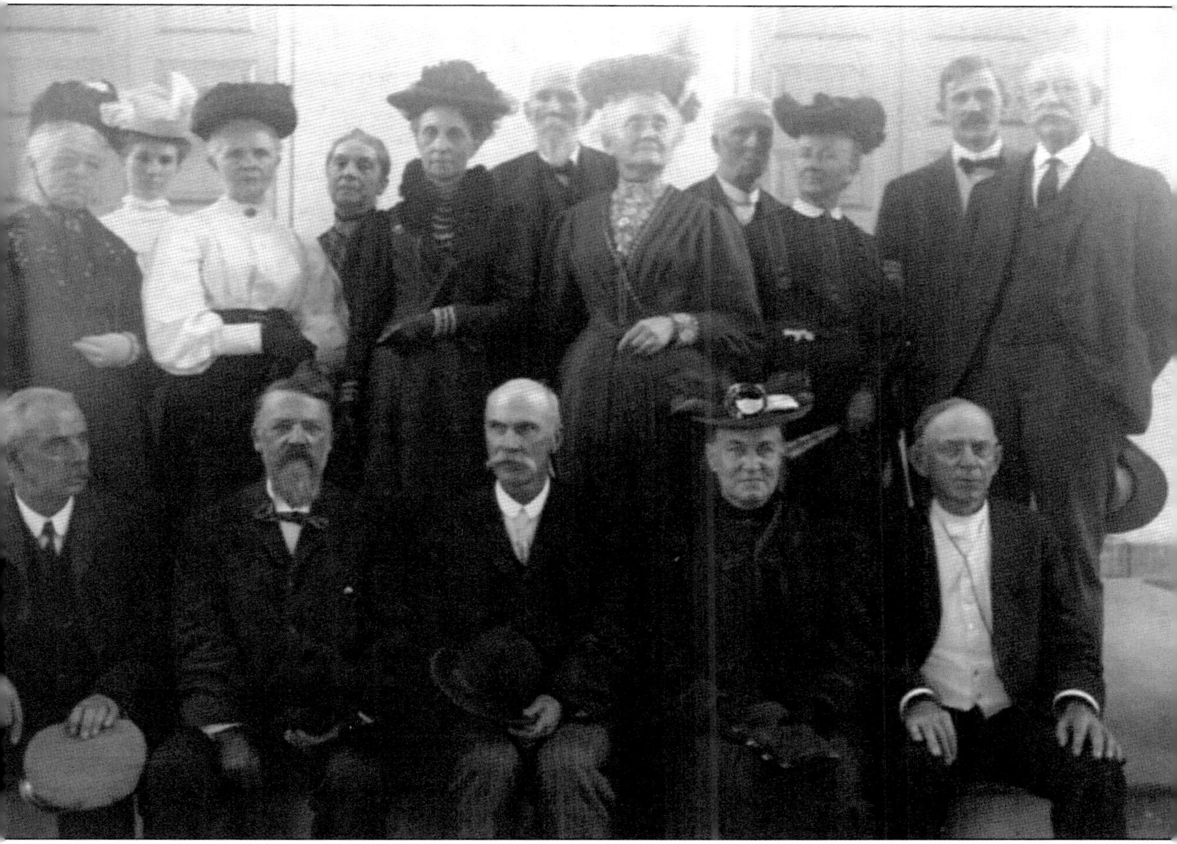

The Seneca Falls Historical Society is pictured on an outing to Romulus. The members of the society were very interested in the preservation of the history of Seneca County as well as Seneca Falls. Founded in 1896 and chartered by the New York State Board of Regents in 1906, the society selected topics, and each member would write a paper and present it at the monthly meetings. Without the foundation laid by these early historians, the story of Seneca Falls could not be told today.